The Americanization of Edward Bok

Edward W. Bok

The Lakeside Classics

THE AMERICANIZATION
OF EDWARD BOK

The Autobiography of a
Dutch Boy Fifty Years After

By
Edward W. Bok

EDITED BY
W. DAVID LEWIS

The Lakeside Press

R.R. DONNELLEY & SONS COMPANY

CHICAGO

December, 2000

PUBLISHERS' PREFACE

THIS YEAR'S Lakeside Classic is the first to focus on our own industry since the initial volume in 1903. The series began with the *Autobiography of Benjamin Franklin*, writer, printer, publisher, scientist, patriot, diplomat, and statesman. Ninety-eight years later, we are pleased to present another remarkable American, Edward Bok, who also served his adopted country while pursuing a distinguished career in the publishing industry, culminating with the Pulitzer Prize in 1921 for this autobiography.

The Americanization of Edward Bok offers two themes: the rags-to-riches tale of a Dutch immigrant boy combined with the story of one of America's most successful magazines, *The Ladies' Home Journal*.

Bok worked his way from poverty to national recognition as the leading editor of his day. In between he did everything from hawking ice water to selling advertising for *Scribner's Magazine*. When Cyrus Curtis invited him to edit a new magazine for women, Bok used the publication to crusade for social causes, to introduce Americans to the finest writers of the day, and to offer service features that women throughout America found invaluable.

Although R.R. Donnelley is a major printer of magazines today, we did not enter this business until 1928, with our first contract for *Time* magazine. During the period in our book, Curtis Publishing maintained its own manufacturing facilities for its publications. R.R. Donnelley began printing the *Journal* in 1982 and continues to serve the magazine's current publisher, Meredith Corporation.

Thomas E. Donnelley, son of the company's founder, introduced the Lakeside Classics series. T.E. believed that a simple, well-designed, and expertly manufactured book would be an appropriate gift from a company that prided itself, then as it does now, on high-quality service to the publishing industry.

W. David Lewis, Distinguished University Professor at Auburn University, Alabama, served as our editor. Among his honors are the Leonardo da Vinci Medal, the highest honor of the Society for the History of Technology, and appointment in 1993–94 as the Charles A. Lindbergh Professor, National Air and Space Museum. A former National Humanities Fellow at the University of Chicago, he has a long-standing interest in women's history and American social reformers.

Preparing a new edition of an historical work requires the help of many. We would especially like to thank the University of Chicago Library, which offered the use of its collection. The editor thanks Karl Hambsch, research associate; Jerry Snead, software consultant, and Marcia Boosinger, Timothy Dodge, and Linda Thornton of the Ralph Brown Draughon Library, Auburn University.

As the century begins, R.R. Donnelley is in the midst of transforming from a company rooted in the printing press to a company focused on providing communications solutions to customers.

The game is much bigger than putting ink on paper. Our role is to digitally capture and store customers' content, convert it to the proper formats and channel it to the desired forms of communication. In doing so, we are a player not only in the traditional world of ink on paper but also in electronic media, such as Web sites.

The reason for this transformation is simple—our customers are changing. Book and magazine publishers, retailers, and catalogers are no longer strictly publishers of printed materials; they are becoming multi-channel communicators who use print, the Internet, and more to get their words and images delivered. They are expanding their content vertically—adding depth to meet the narrow interests of very specific target audiences. At the same time, they are building their delivery systems horizontally through multiple channels, so they can communicate to their audiences at any time, any place.

This transformation is an enormous undertaking that will touch every employee and every customer in every location around the world. To help guide this transformation, the top leaders in the company worked together to develop three complementary business strategies that will guide our plans for the future.

The first strategy is to transform our core printing business. There are dramatic changes ahead for the book, magazine, catalog, and retail insert business. This is the heart of the company and the source of magnificent customers. Our responsibility to these customers is to accelerate process improvements in production and substantially improve capital efficiency.

Our second strategy is to speed growth in existing high-value businesses, which serve markets that are growing faster than core print and generate higher returns because of their focus on service. Markets included in this strategy are premedia, logistics, direct mail, healthcare and investor communications, directory services, and certain international markets.

The third strategy is to extend logically into complementary businesses. We help customers expand their content onto the Internet as well as maximize their Internet presence to meet the needs of their audiences.

In 2000, we achieved many successes in each of these strategies. However, the vitality of the core print businesses drove our growth. Our book, catalog, and magazine businesses had a tremendous year. With the adoption of common quality standards, the book group has ensured that each volume of a title matches the identical quality requirements, no matter where it is printed. By printing items in multiple locations we have significantly compressed our production time. No one else in the industry can do this.

Through a comprehensive continuous improvement program, core print implemented Six Sigma and analytic skills. Employees in all of our locations are enhancing their knowledge and capabilities in order to provide greater benefits to our customers and shareholders.

Businesses in our second strategy made strong

progress this year. These businesses have achieved annual double-digit growth rates since 1997.

Premedia Technologies introduced a digital asset management platform called Image Merchant™. This cutting-edge technology gives customers the ability to prepare materials simultaneously for either print or online use. By welcoming Omega Studios and Iridio to our premedia family, we now operate the largest network of digital photography studios in the world. Premedia also expanded geographically into Dallas, Seattle, and New York City.

Through the purchase of CTC Distribution Direct (Minneapolis), the largest distributor of consumer parcels in the United States, we doubled the size of our logistics business and added new distribution capabilities with the United States Postal Service, adding value for our high-volume mailer catalog customers.

Donnelley Cochrane's acquisition of Gráfica Circulo, a leading book printer based in Barueri, Brazil, made R.R. Donnelley the largest book printer in South America. We also invested $10 million to expand the Donnelley Hamburg book printing facility in Brazil.

Significant progress was made on the strategy to extend into complementary businesses. In May, we successfully relaunched our online business as Red Rover Digital, which helps customers maximize content to create online brands and businesses. Several other Internet initiatives focused on supplying customer content to different Internet-enabled services.

We help customers bridge the gap between print

and the Internet by working with them to understand which of these channels is the best way to reach their target audiences. Research indicates that the Internet is very effective when used with other communications vehicles. For instance, customers are realizing the complementary nature of magazines and the Internet. By building upon our long-term customer relationships, we offer them a total supply chain solution that includes print, logistics, paper management services, and a broad range of content management services. This is what the future will look like for more and more of our customers.

Our focus on the customer is unparalleled in the industry. Now that we have a clear vision for the future, we are ready to make it happen. We are confident that we have the right people, the right priorities, and the right approach to successfully partner with customers to provide innovative communications solutions.

We would like to thank James R. Donnelley, former vice chairman, who retired in June with thirty-eight years of service. As a current Board member of R.R. Donnelley, Jim will continue his hard work and dedication to the well-being of our employees and the success of our business.

As the new year approaches, we wish you and your families good health and happiness.

THE PUBLISHERS

December 2000

CONTENTS

ILLUSTRATIONS

HISTORICAL INTRODUCTION

D URING the late nineteenth and early twentieth centuries, the American magazine industry achieved
mass markets by selling well-edited, well-written, and
well-illustrated periodicals at prices vast numbers of
readers could afford. Nobody played a more important role in this development than Edward Bok, a
Dutch immigrant who built *The Ladies' Home Journal* into the world's best-selling magazine after he
became its editor in 1889. In February 1903, its circulation reached the unprecedented figure of 1,000,000
and it was receiving as many as 10,000 letters in a single day. By 1908, it had 1,250,000 subscribers; fifty
mail cars were needed to take one monthly issue to
the post office.[1]

The success of the *Journal* can be traced partly to
the remarkable business ability of its publisher, Cyrus
H. K. Curtis, an entrepreneur with a genius for conceiving managerial strategies, devising sales tactics,
and winning advertising revenue. But the driving force
behind the magazine's phenomenal popularity was
Bok, who masterminded its content. Bok displayed
acute sensitivity to what women wanted to read at a
time when the rise of an urban, industrial civilization

[1]Salme Harju Steinberg, *Reformer in the Market Place: Ed-
ward W. Bok and* The Ladies' Home Journal (Baton Rouge:
Louisiana State University Press, 1979), 12; James Playsted Wood,
The Curtis Magazines (New York: Ronald Press, 1971), 28, 50.

was sweeping away an era of small enterprises and largely agricultural pursuits. The end of the Gilded Age, the entire course of the Progressive Era, and the onset of the Lost Generation unfolded in the three turbulent decades in which he edited a magazine that served as a leading barometer of changing attitudes and tastes. For this reason alone his autobiography, *The Americanization of Edward Bok,* would be an important work. Its literary merits—it won a Pulitzer Prize in 1921—make it all the more worth reading.

Eduard Willem Gerard Cesar Hidde Bok, as Edward Bok was originally named, was born at Den Helder, The Netherlands, on 9 October 1863. His account of his Dutch ancestry, which begins the book, is romanticized. Texel, which he calls "The Island of Nightingales," lies off the coast of North Holland. Together with the nearby town of Den Helder on the mainland, Texel was a roadstead from which the Dutch East India Company's ships once sailed to the Far East in quest of spices and other commodities. Contrary to what Bok says, it was neither barren nor a den of pirates before his grandfather arrived there. The worst that could be said of its inhabitants is that they sometimes failed to report goods washed ashore from shipwrecks to avoid sharing the proceeds with the government.[2]

[2]J. A. van der Vils, *'t Lant van Texsel: Een geschiedschrijving* (Den Burg-Texel, 1975). Information from this and other Dutch-language sources that follow was kindly supplied and translated by Hans van Felius, Head of the Search Room and Public Informa-

Bok's grandfather, Willem Bok, who was born in 1800, was descended from Hidde Bok, an admiral in the Dutch navy. The Bok family (whose name means "goat" in Dutch) had patrician status. Edward's account of his grandfather's achievements came from memories that his grandmother, Welmoet Tideman Bok, had passed on to her children. Such traditions are likely to be distorted by legitimate family pride. Willem, however, did become a deputy judge on the island of Texel, and ended his career there as inspector of primary education.

Edward's father, Willem Jan Hidde Bok, was a notary at Den Helder from 1858 to 1862 and held the same position at Nieuwediep. He married Edward's mother, Sieke Geertruida van Herwerden, a native of Den Helder. Details of his life are obscure, but he was at one time a person of consequence. Edward later dimly recalled being at a reception for notables when he was a toddler, where he sat on the lap of the great German statesman, Otto von Bismarck. He amused onlookers by innocently knocking a wineglass out of Bismarck's hand and spilling it on his shirt.

Edward had vivid memories of the wealth and the comfort his family enjoyed during his childhood. Unfortunately his father, whose fortune was at one time

tion Department, Rijksarchif in Noord-Holland, Harlem, The Netherlands. I am most grateful to Mr. van Felius for his help. I am also indebted to Wybren Verstegen, a Dutch historian, for advising me to contact the Rijksarchif.

estimated at 150,000 Dutch florins, became involved
in disastrous financial speculations, lost his wealth,
and went to England to escape his creditors. When
things failed to improve, the Boks sailed to America
in 1870 and rented an inexpensive third-floor apartment in Brooklyn. Edward was seven years old, an
impressionable age for a child to be uprooted and see
his family reduced to poverty. His father found a job as
a translator for the Western Union Telegraph Company, making barely enough money to support his family. Both in *The Americanization of Edward Bok* and in
a later memoir, *Twice Thirty,* Edward Bok wrote feel-
ingly about the straitened circumstances in which he
lived after coming to America. He helped his family
survive by scavenging for rags, empty bottles, and
pieces of tinfoil that he sold to a junk dealer. "A nickel
represented ofttimes days of saving," he recalled.[3]

A boyhood hobby put Edward on a path leading
from rags to riches. Starting on a small scale, he became an autograph collector. Noticing him looking at
a signature he had received in the mail, his father
counseled that he go beyond what he was doing by so-
liciting advice from famous people, asking for their
reflections about important subjects. This advice had

[3]Edward W. Bok, *Twice Thirty: Some Short and Simple An-
nals of the Road* (New York: Charles Scribner's Sons, 1925), 15–26,
31–34. Bok wrote this book, a second autobiography, primarily
for his children. Unlike *The Americanization of Edward Bok,* it is
written in the first person. It is valuable as a supplementary source
of information about Bok's life and career.

Bok's grandfather,
Willem Bok

Bok's grandmother,
Wilmoet Tideman Bok

Bok's father,
Willem Jan Hidde Bok

Bok's mother, Sieke Geertruida
van Herwerden Bok

Edward Bok's birthplace, Den Helder, The Netherlands

unpredictable and far-reaching results. Soon Edward would dine with presidents and ex-presidents of the United States and visit eminent poets and essayists like Longfellow and Emerson—all because he had the temerity to write some of the most important figures of his time and dare to believe that they would pay heed. It is a heartwarming story that says much about the openness of American society and the lack of pretense shown by some of its greatest public figures.

What makes Bok's personal saga all the more compelling is the success he achieved with just a meager formal education, characteristic of a culture that rewarded ambition without asking much about a man's credentials as long as he demonstrated ability. Bok had little formal schooling beyond the elementary level. Stenography, aptitude for writing, and a talent for entrepreneurship were his passports to advancement.

Because Bok's adopted land gave so much to him, it is not accidental that he included the word "Americanization" in the title of his autobiography. Nor is it strange that he prominently mentioned Andrew Carnegie's *Triumphant Democracy,* written by a Scottish immigrant who rose from being a bobbin boy in a textile factory to become the wealthiest man in the world and the creator of philanthropic institutions that flourish today. *The Americanization of Edward Bok* and *Triumphant Democracy* are hymns of praise to a Land of Opportunity, and both reflect a strong sense of individualism and an intense drive to climb the ladder of success.

Bok's father's death left Edward's mother, Sieke, in penury. Assuming a role evoking the plot of a Horatio Alger story, Edward kept her from having to work by writing theater reviews for the *Brooklyn Eagle*. He also showed a keen eye for opportunity by noticing the deficiencies of a theater program; he launched his first publishing venture by producing a more attractive program and turning it into a paying proposition.

Bok amassed wealth as he pursued the American Dream. When he died in 1930, he left an estate valued at more than $16 million.[4] But money, however important to him, was not his main goal. He turned his back on a career devoted solely to pecuniary gain when he left a position as secretary to Jay Gould, the telegraph and railroad titan who taught Bok how to play the stock market and predicted a bright future for him in the financial world. Gould belonged to a generation that dominated what Mark Twain, who shared its acquisitive instincts but mocked its ethics, enduringly called the "Gilded Age."[5] Having had the good luck to survive the cataclysmic Civil War, many of its members turned their backs on noble aims. They presided over a period of massive industrialization and left a legacy of economic growth that is too complex to deserve branding them simply as "Robber Barons." But they tended to measure achievement in

[4]Wood, *The Curtis Magazines,* 121.
[5]See Mark Twain and C. D. Warner, *The Gilded Age: A Tale of To-Day,* a satirical novel published in 1873 and reprinted many times since.

quantitative terms. Bok, who belonged to the next generation, which had not fought in the war and reacted against the values of the Gilded Age, wanted something more ethically and spiritually satisfying than mere dollars.[6]

In recounting his Americanization, Bok wrote that he left his job with Gould because he was offended by his inconsiderate behavior. He may also have spurned the type of career into which Gould beckoned him because he had seen from his father's example that fortune is a fickle mistress. Most likely, however, he had been deeply attracted by the idealism of the persons whose autographs he had collected, most of whom were survivors of a pre-Civil War generation that regarded a bloody fratricidal conflict as preferable to surrendering high moral values. Instead of heeding Gould's call to become a financier, Bok became a clerk with a publisher, Henry Holt, who had a strong list of quality books and a strict sense of professional ethics.

[6]On the interpretation advanced here, see William Strauss and Neil Howe, *Generations: The History of America's Future* (New York: William Morrow and Company, Inc., 1991), 190–227. Despite criticism this book has received because of its sweeping generalizations, it makes good sense as a guide to interpreting Bok's life and career. On generation theory, see also Arthur M. Schlesinger, Jr., *The Cycles of American Politics* (New York: Houghton Mifflin paperback, 1999), 23–48. For a sympathetic view of Gould by an eminent historian, denying that he was the arch-villain depicted in the "Robber Baron" tradition, see Maury Klein, *The Life and Legend of Jay Gould* (Baltimore: Johns Hopkins University Press, 1986).

The eloquent preaching of Henry Ward Beecher, Brooklyn's most famous Protestant minister, also attracted Bok. Beecher had abandoned the Calvinist emphasis on sin for a theology of moral freedom and divine love. His cavernous Plymouth Congregational Church was packed with thousands of worshipers on any given Sunday. Bok was impressed by his assertions, evoking the teachings of Adam Smith, that "self-interest and altruism are not incompatible."[7] Thus Beecher helped set Bok on a path that satisfied both the idealist and the upward striver in his personal makeup.

Joining a debating society at Plymouth Church, Bok used it as a springboard for creating *The Brooklyn Magazine,* a journal of opinion that included copies of Beecher's sermons. Thinking that some of the articles he was writing might appeal to a broader readership, Bok became a pioneer in syndication, selling his essays for simultaneous publication in newspapers across the country. As profits accrued from this part-time venture, which Bok pursued in the evenings while continuing to work for Holt, he conceived an idea that foreshadowed his eventual career of editing a woman's magazine. Capitalizing on the popularity of Ella Wheeler Wilcox, a temperance advocate who had become known as the "Poetess of Passion" by writing sensuous but quite genteel romantic

[7]Stated in this manner in Chris Rohmann, *A World of Ideas: A Dictionary of Important Theories, Concepts, Beliefs, and Thinkers* (New York: Ballantine Books, 1999), 361–362.

verse, Edward hired her to offer a "weekly letter on women's topics" to his enterprise, Bok Syndicate Press. Meanwhile, his association with Holt, who published American editions of works by leading European authors, led Bok to begin writing a literary column for New York newspapers. It too became part of his nationally syndicated output.

After spending two years with Holt, Bok accepted a stenographic position in 1884 with Charles Scribner's Sons, a publisher of high-quality books that would soon launch a premier magazine. In 1881, the firm had sold an earlier periodical, *Scribner's Monthly,* to the Century Company and agreed not to use its corporate name on another magazine for at least five years. When this term expired, Scribner's created a new journal for the cultural elite and hired Edward L. Burlingame, son of a distinguished diplomat, to edit it. Educated in outstanding American and European universities, and having a background in both newspaper and book publishing, Burlingame combined an aggressive entrepreneurial spirit with an insistence on high literary and artistic standards. Only by demanding the best could he compete with his chief rivals, *Atlantic Monthly*, *Century*, and *Harper's New Monthly Magazine.* Like Beecher, Burlingame became a mentor to Bok at a crucial stage in his development.

Bok's experience with *Scribner's* had a significant impact on his later career. Elegantly printed and superbly illustrated, and featuring well-written articles

on a wide variety of subjects, it exuded sophistica-
tion. Bok quickly learned to tell good writing from
bad. He also became advertising director for *Scribner's,* giving him a firm grasp on consumer tastes.
Meanwhile, he tuned his literary instincts by having
personal contacts with eminent authors like the
sallow-faced, chain-smoking Robert Louis Stevenson.

Bok's work for *Scribner's,* and the syndicated material he wrote, were noted with interest by Cyrus H.
K. Curtis, a Philadelphia publisher who became his
supreme mentor in 1889.[8] Curtis had been born in
1850 in Portland, Maine. He became a newsboy and
aspired to a career in journalism at an early age. His
formal education ended in grammar school. Buying a
small hand press in 1865, he published a four-page
newspaper, *The Young America,* filling it with stories
and miscellaneous tidbits entitled "Enigmas" and
"Conundrums." ("What is the difference between a
cat and a catalogue?" asked one of his conundrums.
"One has claws at the end of its paws, and the other
has pauses at the end of its clauses.")

Curtis's paper went out of business in 1866 when
his family's home was destroyed by fire. After clerking
for dry goods stores in Portland, Maine, and Boston,
he became an advertising agent for newspapers and
established his own journal, *The People's Ledger.* In
Boston, he married Louisa Knapp, who worked as a
secretary for Samuel Gridley Howe, a well-known

[8]Curtis's middle names, Hermann Kotzschmar, were given to
him in honor of a musician to whom his father was devoted.

physician and reformer whose work with severely handicapped children was famous throughout the world.[9] In August 1876, Cyrus and Louisa had a daughter, Mary Louise; she ultimately became Bok's wife.

Curtis moved *The People's Ledger* to New York City seeking lower costs and relocated to Philadelphia for the same reason. Pennsylvania's largest city was a publishing hotbed in which Curtis found it difficult to compete. Selling his paper, he became advertising manager for the Philadelphia *Press*, and promoted it in the surrounding countryside by touting its coverage of agricultural news. Dissatisfied with working for a firm that he did not own, he borrowed $2,000 and started a four-page weekly, *The Tribune and Farmer*. It contained a "Women and Home" department designed to attract female subscribers. Curtis's wife, Louisa, who was unimpressed by its contents, took it over and transformed it into an eight-page magazine that appeared for the first time in December 1883. Its name was *The Ladies' Journal and Practical Housekeeper*, but an artistic embellishment in the title featured the word "Home." Readers called it *The Ladies' Home Journal*, and the name stuck.

Curtis, a relentless promoter, had achieved a circulation of 48,000 for *The Tribune and Farmer* within

[9]Wood, *The Curtis Magazines*, 3–10; Edward W. Bok, *A Man from Maine* (New York: Charles Scribner's Sons, 1925), 3–96. Howe was famous for educating the visually, vocally, and aurally impaired. His best-known student was Laura Bridgman, the Helen Keller of her day.

five years, but Louisa quickly outdid him. Only one year after its first appearance, *The Ladies' Home Journal* had 25,000 subscribers. Besides featuring serial stories, it included "articles on flower culture, fashion notes, and advice on the care of children," and "carried instructive pieces on cooking, needlework, and handicrafts." Encouraged by its popularity, Curtis hired a Philadelphia advertising firm, N. W. Ayer & Son, to help him push it even more energetically. Within a year its circulation burgeoned to 200,000, prompting Curtis to rent larger facilities and solicit stories from popular writers including Louisa May Alcott, the renowned author of *Little Women,* who was persuaded to contribute to the magazine by a promise to pay $100 to her favorite charity. Borrowing heavily, Curtis spent lavishly on advertising and had a circulation of 488,000 by 1889.[10]

At this point Louisa decided to give up editing the *Journal* to devote more time to her daughter, Mary Louise. Having already created the nation's first mass-circulation periodical, Curtis wanted to push sales even higher by making it a "high-class magazine" aimed at growing numbers of affluent persons, both male *and* female, in a rapidly urbanizing American society. *Scribner's* offered a good model for what he wished to accomplish, and he already knew what type of individual he was looking for to succeed his wife.

---

[10]On the early history of the *Journal,* see also Frank Luther Mott, *A History of American Magazines, 1885–1905* (Cambridge, Mass.: Harvard University Press, 1957), 536–539.

Cyrus H.K. Curtis *Louisa Knapp Curtis*

Going to New York City, he interviewed Bok, who was only twenty-six years old, and offered him the job. Bok accepted, but not before being satisfied Curtis intended to seek as broad a readership as was possible. "Because women were the leading purchasers of consumer goods by the 1890s," a perceptive scholar has noted, "it was clear that a magazine ostensibly edited for them would affect the whole family's purchasing power. Both Curtis and Bok ... viewed the *Journal* as more than merely a women's magazine. They hoped it would appeal to every family member."[11]

Curtis's desire for the *Journal* to be read by men as well as women helps explain why he appointed a man to replace his wife as editor. Bok's pioneering of a syndicated column, his association with a "first-class magazine," and his experience as director of advertising for *Scribner's* all counted in his favor. Curtis obviously considered Bok's youth not as a liability but an asset. Although Bok would write advertising copy for the *Journal,* he was willing to leave decision-making power over this critical matter in the hands of Curtis, whose business acumen Bok recognized as superior to his own. Curtis reciprocated by giving Bok a free hand in setting editorial policy, and Bok had no hesitation about using this authority as he saw fit. From the beginning, Bok molded the style of the magazine in his own image, with results that soon became apparent in its rapidly growing circulation.

[11]Steinberg, *Reformer in the Marketplace,* 2.

Historians have already examined many of his editorial strategies in depth, typically by focusing on the *Journal* as a highly profitable business enterprise or on what it reveals as a barometer of attitudes and values prevalent among women during the era in which Bok shaped its content. On the other hand, they have paid too little attention to Bok's unrelenting efforts to elevate the literary tastes of his readers, which will be highlighted in this essay.[12]

Bok's literary crusade was rooted in his convictions about the civilizing role that he thought women should play in American culture. Historians have recognized that he took a conservative view of the place of women in American society but have not explained how his attitudes evolved over time or were related to his own personal experiences. One scholar, for example, cites Bok's statement in 1923 that "he neither liked women nor understood them; nor had he any wish

---

[12]In addition to Steinberg's *Reformer in the Marketplace,* works dealing mainly or partly with Bok and *The Ladies' Home Journal* include Helen Damon-Moore, *Magazines for the Millions: Gender and Commerce in* The Ladies' Home Journal *and* The Saturday Evening Post (Albany: State University of New York, 1994); Kathleen L. Endres and Therese L. Lueck, eds., *Women's Periodicals in the United States: Consumer Magazines* (Westport, Conn.: Greenwood Press, 1995), particularly pp. 172–180; Jennifer Scanlon, *Inarticulate Longings:* The Ladies' Home Journal, *Gender, and the Promise of Consumer Culture* (New York: Routledge, 1995); David Shi, "Edward Bok & The Simple Life," *American Heritage,* XXXVI, 1 (December, 1984), 100–109; and Helen Woodward, *The Lady Persuaders* (New York: Ivan Oblensky, Inc., 1960), particularly pp. 63–101.

to," without realizing that it reveals more about how Bok felt at the end of his editorial career than about the spirit in which he started it.[13] "From my earliest years I have ever believed in woman," Bok stated in 1892. But he added significantly, "I believe that women are better than men—better in their lives, purer in their thoughts, more conscientious in their motives, and morally stronger in every respect."[14]

Between 1892 and 1923, Bok went through a long process of disillusionment about American women.

Bok had derived his notions about womanhood from his mother, "the confidante of my boyhood, the greatest joy and blessing of my life."[15] Her values came from The Netherlands, where women led sheltered and circumscribed lives. A Dutch poem, "The Heroic Housewife," declared that ". . . a wife must stay at home to be in the kitchen. . . ."[16]

Edward absorbed these values, explaining why he exerted himself so unsparingly to support his mother after his father died. In a book that he later wrote for his two sons, he recounted how his widowed mother

[13]Nancy Woloch, *Women and the American Experience,* Volume Two: from 1860, the 2nd ed. (New York: McGraw Hill, 1994), 410.
[14]Edward W. Bok, "At Home With the Editor," *The Ladies' Home Journal* [hereafter cited LHJ], IX, 9 (August 1892), 12.
[15]Ibid.
[16]Jacob Cats, "The Heroic Housewife," as quoted in Simon Schama, *An Embarrassment of Riches: An Interpretation of Dutch Culture in the Heroic Age* (New York: Alfred A. Knopf, 1987), 400.

"had broken down from the housework to which she was unaccustomed," causing him and his brother to pool their meager savings to send her to the mountains for a vacation. While she was away the brother became ill, but the two boys decided not to tell her. "It was unthinkable," Edward said, "that she should know of my brother's illness, since she would naturally come home immediately, and the anxiety and strain might be fatal to her."[17]

These words reveal Bok's belief that women were frail, delicate creatures who needed protection and should remain anchored in the home. His later disillusionment stemmed from learning that most American women did not conform to his idealized image and that a growing number of females did not want to play the sheltered role he thought best. It is instructive to note that his mother did not die until 1907, when she was eighty—a hearty old age that was well beyond normal life expectancy at the time and an indication that she was, perhaps, less frail, less delicate than Bok might have acknowledged.[18] Indeed, he had not understood her any better than he had understood women in general.

Bok's Dutch heritage was consistent with beliefs about women that were widely held in America when he became editor of the *Journal.* They were part of a "Cult of True Womanhood" to which many middle- and upper-class females subscribed for reasons that

[17]Bok, *Twice Thirty,* 140.
[18]*Nederlands Patriciaat,* jrg. 64, p. 18.

flattered them, despite knowing that they were much tougher than they let on.[19]

Bok opposed female suffrage because he felt that women had too elevated a nature to participate in the hurly-burly of politics. That position earned him the support of conservative feminists like Abby Hamlin Abbott, president of the New York Association Opposed to the Extension of Suffrage to Women. Abbott was the wife of Lyman Abbott, a prominent Christian evolutionist who was a close associate of Henry Ward Beecher. [20] She spoke for untold numbers of females who were comfortable with the conventional values of Victorian America. Such women were content "to live their lives comforting work-weary husbands, devoting themselves to molding young children into moral, upright citizens and fashioning homes that were at once a retreat from the outside world and a material as well as cultural inventory of refinement, social standing, intellect, and honor."[21] Even many suffragists shared most of Bok's conservative views despite disagreeing with him on whether women

[19]For a discussion of the cult, see Barbara Welter, *Dimity Convictions: The American Woman in the Nineteenth Century* (Athens: Ohio University Press, 1976), 21–41.

[20]Ira V. Brown, *Lyman Abbott: Christian Evolutionist* (Cambridge, Mass.: Harvard University Press, 1953), 208. On opposition to suffrage among large numbers of American women, see Carl N. Degler, *At Odds: Women and the Family in America from the Revolution to the Present* (New York: Oxford University Press, 1980), 349–355.

[21]Ellen M. Plante, *Women at Home in Victorian America: A Social History* (New York: Facts On File, Inc., 1997), xi.

should have the right to vote. Bok, in short, understood enough about American women and their attitudes to appeal successfully to a huge audience in 1889. Only after three decades of profound cultural change did he find himself increasingly out of touch with his readers and retire in disillusionment.

Under Bok's editorial guidance *The Ladies' Home Journal* constantly stressed the role of women as mother and homemaker. "A man expects the maternal instinct in a woman," Bok asserted, "and is disappointed if he does not find it." Eugene Field, a humorist who was one of Bok's best friends, enjoyed jesting about the magazine's constant references to toilet soaps and corset covers, lemon pie and angel food cake, cures for chapped lips, and instructions for "pulling out basting threads with forceps instead of with the fingers."[22]

Bok's views would have infuriated later advocates of women's liberation. Women, Bok said, liked a man who could be "strong as a lion when trouble comes," but ready, if his wife was "nervous and tired," to be able to "button up a shoe and do it with an amount of consideration that is a mental and physical bracer-up." And women wanted men who knew their "innocent weaknesses," would "bring home a box of candy," be "the master of the situation," and have "brains enough to help a woman to decide what is the best thing to do under any circumstances." Such men would have "wit

[22]Mott, *American Magazines,* 1885–1905, 541.

enough to realize when one of the fairer sex is slightly stubborn that persuasion is more powerful than all the argument in the world."[23]

Evidently this patronizing outlook was not offensive to readers of the *Journal* when it was set forth in 1890, judging from the magazine's mounting circulation. But times would change as the "New Woman," with an "enhanced sense of self, gender, and mission," became increasingly prevalent, and ideas that had once been acceptable would become less so among subscribers by the end of Bok's editorial reign.[24]

Even in 1890, Bok was willing to sanction a limited sphere of female employment outside the home. He hired women to edit sections of the *Journal* and welcomed them into nursing, as well as the practice of medicine, particularly pediatrics, for which their sensitive, compassionate natures peculiarly fitted them. He also condoned their working as secretaries and stenographers, but always with concern that such occupations were full of dangers for females to which men who pursued them were not exposed. If a woman needed to earn money, it was safer and more consistent with her special gifts to work at or near the family hearthside. In 1891, an article in the *Journal* recommended bee keeping as a suitable female occupation because women had "a gentler, finer touch than men."

[23]"Just Between Ourselves," LHJ, VIII, 5 (April 1890), 8. The articles mentioned appeared in the issue of June 1890.
[24]See particularly "The Rise of the New Woman, 1860–1920," in Woloch, *Women and the American Experience,* II, 269–307.

Bee keeping was also consistent with feminine modesty, leaving the body unexposed. "Nearly all beekeepers wear veils, and all beginners should wear gloves of rubber," the article stated. "The dress is a divided skirt, but made so full that it is not noticed. Each part of the skirt is gathered at the bottom into a hem or band to button around the ankle below the top of the boot."[25]

Bok's conviction that women were natural custodians of cultural uplift led him to stress literature as a realm they should cultivate. Writing, which could be done at home, was a highly suitable occupation to pursue, and the *Journal* offered much advice about how to become a successful author. Continuing with themes already sounded in his syndicated essays, Bok established a regular column, "In Literary Circles," in which he provided counsel on the art of conceiving fresh ideas, designing effective plots, creating good titles, and being patient with overworked editors who kept manuscripts longer than many novice writers might, in good conscience, expect.

He also warned that "fancy writing is a grave into which hundreds of young writers are being buried," stating that "literary sunsets and moonlights are all very pretty, but there is just about one author in every fifty years who makes a reputation on them." He cautioned against writing poetry too early in one's career,

[25]Julia Allyn, "Bee-Keeping for Women," LHJ, IX, 5 (April 1891), 4.

saying that it was an inherently difficult form of literature to master for all but the most talented of writers. [26]

Not all women could write, but they could read,
and Bok urged them to do so without neglecting other
worthwhile activities. Numerous articles praised the
works of contemporary authors, both male and female, upholding them as role models for readers of
the *Journal* to admire. [27] "It is always well for every
woman to remember that her reading is the greatest
key to her character," Bok declared. "Read good
books, and they will unconsciously make you speak
better English, systematize your mind, give you a better knowledge of the world, and tend to make you in
every respect a brighter, more interesting, more broad,
and more considerate woman." [28]

The zeal with which Bok pursued articles and stories by some of the most famous authors of his day
for publication in the *Journal* stemmed from deeper
impulses than a mere desire to boost circulation. It
reflected his undying faith in the power of eloquent

[26] Among many other articles too numerous to cite here, see
Edward W. Bok, "An Informal Literary Talk," LHJ, VII, 12 (November 1890), 16, and "The Girl Who Writes Poetry," IX, 5 (April
1892), 18.

[27] See Marguerite Merington, "Margaret Deland," LHJ, IX, 11
(October 1892), 7; H. H. Boyesen, "Mr. Howells at Close Range,"
X, 12 (November 1893), 7; "Four Famous Young Authors," XI, 9
(August 1894), 5, and Emma B. Kaufman, "The Personality of a
Charming Writer" [Kate Douglas Wiggin], XII, 5 (April 1895), 5.
Many other articles in LHJ could be cited if space permitted.

[28] Edward W. Bok, "The Book in a Woman's Hand," LHJ, VII,
6 (May 1890), 8.

speech and writing to raise the moral virtue of the nation. He was particularly concerned about what he saw happening to popular culture in an era when millions of Americans were moving from the country to the city, buying new homes, and earning unaccustomed amounts of money without making equivalent progress in cultural awareness. It troubled him terribly, as he said in one of his editorials, that women were reading "trashy novels."[29]

An early sign of the literary mission Bok assumed when he took the helm of the *Journal* was a long series of autobiographical articles by William Dean Howells, America's chief standard-bearer of what Henry F. May has aptly called "practical idealism." An article in the *Journal* called Howells "the foremost man of letters in the United States."[30] As Howells indicated in his novel *The Rise of Silas Lapham*, cultivating an appreciation of literature was crucial among millions of Americans who were becoming upwardly mobile without becoming well read. Bok agreed, feeling that nothing less was at stake than the cultural welfare of a nation he loved and wanted to protect from philistines.

Howells ultimately became so repelled by industrial capitalism that by the time he published *A Hazard of New Fortunes*, in 1890, he had rejected it to

[29]Bok, "Are Women Reading Our Trashy Novels?" in ibid.
[30]Henry F. May, *The End of American Innocence* (Chicago: Quadrangle Books, 1964), 3-19; Boyesen, "Mr. Howells at Close Range," previously cited.

become "the first distinguished American man of letters to espouse Marxian socialism."[31] However deeply
Bok admired Howells, and despite the encouragement
he gave to Edward Bellamy, who preached a non-
Marxian utopianism in his 1888 novel *Looking Backward,* Bok never strayed very far from conventional
American business values. Had he done so, he would
not have thrived at the helm of a magazine that depended heavily upon advertising revenue, nor could
he have maintained his relationship with Curtis.

Instead, Bok poured his idealism into reforms that
were economically and ideologically compatible with
middle-class respectability and a capitalist economy.
His crusade against patent medicines, his support for
the kindergarten movement, his constant concern for
child welfare, and his campaign for urban beautifica-
tion were consistent with the Progressive spirit in trying to create a more virtuous and principled nation
while leaving its business institutions intact. Many of
his activities, including his advocacy of architectural
renewal in the "City Beautiful" movement, were calculated to promote economic growth. His reformism
reflected a growing realization among entrepreneurs
that unregulated competition was inimical to the best
interests of a capitalist civilization. He participated in
what historian Robert Wiebe has called a "search for
order" in a country trying to escape seemingly endless

[31]Vernon Louis Parrington, *The Beginnings of Critical Realism
in America,* Vol. 3 of *Main Currents in American Thought* (New
York: Harcourt, Brace and Company, 1930), 245.

Cary William Bok
Courtesy The Hill School

The Lea home in Merion, Pennsylvania

William Curtis Bok
Courtesy The Hill School

Edward Bok *Mary Louise Curtis Bok*

Courtesy Bruccoli, Clark, Layman

cycles of boom and bust that had played havoc with fiscal responsibility and economic progress since the Civil War.[32] It was for this main reason, as well as for Theodore Roosevelt's literary attainments, that Bok admired the twenty-sixth president's "New Nationalism" and the type of Progressive Republicanism he espoused.

Curtis, who was an extremely successful entrepreneur, shared the same concern for mixing profit seeking with practical idealism. Bok and Curtis cemented their business relationship at an even deeper level on 22 October 1896, when Bok married Curtis's only child, Mary Louise. The union resulted in two sons (William Curtis Bok and Cary William Bok). Bok also wrote an admiring biography of Curtis, *A Man from Maine,* praising his commitment to ethical standards that went above mere money mongering. Bok deeply admired Curtis's genius as a visionary promoter. "The fact must never be forgotten," Bok declared in one of his editorials, "that no magazine published in the United States could give what it is giving to the reader each month if it were not for the revenue which the advertiser brings the magazine. It is the growth of advertising in this country which . . . has brought the American magazine to its present enviable position in literary, illustrative, and mechanical excellence. The

[32]Robert Wiebe, *Businessmen and Reform: A Study of the Progressive Movement* (Cambridge, Mass.: Harvard University Press, 1962).

American advertiser had made the superior American magazine of today possible."[33]

Curtis's ethical sense was epitomized by twenty-one principles he set forth in 1910 about the quality of advertising he would permit in the magazines that he owned. The principles he espoused were characteristic of the "search for order" in which he and like-minded businessmen were engaged in the high noon of the Progressive Era:[34]

1. Exclusion of all advertising intended to defraud.
2. Exclusion of all extravagantly worded advertisements.
3. Exclusion of all knocking copy.[35]
4. No medical or curative advertisements.[36]
5. No advertisements for alcoholic liquors.
6. No general mail-order advertising.
7. Scrutiny of all installment advertisements.
8. No immoral or suggestive advertisements.
9. No cheap or vulgar advertisements.
10. No blind advertisements.[37]
11. No answers to advertisements to be sent to publisher.

[33] Quoted in Wood, *The Curtis Magazines,* 27.
[34] These principles are taken *verbatim* from ibid, 65–66.
[35] Advertising intended to reflect adversely on competitors.
[36] Consistent with Bok's outspoken attacks against the patent medicine industry.
[37] Advertisements that do not reveal the identity of the advertiser.

12. No quotes from the editorial matter in Curtis magazines to be used in any advertising copy.
13. No advertisements for boys or girls to work as agents.
14. "Free" to be used only if an advertising offer is actually free.
15. Prize competition terms to be submitted in advance for inspection by the publisher.
16. No illustrations of stamps or coins.
17. No use of copyrighted material unless permission obtained in advance.
18. No speculative real estate advertisements.
19. No use of the name of The Curtis Publishing Company as a responsible reference.
20. No use of the names of Curtis publications as endorsements.
21. No insertion of foreign matter between the pages of any Curtis magazines.

These standards governed what had become a much larger publishing empire than the one Bok had joined in 1889. In 1897, wishing to create a new periodical that would emulate the achievements of the *Journal,* Curtis decided to buy a floundering magazine, *The Saturday Evening Post,* and transform it into a mass circulation bonanza. He wanted the *Post* to be ostensibly for men but actually for both men and women, making it a mirror image of the *Journal.*[38]

[38]Wood, *The Curtis Magazines,* 37.

To edit the *Post,* Curtis chose George Horace Lorimer, a man with a background similar to that of Bok except for his American nativity. Born in Kentucky in 1867, Lorimer had worked for Chicago meat packer Philip D. Armour just as Bok had clerked for Jay Gould. Like Bok, Lorimer had a flair for advertising. Despite having spent some time in college, he was basically self-educated. Most of his knowledge of books came from browsing in the well-stocked library of his father, a Baptist minister. Lorimer also shared Bok's background in journalism, having held a job as a newspaper reporter in Boston. Like Bok, he joined Curtis's publishing empire at a young age. He had an evangelical style he had learned from hearing his father preach, and a strongly pro-business attitude similar to that of Bok.

After becoming editor-in-chief of the *Post* in 1899, Lorimer, like Bok, successfully pursued articles by well-known writers including Ring Lardner, Jack London, and Booth Tarkington. The main difference between the two men was that Lorimer wanted action and success stories that would appeal to a masculine audience.

Perhaps because they were too similar to one another, Lorimer and Bok did not get along. Despite Lorimer's best efforts, the *Post* did not initially prosper, and Curtis covered its losses by drawing on profits accrued by the *Journal.* Bok naturally resented this policy. His ill feeling only increased when the *Post* began to succeed, intensifying his rivalry with Lorimer.

The Saturday Evening Post, *boasting
of circulation growth*

George Horace Lorimer, editor,
The Saturday Evening Post

Courtesy The Curtis Publishing Company

xlix

In 1902, after incurring losses of $1,350,000, all paid by the *Journal*, the *Post* suddenly took off and became the mass circulation magazine for which Curtis had hoped. By 1908, it had a circulation of 1,000,000.

Still, the growth of Curtis's empire, which expanded with the purchase of yet another magazine, *Country Gentleman*, brought fresh rewards for Bok. Buoyed by the sensational success of the *Journal* and *Post*, Curtis built an enormous new building on Philadelphia's Independence Square, covering an entire city block. Bok, entrusted with decorating the building, secured the joint services of Louis C. Tiffany and Maxfield Parrish. Bok's reward for persistence was a large walnut-paneled office on the corner of the seventh floor with a massive fireplace, the only one in the building that actually worked. Other visual accoutrements showed how far a poor young immigrant had come from his early days in Brooklyn. An impressive Chinese court rug covered the floor. One of the walls featured a large reproduction in oil of Rembrandt's "Dutch Masters," forming a fitting picture for a boy from The Netherlands who had made a fortune in America. "Hair parted boyishly in the middle, white handkerchief protruding from his breast pocket, stickpin in the cravat tied with something of a flourish," stated a historian of The Curtis Publishing Company, "Edward Bok worked at a graceful desk with delicately carved legs."[39]

[39]Ibid., 57.

Bok had reached the pinnacle of his career, but frustrations continued to detract from the satisfactions he felt in his work. His resentment toward Lorimer and the *Post* was only one source of discontent. He was disillusioned by the way women had responded to one of his reformist crusades, an effort to spare the lives of baby egrets by having the importation of ai-grettes (plumes used to adorn ladies' hats) legally banned. He had counted on maternal instincts to sway female readers, only to find that they were more con-cerned about being stylishly dressed than about the slaughter of mother egrets, leaving their babies to starve. Bok was not a misogynist. Had this been true he could not have succeeded in building the *Journal* into a mass circulation magazine. As usual, he had merely taken too idealistic a view of women, who were only human. Failing to persuade them to spare the lives of baby egrets, he took satisfaction in mustering support for his humanitarian crusade among men, re-sulting in the passage of legislation aimed at stopping a cruel process he rightly abhorred.

The growing power of the woman's suffrage move-ment also distressed Bok, who continued, albeit more and more privately, to think that a proper lady should shun something as degrading as the political process. Only recently this attitude had even been manifested in upper-class society toward males who took part in partisan activities that seemed unsuitable for persons of refinement. Theodore Roosevelt had encountered strong opposition among his patrician relatives in the

1880s when he started to attend Republican meetings
at Morton Hall, a "grimy, smelly clubhouse above a
saloon on Fifty-ninth Street" in New York City, per-
vaded by cigar smoke, ribaldry, and uncouth behavior.[40] Why, Bok wondered, should women of quality
sully themselves when they could more suitably elevate society by setting an example of civilized conduct? Even though he stopped overtly opposing
granting women the right to vote, his convictions remained unchanged. He was increasingly out of step
with the times.

Bok had planned to retire in 1913 when he reached
age fifty, but the onset of World War I and America's
ultimate entry into that conflict led him to persevere in
his post. When German forces invaded and overran
Belgium in 1914, he became an ardent supporter of
Herbert Hoover's efforts to feed and clothe its people.
After the United States formally became a belligerent
in April 1917, Bok devoted himself and the *Journal*
unreservedly to the war effort. Because the magazine
had always been intended to appeal to both women
and men, there was nothing anomalous about distributing it among American troops in France. Nor was it
surprising that articles dealt with such subjects as the
heroic record of an elite French fighter squadron, the
Cignones (storks), and the exploits of pilots who belonged to the unit. By the time the article appeared in

---

[40]H. W. Brands, *T. R.: The Last Romantic* (New York: Basic
Books, 1997), 123.

September 1918, Bok was in France observing conditions on the Western Front as the guest of Lord Northcliffe, the British information minister.

Bok's tenure at the helm of the *Journal* was almost over when he came home from France. His name appeared for the last time as editor on the December 1919 issue, at which time the magazine had a circulation of more than 2,000,000. It was an opportune moment for him to step down. Throughout his career he had stood for a practical idealism that was no longer in vogue. The Flapper Era had begun and a Lost Generation had emerged, one whose members had "grown up to find all gods dead, all wars fought, all faith in man shaken," as F. Scott Fitzgerald declared in his novel *This Side of Paradise.* There was little cultural breathing room for Bok in an ambiance in which women wore short skirts, danced the Charleston, smoked publicly, and violated sexual mores that he and his peers had considered sacred.

The literary scene was also changing for the worse as far as Bok was concerned. The tough, staccato prose of Hemingway's *A Farewell to Arms* and the hard-boiled crime stories of Dashiell Hammett, filled with the "gritty argot of the streets,"[41] came from a different world from the one to which Bok was accustomed. Strewn throughout the pages of *The Americanization of Edward Bok* are the names of writers

[41] William F. Nolan, Introduction to Kirby McCauley et al., *Nightmare Town: Dashiell Hammett Stories* (New York: Alfred A. Knopf, 1999), xi.

whom he admired and with whom he had been proud
to associate: Eugene Field, Hamilton Mabie, James
Whitcomb Riley, and Henry van Dyke, to name but a
few. Virtually all of them passed quickly into oblivion
with what Henry F. May aptly described as "The End
of American Innocence."

Still, Bok remained a power in the Curtis publishing empire. "His tailored English jackets were much
in evidence about Independence Square," wrote
James Playsted Wood. "His voice was loud and clear
at the head table in the executive dining room."[42] *The
Americanization of Edward Bok* won the Pulitzer Prize
in 1921, adding further luster to his image.

Bok's friends wondered how he could retire in his
mid-fifties, when his health was still robust, and avoid
a life of boredom. They need not have worried. In
1925, six years after he had stepped down from his editorial responsibilities, he reported that he had enjoyed "unexampled activity, better health, more vigor
at the end than at the beginning, and a satisfaction
with life not known before." Looking ahead in 1919, he
had entertained "wonderful dreams of leisure time
when I would read and study and idle and travel." Instead, he poured his energy into a multitude of causes
like the University Extension Society, which provided
Philadelphians an annual series of cultural events offering "the best in music, the drama, the opera, liter-

[42]Strauss and Howe, *Generations,* 247–260; Wood, *The Curtis
Magazines,* 84.

ature, and the highest form of entertainments of all kinds." He also supported the City Club, an organization for men, the Civic Club, a similar entity for women, and the Academy of Music Corporation, which owned the building in which the Forum held its events. He endowed prizes for firefighters and police officers who had displayed conspicuous bravery. He created an annual $10,000 award for distinguished public service to Philadelphia, which he proudly called "a Nobel Prize adapted to the interests of a city." He gave Harvard University funding for yet another series of prizes recognizing excellence in advertising. In 1922, he established the American Peace Award, a $50,000 prize for the best plan submitted to a distinguished twelve-person jury for bringing an end to war.[43]

Bok also created a permanent physical monument to his ideals. In 1914, Frederick Law Olmsted, Jr., son of America's foremost landscape architect, had visited a desolate eminence, "Iron Mountain," near Lake Wales, Florida, midway between the Atlantic Ocean and the Gulf of Mexico. Eight years later, with Bok's financial support, Olmsted started laying out what became the Mountain Lake Sanctuary and Singing Tower, beginning with bringing copious quantities of water to the site. Soon the property was covered with thousands of azaleas, irises, dogwoods, and magnolia

[43]Bok, *Twice Thirty*, 421–479. Eleanor Roosevelt was a member of the jury that decided the winner of the Peace Award.

Former President Calvin Coolidge and Mrs. Coolidge and the
Boks at the dedication of Bok Tower Gardens, 1929

Courtesy Bok Tower Gardens, Lake Wales, Florida

Carillon Tower at Bok Tower Gardens

Courtesy Temple University Libraries/Urban Archives

trees. Ducks swam in the two man-made lakes and flamingoes lived along the banks. The forty-mile view from the site, the highest point in Florida, presented a "wonderful panorama" of the surrounding country-side, with the Atlantic Ocean to the east and the Gulf of Mexico on the west.

Dominating the grounds was what Bok called "the most beautiful Carillon Tower in the world, with a carillon of bells second to none in the United States or Europe." Two hundred and five feet high, and resting on 160 reinforced concrete piles, it was built in Gothic style and faced with Georgia pink marble and Florida coquina rock of the type used by the Spanish to build their original fortifications in Florida. Eight windows in the octagonal top of the structure were of a "Gothic lace pattern worked in faience," behind which were the bells. "When you hear the carillon at the Sanctuary send out its glorious melodies from the Tower's heights," Bok wrote, "you lose the idea of the Tower as just a building, or of the bells as bells. Instead you feel the whole unit alive, a wonderful singing force, the noblest expression of democratic music, a true Singing Tower."[44]

Bok's description of the sanctuary appeared in a 1929 issue of *Scribner's,* the magazine he had helped create in the now distant past. His words suggest that the "Island of Nightingales" about which he wrote in

---

[44]Edward W. Bok, *America's Taj Mahal: The Singing Tower of Florida,* republished ed. (Lake Wales, Fla: Bok Tower Gardens Foundation, 1989).

the opening pages of *The Americanization of Edward Bok* did not really depict a nonexistent Dutch paradise that his grandfather had created off the Dutch coast. Instead, his "Introduction of Two Persons" was a forecast of the earthly paradise he was planning with Olmsted. On 1 February 1929, former President Calvin Coolidge and his wife, Grace, dedicated the sanctuary and signed their names in a maroon leather guest book. Among later signatories was Bok's two-year-old grandson, Derek, who inscribed a trembling "X" in place of a signature he was incapable of writing. Derek Bok later became president of Harvard University.

Edward Bok died on 9 January 1930. Curtis survived only a short while longer, dying in 1932. Both men were giants of American journalism who effectively complemented each other's talents in building a great publishing empire. Curtis, a visionary entrepreneur, had founded the venture, but Bok's creative contribution was no less fundamental. His Florida sanctuary would honor his name among future generations, fulfilling his motto, "Make you the world a bit more beautiful and better because you have been in it."

W. David Lewis

Auburn University
April 2000

The Americanization of Edward Bok

AN EXPLANATION

THIS BOOK was to have been written in 1914, when I foresaw some leisure to write it, for I then intended to retire from active editorship. But the war came, an entirely new set of duties commanded, and the project was laid aside.

Its title and the form, however, were then chosen. By the form I refer particularly to the use of the third person. I had always felt the most effective method of writing an autobiography, for the sake of a better perspective, was mentally to separate the writer from his subject by this device.

Moreover, this method came to me very naturally in dealing with the Edward Bok, editor and publicist, whom I have tried to describe in this book, because in many respects he has had and has been a personality apart from my private self. I have again and again found myself watching with intense amusement and interest the Edward Bok of this book at work. I have, in turn, applauded him and criticized him, as I do in this book. Not that I ever considered myself bigger or broader than this Edward Bok: simply that he was different. His tastes, his outlook, his manner of looking at things were totally at variance with my own. In fact, my chief difficulty during Edward Bok's directorship of *The Ladies' Home Journal* was to abstain from breaking through the editor and revealing my real self.

Several times I did so, and each time I saw how

different was the effect from that when the editorial Edward Bok had been allowed sway. Little by little I learned to subordinate myself and to let him have full rein.

But no relief of my life was so great to me personally as his decision to retire from his editorship. My family and friends were surprised and amused by my intense and obvious relief when he did so. Only to those closest to me could I explain the reason for the sense of absolute freedom and gratitude that I felt.

Since that time my feelings have been an interesting study to myself. There are no longer two personalities. The Edward Bok of whom I have written has passed out of my being as completely as if he had never been there, save for the records and files on my library shelves. It is easy, therefore, for me to write of him as a personality apart: in fact, I could not depict him from any other point of view. To write of him in the first person, as if he were myself, is impossible, for he is not.

The title suggests my principal reason for writing the book. Every life has some interest and significance; mine, perhaps, a special one. Here was a little Dutch boy unceremoniously set down in America, unable to make himself understood or even to know what persons were saying; his education was extremely limited, practically negligible; and yet, by some curious decree of fate, he was destined to write, for a period of years, to the largest body of readers ever addressed by an American editor—the circulation of the magazine he edited running into figures previously unheard of in periodical literature. He made no pretense to style or even to composition: his grammar was faulty, as it was natural it should be, in a language not his own. His roots never went deep, for the intellectual soil had not been favorable to their growth—yet, it must be confessed, he achieved.

But how all this came about, how such a boy, with every disadvantage to overcome, was able, apparently, to "make good"—this possesses an interest and for some, perhaps, a value which, after all, is the only reason for any book.

EDWARD W. BOK

Merion, Pennsylvania
1920

AN INTRODUCTION OF
TWO PERSONS

A LONG an island in the North Sea, five miles from the Dutch coast, stretches a dangerous ledge of rocks that has proved the graveyard of many a vessel sailing that turbulent sea. On this island once lived a group of men who, as each vessel was wrecked, looted the vessel and murdered those of the crew who reached shore. The government of The Netherlands decided to exterminate the island pirates, and for the job King William selected a young lawyer at The Hague.[1]

"I want you to clean up that island," was the royal order. It was a formidable job for a young man of twenty-odd years. By royal proclamation he was made mayor of the island, and within a year, a court of law

---

[1]The young lawyer is Bok's grandfather, Willem Bok (1800-1872). He was appointed notary public (a post that required a royal decree) in a village on the island of Texel ("this island") in 1827. After that he was secretary of the municipality and *opper-strandvonder* (head wreckmaster). Contrary to the impression given by Bok, the island of Texel was well developed before the nineteenth century. Under Dutch law, goods that washed ashore from shipwrecks were sold by an official for the benefit of the government, but a modest part of the proceeds went to the finders. Because the finder's share was small, people were motivated to keep the goods for themselves, but this activity is hardly the piracy Bok describes in his highly romanticized account, nor is it likely that murders took place in connection with it. Willem Bok also studied at the University of Leiden, graduated in 1833, and became an attorney at the Dutch Supreme Court and held various other important regional governmental posts in his lifetime.

7

being established, the young attorney was appointed judge; and in that dual capacity he "cleaned up" the island.

The young man now decided to settle on the island, and began to look around for a home. It was a grim place, barren of tree or living green of any kind; it was as if a man had been exiled to Siberia. Still, argued the young mayor, an ugly place is ugly only because it is not beautiful. And beautiful he determined this island should be.

One day the young mayor-judge called together his council. "We must have trees," he said, "we can make this island a spot of beauty if we will!" But the practical seafaring men demurred; the little money they had was needed for matters far more urgent than trees.

"Very well," was the mayor's decision—and little they guessed what the words were destined to mean— "I will do it myself." And that year he planted 100 trees, the first the island had ever seen.

"Too cold," said the islanders, "the severe north winds and storms will kill them all."

"Then I will plant more," said the unperturbed mayor. And for the fifty years that he lived on the island he did so. He planted trees each year; and, moreover, he had deeded to the island government land which he turned into public squares and parks, and where each spring he set out shrubs and plants.

Moistened by the salt mist, the trees did not wither but grew prodigiously. In all that expanse of turbulent sea—and only those who have seen the North Sea in a storm know how turbulent it can be—there was not a foot of ground on which the birds, storm-driven across the water waste, could rest in their flight. Hundreds of dead birds often covered the surface of the sea. Then one day the trees had grown tall enough to look over the sea, and, spent and driven, the first birds came and rested in their leafy shelter. And others came and found protection, and gave their gratitude vent in song. Within a few years so many birds had discovered the trees on this new island home that they attracted the attention not only of the native islanders but also of the people on the shore fives miles distant, and the island became famous as the home of the rarest and most beautiful birds. So grateful were the birds for their resting place that they chose one end of the island as a special spot for the laying of their eggs and the raising of their young, and they fairly peopled it. It was not long before ornithologists from various parts of the world came to "Eggland," as the farthermost point of the island came to be known, to see the marvelous sight, not of thousands but of hundreds of thousands of bird eggs.

A pair of storm-driven nightingales had now found the island and mated there; their wonderful notes thrilled even the souls of the natives; and as dusk fell upon the seabound strip of land, the women and children would come to listen to the evening notes of the birds of golden song. The two nightingales soon grew into a colony, and within a few years so rich was the island in its nightingales that over to the Dutch coast and throughout the land and into other countries spread the fame of "The Island of Nightingales."

Meantime, the young mayor-judge, grown to manhood, had kept on planting trees each year, setting out his shrubbery and plants, until their verdure now beautifully shaded the quaint, narrow lanes, and transformed into cool wooded roads what once had been only barren sun-baked wastes. Artists began to hear of the place and brought their canvases, and on the walls of hundreds of homes throughout the world hang today bits of the beautiful lanes and wooded spots of "The Island of Nightingales." The American artist William M. Chase took his pupils there almost annually. "In all the world today," he declared to his students, as they exclaimed at the natural restfulness of the island, "there is no more beautiful place."

The trees are now majestic in their height of forty or more feet, for it is nearly a hundred years since the young attorney went to the island and planted the first tree; today the churchyard where he lies is a bower of cool green, with the trees that he planted dropping their moisture on the lichen-covered stones on his grave.

This much did one man do. But he did more.

After he had been on the barren island two years, he went to the mainland one day, and brought back with him a bride. It was a bleak place for a bridal home, but the young wife had the qualities of the husband. "While you raise your trees," she said, "I will raise our children." And within a score of years the young bride sent thirteen happy-faced, well-brought-up children over that island, and there was reared a home such as is given to few. Said a man who subsequently married a daughter of that home: "It was such a home that once you had been in it you felt you must be of it, and that if you couldn't marry one of the daughters you would have been glad to have married the cook."

One day when the children had grown to man's and woman's estate, the mother[2] called them all together and said to them, "I want to tell you the story of your father and of this island," and she told them the simple story that is written here.

"And now," she said, "as you go out into the world I want each of you to take with you the spirit of your father's work, and each in your own way and place, to do as he has done: make you the world a bit more beautiful and better because you have been in it. That is your mother's message to you."

The first son[3] to leave the island home went with a band of hardy men to South Africa, where they settled and became known as "the Boers." Tirelessly they worked at the colony until towns and cities sprang up and a new nation came into being: The Transvaal Republic. The son became secretary of state of the new country, and today the United States of South Africa

[2]the mother: Bok's grandmother was Welmoet Tideman, whose father was a Dutch civil servant.
[3]first son: Willem Eduard Bok (fourth son in birth order) became a commissioner in Zaandam before emigrating in 1876 to Pretoria in South Africa. There he became secretary of state of the Republic of South Africa and received various honors.

bears tribute, in part, to the mother's message to all of her children "make the world a bit more beautiful and better."

The second son[4] left home for the Dutch mainland, where he took charge of a small parish; and when he had finished his work he was mourned by king and peasant as one of the leading clergymen of his time and people.

A third son,[5] scorning his own safety, plunged into the boiling surf on one of those nights of terror so common to that coast, rescued a half-dead sailor, carried him to his father's house, and brought him back to a life of usefulness that gave the world a record of imperishable value. For the half-drowned sailor was Heinrich Schliemann, the famous explorer of the dead cities of Troy.[6]

The first daughter[7] now left the island nest; to her inspiration her husband owed, at his life's close, a shelf of works in philosophy which today are among the standard books of their class.

[4]second son: Dr. Johannes Wilhelmus Bok became a minister in the *Remonstrantse Broedershap* (the Brotherhood of Remonstrants), an upper-class church.

[5]third son: refers to Willem Eduard Bruno Bok, born in 1833.

[6]German Archeologist Heinrich Schliemann discovered the royal tombs at Mycenae and located the site of the ancient city of Troy.

[7]first daughter: refers to Welmoet Pauline Bok (actually the third daughter and sixth child in birth sequence). She married Dr. Thomas Theodorus Hendrikus Jorissen, who won an honorary doctorate in letters from the University of Leiden and taught history at the University of Amsterdam.

The second daughter[8] worked beside her husband until she brought him to be regarded as one of the ablest preachers of his land, speaking for more than forty years the message of man's betterment.

To another son it was given to sit wisely in the councils of his land; another followed the footsteps of his father.[9] Another daughter, refusing marriage for duty, ministered unto and made a home for one whose eyes could see not.[10]

So they went out into the world, the girls and boys of that island home, each carrying the story of their father's simple but beautiful work and the remembrance of their mother's message. Not one from that home but did well his or her work in the world; some greater, some smaller, but each left behind the traces of a life well spent.

[8]second daughter: presumably Alida Johanna Geertruida Welmoet Bok, who married Dr. Johannes Dyserinck, who received an honorary doctorate in theology from the University of Leiden and was a preacher in Dutch Baptist churches at Den Helder, Vlissingen, and Rotterdam.

[9]The son who sat "wisely in councils of his land" was Edward Bok's father, Willem Jan Hidde Bok; and the son who "followed the footsteps of his father" was Willem Henri Bruno Bok, who became a notary at Den Burg.

[10]The daughter who refused marriage was presumably Henrietta Elisabeth Welmoet Bok, twin sister of Alida. Other sisters included Welmoet Catharina Bok, the eldest of the daughters, who married a commissioner of grain in Zaandam; Maria Geertruida Welmoet Bok, second daughter, who married a marine engineer; Theodora Joanna Welmoet Bok, who married a distinguished Amsterdam merchant; and Anna Elisabeth Welmoet Bok, who died within a year of her birth.

And, as all good work is immortal, so today all over the world goes on the influence of this one man and one woman, whose life on that little Dutch island changed its barren rocks to a bower of verdure, a home for the birds and the song of the nightingale. The grandchildren have gone to the four corners of the globe, and are now the generation of workers— some in the far East Indies; others in Africa; and still others in our own land of America. But each has tried, according to the talents given, to carry out the message of that day, to tell the story of the grandfather's work; just as it is told here by the author of this book, who, in the efforts of his later years, has tried to carry out, so far as opportunity has come to him, the message of his grandmother:

"Make you the world a bit more beautiful and better because you have been in it."

I

The First Days in America

THE LEVIATHAN of the Atlantic Ocean, in 1870, was
The Queen, and when she was warped into her
dock on 20 September of that year, she discharged,
among her passengers, a family of four from The
Netherlands who were to make an experiment of
Americanization.

The father,[1] a man bearing one of the most respected names in The Netherlands, had acquired
wealth and position for himself; unwise investments,
however, had swept away his fortune, and in preference to a new start in his own land, he had decided to
make the new beginning in the United States, where
a favorite brother-in-law had gone several years before. But that, never a simple matter for a man who has
reached forty-two, is particularly difficult for a foreigner in a strange land. This fact he and his wife were

---

[1]father: Willem Jan Hidde Bok, Edward's father, made a large
fortune in investments but lost it in disastrous speculations. Two
of Bok's brothers advanced him funds, but he lost these too and
was forced to flee to London to escape creditors. He emigrated in
1870 to Brooklyn, New York, where he and his family found lodg-
ings in an apartment building. His remaining European assets
were sold in 1871 to pay his debts. After failing to succeed as an insurance salesman, he became a translator for Western Union in
New York City. He died in 1881.

to find out. The wife,[2] also carefully reared, had been accustomed to a scale of living which she had now to abandon. Her Americanization experiment was to compel her, for the first time in her life, to become a housekeeper without domestic help. There were two boys: the elder, William,[3] was eight and a half years of age; the younger, in nineteen days from his landing date, was to celebrate his seventh birthday.

This younger boy was Edward William Bok. He had, according to the Dutch custom, two other names, but he had decided to leave those in The Netherlands. And the American public was, in later years, to omit for him the "William."

Edward's first six days in the United States were spent in New York, and then he was taken to Brooklyn,[4] where he was destined to live for nearly twenty years.

Thanks to the linguistic sense inherent in the Dutch, and to an educational system that compels the

[2]wife: Sieke Geertruida van Herwerden Bok, Edward's mother, was born at Den Helder in 1837. She died in Philadelphia, Pennsylvania, in 1907.

[3]Edward Bok's elder brother, Willem Joannes Bruno Eduard Hidde Bok, was born at Den Helder in 1861. In the United States he became known as William John Bok. In Brooklyn, he was manager of the Bok Syndicate Press established by his brother Edward. He died in Philadelphia in 1935.

[4]Brooklyn was an independent municipality and the nation's third-largest city (after New York and Philadelphia) until 1898, when it became a borough of New York City. Its history can be traced to the Dutch settlement of Breuckelyn in 1636. Completion in 1883 of the Brooklyn Bridge hastened its annexation to New York City.

Edward Bok, six years old

study of languages, English was already familiar to the father and mother. But to the two sons, who had barely learned the beginnings of their native tongue, the English language was as a closed book. It seemed a cruel decision of the father to put his two boys into a public school in Brooklyn, but he argued that if they were to become Americans, the sooner they became part of the life of the country and learned its language for themselves, the better. And so, without the ability to make known the slightest want or to understand a single word, the morning after their removal to Brooklyn, the two boys were taken to a public school.

The American boy of 1870 is not a whit less cruel than is the American boy of 1920; and he was none the loath to show that cruelty. This trait was evident at the first recess of the first day at school. At the dismissal, the brothers naturally sought each other, only to find themselves surrounded by a group of tormentors. Edward seemed to look particularly inviting, and nicknaming him "Dutchy" they devoted themselves at each noon recess and after school to inflicting their cruelties upon him.

Louis XIV may have been right when he said that "every new language requires a new soul," but Edward Bok knew that while spoken languages might differ, there is one language understood by boys the world over. And with this language Edward decided to do some experimenting. After a few days at school he cast his eyes over the group of his tormentors, picked out one who seemed to him the ringleader, and before the boy was aware of what had happened Edward Bok was in the full swing of his first real experiment with Americanization. Of course the American boy retaliated. But the boy from The Netherlands had not been born and brought up in the muscle-building air of the Dutch dikes for nothing, and after a few moments he found himself looking down on his tormentor and into the eyes of a crowd of very respectful boys and giggling girls who readily made a passageway for his brother and himself.

At the best, they were difficult days at school for a young boy without the language. But the national linguistic gift inherent in the Dutch race came to the boy's rescue, and as the roots of the Anglo-Saxon lie in the Frisian tongue, and thus in the language of his native country, Edward soon found that with a change of vowel here and there the English language was not so difficult a conquest. At all events, he then set out to master it.

But his fatal gift of editing, although its possession was unknown to him, began to assert itself when, just as he seemed to be getting along fairly well, he balked at following the Spencerian style of writing in his copy-books. Instinctively he rebelled at the flourishes which embellished that form of handwriting. He seemed to divine somehow that such penmanship could not be useful or practicable for after life, and so, with that Dutch stolidity that, once fixed, knows no altering, he refused to copy his writing lessons.

Sample of Spencerian style in vogue at this period

Trouble immediately ensued between Edward and his teacher. Finding herself against a literal blank wall—for Edward simply refused, but had not the gift of English with which to explain his refusal—the teacher decided to take the matter to the male principal of the school. She explained that she had kept Edward after school for as long as two hours to compel him to copy his Spencerian lesson, but that the boy simply sat quiet. He was perfectly well-behaved, she explained, but as to his lesson, he would attempt absolutely nothing.

It was the prevailing custom in the public schools of 1870 to punish boys by making them hold out the palms of their hands, upon which the principal would inflict blows with a rattan. The first time Edward was punished in this way, his hand became so swollen he wondered at a system of punishment which rendered him incapable of writing, particularly as the discerning principal had chosen the boy's right hand upon which to rain the blows. Edward was told to sit down at the principal's own desk and copy the lesson. He sat, but he did not write. He would not for one thing, and he could not if he would. After half an hour of purposeless sitting, the principal ordered Edward again to stand up and hold out his hand; and once more the rattan fell in repeated blows. Of course it did no good, and as it was then five o'clock, and the principal had inflicted all the punishment that the law allowed, and as he probably wanted to go home as much as Edward did, he dismissed the sore-handed but more-than-ever determined Dutch boy.

Edward went home to his father, exhibited his swollen hand, explained the reason, and showed the penmanship lesson which he had refused to copy. It is a singular fact that even at that age he already understood Americanization enough to realize that to cope successfully with any American institution, one must be constructive as well as destructive. He went to his room, brought out a specimen of Italian handwriting he had seen in a newspaper, and explained to his father that this simpler penmanship seemed to him better for practical purposes than the curlicue fancifully embroidered Spencerian style; that if he had to learn penmanship, why not learn the system that was of more possible use in after life?

Now, your Dutchman is nothing if not practical. He is very simple and direct in his nature, and is very likely to be equally so in his mental view. Edward's father was distinctly interested—very much amused, as he confessed to the boy in later years—in his son's discernment of the futility of the Spencerian style of penmanship. He agreed with the boy and, next morning, accompanied him to school and to the principal. The two men were closeted together, and when they came out Edward was sent to his classroom. For some weeks he was given no penmanship lessons, and then a new copy-book was given him with a much simpler style. He pounced upon it and within a short time stood at the head of his class in writing.

The same instinct that was so often to lead Edward aright in his future life, at its very beginning, served him in a singularly valuable way in directing his attention to the study of penmanship; for it was through his legible handwriting that later, in the absence of the typewriter, he was able to secure and satisfactorily fill three positions which were to lead to his final success.

Unbusy Unchary Yearling

Sample of Spencerian style now in vogue

Years afterward Edward had the satisfaction of seeing public-school pupils given a choice of penmanship lessons: one along the flourish lines and the other of a less ornate order. Of course, the boy never associated the incident of his refusal with the change until later when his mother explained to him that the principal of the school, of whom the father had made a warm friend, was so impressed by the boy's simple but correct view, that he took up the matter with the board of education, and a choice of systems was considered and later decided upon.

From this it will be seen that, unconsciously, Edward Bok had started upon his career of editing!

II

The First Job:
Fifty Cents a Week

THE ELDER Bok did not find his "lines cast in pleasant places"[1] in the United States. He found himself, professionally, unable to adjust the methods of his own land of a lifetime to those of a new country. As a result the fortunes of the transplanted family did not flourish, and Edward soon saw his mother physically failing under burdens to which her nature was not accustomed nor her hands trained. Then he and his brother decided to relieve their mother in the housework by rising early in the morning, building the fire, preparing breakfast, and washing the dishes before they went to school. After school they gave up their play hours, and swept and scrubbed, and helped their mother to prepare the evening meal and wash the dishes afterward. It was a curious coincidence that it should fall upon Edward thus to get a first-hand knowledge of woman's housework, which was to stand him in such practical stead in later years.

It was not easy for the parents to see their boys thus forced to do work which only a short while before had been done by a retinue of servants. And the capstone

[1]Reference is to Psalm 16, v. 6: "The lines are fallen unto me in pleasant places; yea, I have a goodly heritage."

of humiliation seemed to be when Edward and his brother, after having for several mornings found no kindling wood or coal to build the fire, decided to go out of evenings with a basket and pick up what wood they could find in neighboring lots, and the bits of coal spilled from the coal-bin of the grocery store, or left on the curbs before the houses where coal had been delivered. The mother remonstrated with the boys, although in her heart she knew that the necessity was upon them. But Edward had been started upon his Americanization career and answered: "This is America, where one can do anything if it is honest. So long as we don't steal the wood or coal, why shouldn't we get it?" And, turning away, the saddened mother said nothing.

But while the doing of these homely chores was very effective in relieving the untrained and tired mother, it added little to the family income. Edward looked about and decided that the time had come for him, young as he was, to begin some sort of wage-earning. But how and where? The answer he found one afternoon when standing before the shop window of a baker in the neighborhood. The owner of the bakery, who had just placed in the window a series of trays filled with buns, tarts, and pies, came outside to look at the display. He found the hungry boy wistfully regarding the tempting-looking wares.

"Look pretty good, don't they?" asked the baker.

"They certainly would," answered the Dutch boy with his national passion for cleanliness and order, "if only your window were just a bit cleaner, I'd say."

"That's so, too," mused the baker. "Perhaps you'll clean it."

"I will," was the laconic reply. And Edward Bok, there and then got his first job. He went in, found a step-ladder, and put so much Dutch energy into the cleaning of the large show window that the baker immediately arranged with him to clean it every Tuesday and Friday afternoon after school. The salary was to be fifty cents per week!

But one day, after he had finished cleaning the window, and the baker was busy in the rear of the store, a customer came in, and Edward ventured to wait on her. Dexterously he wrapped up for another the fragrant currant-buns for which his young soul—and stomach—so hungered! The baker watched him, saw how quickly and smilingly he served the customer, and offered Edward an extra dollar per week if he would come in afternoons and sell behind the counter. He immediately entered into the bargain with the understanding that, in addition to his salary of a dollar and a half per week, he should each afternoon carry home from the good things unsold a moderate something as a present to his mother. The baker agreed, and Edward promised to come each afternoon except Saturday.

"Want to play ball, hey?" said the baker.

"Yes, I want to play ball," replied the boy, but he was not reserving his Saturday afternoons for games although, boy-like, that might be his preference.

Edward now took on for each Saturday morning—when, of course, there was no school—the delivery route of a weekly paper called the *South Brooklyn Advocate.* He had offered to deliver the neighborhood edition of the paper for one dollar, thus increasing his earnings to two dollars and a half per week.

Transportation, in those days in Brooklyn, was by horse cars, and the car line on Smith Street nearest Edward's home ran to Coney Island. Just around the corner where Edward lived the cars stopped to water the horses on their long haul. The boy noticed that the men jumped from the open cars in summer, ran into the cigar store before which the watering trough was placed, and got a drink of water from the ice-cooler placed near the door. But that was not so easily possible for the women, and they, and especially the children, were forced to take the long ride without a drink. It was this that he had in mind when he reserved his Saturday afternoon to "play ball."

Here was an opening, and Edward decided to fill it. He bought a shining new pail, screwed three hooks on the edge from which he hung three clean shimmering glasses. One Saturday afternoon when a car stopped, the boy leaped on, tactfully asked the conductor if he did not want a drink, and then proceeded to sell his water, cooled with ice, at a cent a glass to the passengers. A little experience showed that he exhausted a pail with every two cars, and each pail netted him thirty cents. Of course Sunday was a most profitable day; and after going to Sunday school in the morning, he did a further Sabbath service for the rest of the day by refreshing tired mothers and thirsty children on the Coney Island cars—at a penny a glass!

But the profit of six dollars which Edward was now reaping in his newly found "bonanza" on Saturday and Sunday afternoons became apparent to other boys, and one Saturday the young ice-water boy found that he had a competitor; then two and soon three. Edward immediately met the challenge; he squeezed half a dozen lemons into each pail of water, added some sugar, tripled his charge, and continued his monopoly by selling "Lemonade, three cents a glass." Soon more passengers were asking for lemonade than for plain drinking water!

One evening Edward went to a party of young people, and his latent journalistic sense whispered to him that his young hostess might like to see her social affair in print. He went home, wrote up the party, being careful to include the name of every boy and girl present, and next morning took the account to the city editor of the *Brooklyn Eagle*,[2] with the sage observation that every name mentioned in that paragraph represented a buyer of the paper who would like to see his or her name in print, and that if the editor had enough of these reports he might very advantageously strengthen the circulation of *The Eagle*. The editor

[2] A Democratic newspaper that began publication in 1841 and was edited for two years by Walt Whitman. By the Civil War it was perhaps the most widely read afternoon newspaper in the United States.

was not slow to see the point and offered Edward three dollars a column for such reports. On his way home, Edward calculated how many parties he would have to attend a week to furnish a column, and decided that he would organize a corps of private reporters himself. Forthwith, he saw every girl and boy he knew, got each to promise to write for him an account of each party he or she attended or gave, and laid great stress on a full recital of names. Within a few weeks, Edward was turning in to *The Eagle* from two to three columns a week; his pay was raised to four dollars a column; the editor was pleased in having started a department that no other paper carried, and the "among those present" at the parties bought the paper and were gratified to see their names.

So everybody was happy, and Edward Bok, as a full-fledged reporter, began his journalistic career.

It is curious how deeply embedded in his nature, even in his earliest years, was the inclination toward the publishing business. The word "curious" is used here because Edward is the first journalist in the Bok family in all the centuries through which it extends in Dutch history. On his father's side, there was a succession of jurists. On the mother's side, not a journalist is visible.

Edward attended the Sunday school of the Carroll Park Methodist Episcopal Church, in Brooklyn, of which a Mr. Elkins was superintendent. One day he learned that Mr. Elkins was associated with the publishing house of Harper and Brothers. Edward had

heard his father speak of *Harper's Weekly*. His father
also brought home an occasional copy of *Harper's
Weekly* and also of *Harper's Magazine*. He had seen
Harper's Young People; the name of Harper and Brothers was on some of his school books; and he pictured
in his mind how wonderful it must be for a man to be
associated with publishers of periodicals that other
people read and books that other folks studied. The
Sunday school superintendent henceforth became a
figure of importance in Edward's eyes. Many a morning the boy hastened from home long before the hour
for school. He seated himself on the steps of the Elkins
house under the pretext of waiting for Mr. Elkins' son
to go to school, but really for the secret purpose of
seeing Mr. Elkins set forth to engage in the momentous
business of making books and periodicals.

But what with helping his mother, tending the
baker's shop in after-school hours, serving his paper
route, plying his street-car trade, and acting as social
reporter, it soon became evident to Edward that he
had not much time to prepare his school lessons. By
a supreme effort, he managed to hold his own in his
class, but no more. Instinctively, he felt that he was
not getting all that he might from his educational opportunities, yet the need for him to add to the family
income was, if anything, becoming greater. The idea
of leaving school was broached to his mother, but she
rebelled. She told the boy that he was earning something now and helping much. Perhaps the tide with
the father would turn and he would find the place to

which his unquestioned talents entitled him. Finally the father did. He associated himself with the Western Union Telegraph Company as translator, a position for which his easy command of languages admirably fitted him. Thus, for a time, the strain upon the family exchequer was lessened.

But the American spirit of initiative had entered deep into the soul of Edward Bok. The brother had left school a year before, and found a place as messenger in a lawyer's office; when one evening Edward heard his father say that the office boy in his department had left, he asked to be allowed to leave school and to apply for the open position, and get the rest of his education in the great world itself. It was not easy for the parents to see the younger son leave school at so early an age, but the boy prevailed.

And so, at the age of thirteen, Edward Bok left school, and on Monday, 7 August 1876, he became office boy in the electrician's department of the Western Union Telegraph Company at six dollars and twenty-five cents per week.

And, as such things will fall out in this curiously strange world, it happened that Edward drew up his chair for the first time to his desk to begin his work on that Monday morning, there had been born in Boston, exactly twelve hours before, a girl-baby who was destined to become his wife. Thus, almost the moment after her birth, Edward Bok started to work for her!

III

The Hunger for Self-Education

WITH SCHOOL DAYS ended, the question of self-education became an absorbing thought with Edward Bok. He had mastered a schoolboy's English, but seven years of public school education was hardly a basis on which to build the work of a lifetime. He saw each day in his duties as office boy some of the foremost men of the time. It was the period of William H. Vanderbilt's[1] ascendancy in Western Union control; and the railroad millionaire and his companions, Hamilton McK. Twombly, James H. Banker, Samuel F. Barger, Alonzo B. Cornell, Augustus Schell, William Orton, were objects of great interest to the young office boy. Then, Alexander Graham Bell and Thomas A. Edison were also constant visitors to the department. He knew that some of these men, too, had been deprived of the advantage of collegiate training, and yet they had risen to the top. But how? The boy decided to read about

[1]William Henry Vanderbilt inherited his father's (Cornelius Vanderbilt) properties, including a controlling interest in the New York Central Railroad. He came to be regarded as the archetypal robber baron, partly because of his famous statement, "The public be damned!" By 1883, he was the richest man in the world, with a fortune approaching $200 million.

these men and others, and find out. He could not, however, afford the separate biographies, so he went to the libraries to find a compendium to authoritatively tell him of all successful men. He found it in Appleton's *Encyclopaedia,* and determining to have only the best, he saved his luncheon money, walked instead of riding the five miles to and from his Brooklyn home, and, after a period of saving, had his reward in the first purchase from his own earnings: a set of the *Encyclopaedia.* He now read about all the successful men, and was encouraged to find that in many cases their beginnings had been as modest as his own, and their opportunities of education as limited.

One day it occurred to him to test the accuracy of the biographies he was reading. James A. Garfield[2] was then spoken of for the presidency; Edward wondered whether it was true that the man who was likely to be president of the United States had once been a boy on the tow-path and, with a simple directness characteristic of his Dutch training, wrote to General Garfield, asking whether the boyhood episode was

[2]James Abram Garfield, twentieth president of the United States, was nominated as a compromise candidate at the 1880 Republican convention. He defeated the Democratic nominee in a closely contested election. After serving less than four months, he was assassinated by Charles J. Guiteau, a disappointed office-seeker. The wording of Bok's passage suggests that he wrote Garfield after his nomination but before his election, because Garfield had not been prominently mentioned for the presidency before being nominated.

true, and explaining why he asked. Of course any public man, no matter how large his correspondence, is pleased to receive an earnest letter from an information-seeking young boy. General Garfield answered warmly and fully. Edward showed the letter to his father, who told the boy that it was valuable and he should keep it. This was a new idea. He followed it further: if one such letter was valuable, how much more valuable would be a hundred! Now, if General Garfield answered him, would not other famous men? Why not begin a collection of autograph letters? Everybody collected something.

Edward had collected postage stamps, and the hobby had, incidentally, helped him wonderfully in his study of geography. Why should not autograph letters from famous persons be of equal service in his struggle for self-education? Not simple autographs— they were meaningless; but actual letters which might tell him something useful. It never occurred to the boy that these men might not answer him.

So he took his *Encyclopaedia*- its trustworthiness now established in his mind by General Garfield's letter—and began to study the lives of successful men and women. Then, with boyish frankness, he wrote on some mooted question in one famous person's life; he asked about the date of some important event in another's, not given in the *Encyclopaedia;* or he asked one man why he did this or why some other man did that.

Most interesting were, of course, the replies. Thus

General Grant[3] sketched on an improvised map the exact spot where General Lee[4] surrendered to him; Longfellow[5] told him how he came to write "Excelsior"; Whittier[6] told the story of "The Barefoot Boy"; Tennyson[7] wrote out a stanza or two of "The Brook," upon condition that Edward would not again use the word "awful," which the poet said "is slang for 'very'" and "I hate slang."

One day the boy received a letter from the Confederate General Jubal A. Early, giving the reason why he burned Chambersburg.[8] A friend visiting Edward's fa-

---

[3]Ulysses S. Grant, Civil War general and eighteenth president of the United States, was in retirement at the time Bok wrote to him.

[4]Robert Edward Lee, the greatest Confederate soldier of the Civil War, accepted the presidency of Washington College, Lexington, Virginia, in the fall of 1865, only a few months after surrendering to Ulysses S. Grant at Appomattox. Lee was convinced that the defeated South should pursue commercial and industrial growth, in contrast to the outlook of ex-Confederate President Jefferson Davis, who believed that the South should remain predominantly agrarian. Lee also advocated peaceful Southern acceptance of the war's outcome and reintegration into the Union.

[5]Henry Wadsworth Longfellow wrote numerous poetic works including "Evangeline," "Hiawatha," "The Courtship of Miles Standish," and "Tales of a Wayside Inn." His verse played a leading role in developing a taste for poetry among the American masses.

[6]John Greenleaf Whittier, a New England Quaker, was a poet and abolitionist. "The Barefoot Boy," beginning with the lines, "Blessings on thee, little man, Barefoot boy, with cheek of tan," was published in 1856.

[7]Alfred, Lord Tennyson, an English poet, was famous for "The Charge of the Light Brigade."

[8]On 30 July 1864, under orders from Major General Jubal A. Early, Confederate raiders led by Brigadier General John McCausland burned Chambersburg, Pennsylvania, in retaliation

ther, happening to see the letter, recognized in it a hitherto-missing bit of history, and suggested that it be published in *The New York Tribune*. The letter attracted wide attention and provoked national discussion.

This suggested to the editor of *The Tribune* that Edward might have other equally interesting letters; so he dispatched a reporter to the boy's home. This reporter was Ripley Hitchcock,[9] who afterward became literary adviser for the Appletons and Harpers.[10] Of course Hitchcock at once saw a "story" in the boy's letters, and within a few days *The Tribune* appeared with a long article on its principal news page giving an

for damage inflicted on the homes of Southern sympathizers by Union forces under Major General David Hunter. Chambersburg sustained damage totaling $1.63 million from the destruction of 559 buildings. Union forces led by Brigadier General William W. Averill pursued the raiders and captured large numbers of them in an attack at Moorefield, West Virginia, on 7 August 1864. Soon after, Union and Confederate forces agreed to stop destroying private property. McCausland went into exile after the war to evade arrest for burning Chambersburg. He returned to the United States in 1867 after warrants against him were cancelled by Ulysses S. Grant, and spent the rest of his life running a farm in West Virginia.

[9]James Ripley Hitchcock, American journalist, was art critic of the New York *Tribune* from 1882–1890, literary adviser of D. Appleton & Co. from 1890–1902, and editor of a seven-volume series, *The Story of the West* (1895–1902).

[10]D. Appleton, a New York publishing firm founded by Daniel Appleton in 1831, issued mainly religious books, British fiction, and children's literature in its early years. After succeeding his father in 1849, William Henry Appleton published works by Charles Darwin, Herbert Spencer, and Edith Wharton. J.J. Harper and Brothers, founded in 1817, expanded rapidly to become the world's largest publishing firm by 1853. It continues to prosper as HarperCollins, one of the world's largest publishing houses.

account of the Brooklyn boy's remarkable letters and how he had secured them. The *Brooklyn Eagle* quickly followed with a request for an interview; the *Boston Globe* followed suit and the *Philadelphia Public Ledger* sent its New York correspondent; before Edward was aware of it, newspapers in different parts of the country were writing about "the well-known Brooklyn autograph collector."

Edward Bok was quick to see the value of the publicity which had so suddenly come to him. He received letters from other autograph collectors all over the country who sought to "exchange" with him. References began to creep into letters from famous persons to whom he had written, saying they had read about his wonderful collection and were proud to be included in it. George W. Childs, of Philadelphia, himself the possessor of probably one of the finest collections of autograph letters in the country, then asked Edward to come to Philadelphia and bring his collection with him—which he did, on the following Sunday, and brought it back greatly enriched.[11]

---

[11]George William Childs was publisher and editor of the *Philadelphia Public Ledger,* which he and a silent partner, Anthony J. Drexel, purchased in 1864. Childs made the *Ledger* a model of excellence in journalism, helped establish Drexel Institute (now Drexel University), and was called "the most notable citizen of Philadelphia since Benjamin Franklin." Like Bok, Childs was an avid autograph collector whose collection included signed documents of every president from George Washington to Benjamin Harrison. Bok devoted much attention to Childs in *The Ladies' Home Journal.*

Several of the writers felt an interest in a boy who frankly told them that he wanted to educate himself, and asked Edward to come and see them. Accordingly, when they lived in New York or Brooklyn, or came to these cities on a visit, he was quick to avail himself of their invitations. He began to note each day in the newspapers the "distinguished arrivals" at the New York hotels; and when any one with whom he had corresponded arrived, Edward would, after business hours, go up-town, pay his respects, and thank him in person for his letters. No person was too high for Edward's boyish approach; President Garfield, General Grant, General Sherman,[12] President Hayes[13]—all

[12]William Tecumseh Sherman, Union general in the Civil War, was best known for his "March to the Sea" through Georgia in 1864.

[13]Rutherford Birchard Hayes, nineteenth president of the United States, served valiantly in the Civil War, in which he was wounded five times and was brevetted as a major general. Elected to the House of Representatives in 1865, he served three years, supported Radical Republican policies, and, as a member of the Joint Committee on the Library, helped develop the Library of Congress into a great institution. He was then elected to three terms as governor of Ohio and played a prominent role in establishing Ohio State University. Nominated by the Republicans for president in 1876, he won the most famous disputed election in American history over Samuel J. Tilden of New York when a fifteen-member bipartisan commission awarded Hayes the electoral votes of Florida, Louisiana, and South Carolina. Despite the controversy aroused by his narrow victory, Hayes was an able chief executive whose greatest achievement was dramatizing the need for awarding federal offices on the basis of merit, resulting ultimately (after he was no longer president) in the passage of the Pendleton Civil Service Reform Act of 1883. Declining to seek reelection in 1880, he spent the rest of his life campaigning for manual and mechanical education, prison reform, and abolition of the death penalty.

were called upon, and all received the boy graciously and were interested in the problem of his self-education. It was a veritable case of making friends on every hand; friends who were to be of the greatest help and value to the boy in his after years, although he had no conception of it at the time.

The Fifth Avenue Hotel, in those days the stopping-place of the majority of the famous men and women visiting New York, represented to the young boy who came to see these celebrities the very pinnacle of opulence.[14] Often while waiting to be received by some dignitary, he wondered how one could acquire enough means to live at a place of such luxury. The dining room, to the boy's mind, was an object of special interest. He would purposely sneak upstairs and sit on one of the soft sofas in the foyer simply to see the well-dressed diners go in and come out. Edward would speculate on whether the time would ever come when he could dine in that wonderful room just once!

One evening he called after the close of business upon General and Mrs. Grant, whom he had met before, and who had expressed a desire to see his collection. It can readily be imagined what a red-letter

[14]The Fifth Avenue Hotel, between 23rd and 24th streets opposite Madison Square, was a six-story building known for its luxurious accommodations. The state Republican Party had its headquarters there, helping account for its popularity with such dignitaries as Mr. and Mrs. Ulysses S. Grant. It was demolished in 1908.

day it made in the boy's life to have General Grant
say: "It might be better for us all to go down to dinner
first and see the collection afterward." Edward had
purposely killed time between five and seven o'clock
thinking that the general's dinner hour, like his own,
was at six. He had allowed an hour for the general to
eat his dinner, only to find that he was still to begin it.
The boy could hardly believe his ears, and unable to
find his voice, he failed to apologize for his modest
suit or his general after-business appearance.

As in a dream he went down in the elevator with his
host and hostess, and when the party of three faced toward the dining-room entrance, so familiar to the boy,
he felt as if his legs must give way under him. There
have since been other red-letter days in Edward Bok's
life, but the moment that still stands out pre-eminent
is when two colored head waiters at the dining-room
entrance, whom he had so often watched, bowed low
and escorted the party to its table. At last, he was in
that sumptuous dining-hall. The entire room took on
the picture of one great eye, and that eye centered on
the party of three—as, in fact, it naturally would. But
Edward felt that the eye was on him, wondering why
he should be there.

What he ate and what he said he does not recall.
General Grant, not a voluble talker himself, gently
drew the boy out, and Mrs. Grant seconded him, until
toward the close of the dinner he heard himself talking. He remembers that he heard his voice, but what
that voice said is all dim to him. Yet one act stamped

Illustration from articles describing Bok's boyhood
encounter with General and Mrs. Grant,
The Ladies' Home Journal, *February 1905*

itself on his mind. The dinner ended with a wonderful dish of nuts and raisins; just before the party rose from the table Mrs. Grant asked the waiter to bring her a paper bag. Into this she emptied the entire dish, and at the close of the evening she gave it to Edward "to eat on the way home." It was a wonderful evening afterward, as upstairs, General Grant smoked the inevitable cigar, and told stories as he read the letters of different celebrities.

Mrs. Grant had asked Edward to send her a photograph of himself, and after one had been taken, the boy took it to the Fifth Avenue Hotel, intending to ask the clerk to send it to her room. Instead, he met General and Mrs. Grant just coming from the elevator, going out to dinner. The boy told them his errand and said he would have the photograph sent upstairs.

"I am so sorry we are just going out to dinner," said Mrs. Grant, "for the general had some excellent photographs just taken of himself, and he signed one for you, and put it aside, intending to send it to you when yours came." Then, turning to the general, she said: "Ulysses, send up for it. We have a few moments."

"I'll go and get it. I know just where it is," returned the general. "Let me have yours," he said, turning to Edward. "I am glad to exchange photographs with you, boy."

To Edward's surprise, when the general returned he brought with him, not a duplicate of the small *carte-de-visite* size which he had given the general—all that he could afford—but a large, full cabinet size.

"They make 'em too big," said the general, as he handed it to Edward.

But the boy didn't think so!

That evening was one that the boy was long to remember. It suddenly came to him that he had read a few days before of Mrs. Abraham Lincoln's arrival in New York at Doctor Holbrook's sanitarium.[15]

Thither Edward went; within half an hour from the time he had been talking with General Grant he was sitting at the bedside of Mrs. Lincoln, showing her the wonderful photograph just presented to him. Edward saw that the widow of the great Lincoln did not mentally respond to his pleasure in his possession. It was apparent even to the boy that mental and physical illness had done their work with the frail frame. But he

[15]Mary Todd Lincoln was the wife of Abraham Lincoln, sixteenth president of the United States. Though well educated and trained in art, music, and dance, she had a combative nature. The death in 1862 of their son, Willie, the assassination of her husband in 1865, and the loss of another son, Tad, in 1871 resulted in unbearable anguish. Her oldest son, Robert, had her committed to a mental institution in 1875, but she was eventually released. It appears that when Bok saw Mary Todd Lincoln, she was staying at "Dr. Miller's Home of Health," on 26th Street between Broadway and 6th Avenue in New York City, where "Turkish vapors, Russian sitz baths, electrical therapy, and nursing care were available at sixty dollars a week." Dr. Lewis Sayre, an expert on bone pathology, had diagnosed her as having kidney, eye, and spinal problems including "spinal sclerosis and hardening of the spinal cord." According to biographer Jean H. Baker, she had to be carried "up and down the stairs on a litter." This information essentially confirms what Bok states about his visit of 13 October 1881, which took place when he was eighteen years old.

had an autograph and the memory, at least, of having got that close to the great president.

Mrs Abraham Lincoln
October 13.Th 1881.

The eventful evening, however, was not yet over. Edward had boarded a Broadway stage to take him to his Brooklyn home when, glancing at the newspaper of a man sitting next to him, he saw the headline "Jefferson Davis arrives in New York."[16] He read enough to see that the Confederate president was stopping at the Metropolitan Hotel,[17] in lower Broadway, and as he looked out of the stage window the sign "Metropolitan Hotel" stared him in the face. In a moment he was out of the stage. He wrote a little note, asked the clerk to send it to Mr. Davis, and within five minutes was talking to the Confederate president and telling of his remarkable evening.

[16]In 1881, D. Appleton and Company published a two-volume work, *Rise and Fall of the Confederate Government,* by Jefferson Davis, formerly president of the Confederate States of America. In August of that year, he and his wife, Varina, made a trip to Europe, returning to the United States in November. Presumably Bok met the Davises in New York City that year, during a visit connected either with a meeting at Appleton's or with their European trip.

[17]The Metropolitan Hotel, which opened in 1852, was one of New York's luxury hotels. It had lavishly furnished public parlors, some 500 guest rooms, and hot and cold running water. The hotel was torn down in 1895.

Mr. Davis was keenly interested in the coincidence and in the boy before him. He asked about the famous collection, and promised to secure for Edward a letter written by each member of the Confederate cabinet. This he subsequently did. Edward remained with Mr. Davis until ten o'clock, and that evening brought about an interchange of letters between the Brooklyn boy and Mr. Davis at Beauvoir, Mississippi, that lasted until the latter passed away.

Edward was fast absorbing a tremendous quantity of biographical information about the most famous men and women of his time, and he was compiling a collection of autograph letters that the newspapers had made famous throughout the country. He was ruminating over his possessions one day and wondering to what practical use he could put his collection. For while it was proving educative to a wonderful degree it was, after all, a hobby, and a hobby means expense. His autograph quest cost him stationery, postage, carfare—all outgo. But it had brought him no income save a rich mental revenue. And the boy and his family needed money. He did not know then, the value of a background.

He was thinking along this line in a restaurant when man sitting next to him opened a box of cigarettes, and taking a picture out of it threw it on the floor. Edward picked it up, thinking it might be a prospect for his collection of autograph letters. It was the picture of a well-known actress. He recalled an advertisement announcing that this particular brand of cigarettes contained, in each package, a lithographed portrait of some famous actor or actress, and that if the purchaser would collect all these he would, in the end, have a valuable album of the greatest actors and actresses of the day. Edward turned the picture over, only to find a blank reverse side. "All very well," he thought, "but what does a purchaser have, after all, in the end, but a lot of pictures? Why don't they use the back of each picture, and tell what each did: a little biography? Then it would be worth keeping." With his passion for self-education, the idea appealed very strongly to him. Believing firmly that there were others possessed of the same thirst, he set out the next day, in his luncheon hour, to find out who made the picture.

At the office of the cigarette company he learned that the making of the pictures was in the hands of the Knapp Lithographic Company. The following luncheon hour, Edward sought the offices of the company, and explained his idea to Mr. Joseph F. Knapp, the president of American Lithograph Company.

"I'll give you ten dollars apiece if you will write me a 100-word biography of 100 famous Americans," was Mr. Knapp's instant reply. "Send me a list, and group them, as, for instance: presidents and vice-presidents, famous soldiers, actors, authors, etc."

"And thus," says Mr. Knapp as he tells the tale today, "I gave Edward Bok his first literary commission, and started him off on his literary career."

And it is true.

But Edward soon found the Lithograph Company

calling for "copy," and, write as he might, he could not supply the biographies fast enough. He, at last, completed the first hundred, and so instantaneous was their success that Mr. Knapp called for a second hundred, and then for a third. Finding that one hand was not equal to the task, Edward offered his brother five dollars for each biography; he made the same offer to one or two journalists whom he knew and whose accuracy he could trust. He was speedily convinced that merely to edit biographies written by others, at one-half the price paid to him, was more profitable than to write himself.

So with five journalists working at top speed to supply the hungry lithograph presses, Mr. Knapp was likewise responsible for Edward Bok's first adventure as an editor. It was commercial, if you will, but it was a commercial editing that had a distinct educational value to a large public.

The important point is that Edward Bok was being led more and more to writing and editorship.

IV

A Presidential Friend
and a Boston Pilgrimage

Edward Bok had not been office boy long before he realized that if he learned shorthand he would stand a better chance for advancement. So he joined the Young Men's Christian Association[1] in Brooklyn and entered the class in stenography. But as this class met only twice a week, Edward, impatient to learn the art of "pothooks" as quickly as possible, supplemented this instruction by a course given on two other evenings at moderate cost by a Brooklyn business college. As the system taught in both classes was the same, more rapid progress was possible, and the two teachers were constantly surprised that he acquired the art so much more quickly than the other students.

Before many weeks Edward could "stenograph" fairly well, and as the typewriter had not then come into its own, he was ready to put his knowledge to practical use.

An opportunity offered itself when the city editor of the *Brooklyn Eagle* asked him to report two speeches at a New England Society dinner. The speakers were

[1]The Young Men's Christian Association was founded in London in 1844 as a nonsectarian Christian lay movement to foster the moral and spiritual condition of young tradesmen.

to be the president of the United States,[2] General
Grant, General Sherman, Mr. Evarts,[3] and General
Sheridan.[4] Edward was to report what General Grant
and the president said, and was instructed to give the
president's speech verbatim.

At the close of the dinner, the reporters came in
and Edward was seated directly in front of the president. In those days when a public dinner included
several kinds of wine, it was the custom to serve the reporters with wine. As the glasses were placed before
Edward's plate he realized that he had to make a decision then and there. He had, of course, constantly
seen wine on his father's table, as is the European custom, but the boy had never tasted it. He decided he
would not begin then, when he needed a clear head.
So, in order to get more room for his notebook, he
asked the waiter to remove the glasses.

It was the first time he had ever attempted to report a public address. General Grant's remarks were
few, as usual, and as he spoke slowly, he gave the
young reporter no trouble. But, alas for his stenographic knowledge, when President Hayes began to
speak! Edward worked hard, but the president was
too rapid for him; he did not get the speech, and

[2] A reference to Rutherford B. Hayes.

[3] William Maxwell Evarts, jurist, statesman, and brilliant public speaker, was best known for his successful defense of President Andrew Johnson in the impeachment trial of 1868.

[4] Philip Henry Sheridan, Union cavalry leader of the Civil War,
was best known for his devastating Shenandoah Valley campaign
in Virginia in 1864.

he noticed that the reporters for the other papers fared no better. Nothing daunted, however, after the speechmaking, Edward resolutely sought the president, and as the latter turned to him, he told him his plight, explained it was his first important "assignment," and asked if he could possibly be given a copy of the speech to "beat" the other papers.

The president looked at him curiously for a moment, and said: "Can you wait a few minutes?"

Edward assured him that he could.

After fifteen minutes or so the president came up to where the boy was waiting, and said abruptly:

"Tell me, my boy, why did you have the wineglasses removed from your place?"[5]

Edward was completely taken aback by the question, but he explained his resolution as well as he could.

"Did you make that decision this evening?" the president asked.

He had.

"What is your name?" the president next inquired.

He was told.

"And you live, where?"

Edward told him.

"Suppose you write your name and address on this card for me," said the president, reaching for one of the place cards on the table.

The boy did so.

[5] Hayes noticed what Bok had done with his wineglasses because his wife, Lucy Webb Hayes, was an ardent temperance advocate.

"Now, I am stopping with Mr. A. A. Low,[6] on Columbia Heights. Is that in the direction of your home?"

It was.

"Suppose you go with me, then, in my carriage," said the president, "and I will give you my speech."

Edward was not quite sure now whether he was on his head or his feet.

As he drove along with the president and his host, the president asked the boy about himself, what he was doing, etc. On arriving at Mr. Low's house, the president went upstairs and in a few moments came down with his speech in full, written in his own hand. Edward assured him he would copy it and return the manuscript in the morning.

The president took out his watch. It was then after midnight. Musing a moment, he said: "You say you are an office boy; what time must you be at your office."

"Half past eight, sir."

"Well, good night," he said, and then, as if it were a second thought, "By the way, I can get another copy of the speech. Just turn that in as it is, if they can read it."

Afterward, Edward found out that, as a matter of

[6] Abiel Abbott Low prospered in trade with the Orient by using clipper ships that delivered goods faster and at lower prices. He eventually served as president of the New York Chamber of Commerce.

fact, it was the president's only copy. Though the boy did not then appreciate this act of consideration, his instinct fortunately led him to copy the speech and leave the original at the president's stopping-place in the morning.

And for all his trouble, the young reporter was amply repaid by seeing that the *Eagle* was the only paper which had a verbatim report of the president's speech.

But the day was not yet done!

That evening, upon reaching home, what was the boy's astonishment to find the following note:

My Dear Young Friend:
I have been telling Mrs. Hayes this morning of what you told me at the dinner last evening, and she was very much interested. She would like to see you, and joins me in asking if you will call upon us this evening at eight-thirty.

Very faithfully yours,
Rutherford B. Hayes

Edward had not risen to the possession of a suit of evening clothes, and distinctly felt its lack for this occasion. But, dressed in the best he had, he set out, at eight o'clock, to call on the president of the United States and his wife!

He had no sooner handed his card to the butler than that dignitary, looking at it, announced: "The President and Mrs. Hayes are waiting for you!" The ring of those magic words still sounds in Edward's ears: "The President and Mrs. Hayes[7] are waiting for you!"—and he a boy of sixteen!

Edward had not been in the room ten minutes before he was made to feel as thoroughly at ease as if he were sitting in his own home before an open fire with his father and mother. Skillfully the president drew from him the story of his youthful hopes and ambitions, and before the boy knew it he was telling the president and his wife all about his precious *Encyclopaedia,* his evening with General Grant, and his efforts to become something more than an office boy. No boy had ever so gracious a listener before; no mother could have been more tenderly motherly than the woman who sat opposite him and seemed so honestly interested in all that he told. Not for a moment during all those two hours was he allowed to remember that his host and hostess were the president of the United States and the first lady of the land!

That evening was the first of many thus spent as the years rolled by; unexpected little courtesies came from the White House, and later from Spiegel Grove;[8] a constant and unflagging interest followed each undertaking on which the boy embarked. Opportunities

[7]Lucy Webb Hayes, wife of President Rutherford B. Hayes, was a staunch Methodist and temperance advocate, who banned alcohol from all state functions and became known as "Lemonade Lucy." After Hayes left the presidency in 1881, they lived for a time in a New York townhouse.

[8]Spiegel Grove was an estate in Fremont, Ohio, owned by Rutherford B. Hayes. He died there in 1893, after suffering a heart attack on a trip to Cleveland.

were opened to him; acquaintances were made possible; a letter came almost every month until that last little note, late in 1892:

> My Dear Friend:
>
> I would write you more fully if I could. You are always thoughtful & kind. Thankfully your friend
>
> Ruth Lucy B. Hayes
>
> Thanks — thanks for your steady friendship.

The passion for autograph collecting was now leading Edward Bok to read the authors whom he had read about. He had become attached to the works of the New England group: Longfellow, Holmes,[9] and, particularly, of Emerson.[10] The philosophy of the sage

[9]Oliver Wendell Holmes, Sr., was a New England Brahmin and physician who became one of America's foremost literary figures. He first achieved recognition by publishing "Old Ironsides" (1830), a poem that helped save the U.S.S. *Constitution* from destruction. He gave James Russell Lowell's *Atlantic Monthly* its name, contributed frequent stories, essays, and poems to its pages, and was in great demand as a public speaker.

[10]Ralph Waldo Emerson, one of America's foremost philosophers and essayists, began his career as minister of Boston's Old Second Church. Shattered by the death of his first wife, Ellen Tucker, he fled to Europe. When he returned, he became the spokesman for Transcendentalism, a school of thought that identified God with Nature and held that every human being shares in the divine essence, or "Oversoul."

of Concord made a peculiarly strong appeal to the young mind, and a small copy of Emerson's essays was always in Edward's pocket on his long stage or horse car rides to his office and back.

He noticed that these New England authors rarely visited New York, or, if they did, their presence was not heralded by the newspapers among the "distinguished arrivals." He had a great desire personally to meet these writers; and, having saved a little money, he decided to take his week's summer vacation in the winter, when he knew he should be more likely to find the people on his quest at home, and to spend his savings on a trip to Boston. He had never been away from home, so this trip was a momentous affair.

He arrived in Boston on Sunday evening; and the first thing he did was to dispatch a note, by messenger, to Dr. Oliver Wendell Holmes, announcing the important fact that he was there, and what his errand was, and asking whether he might come up and see Dr. Holmes any time the next day. Edward naively told him that he could come as early as Dr. Holmes liked— by breakfast time, he was assured, as Edward Bok was all alone!

Within the hour the boy brought back this answer:

My Dear Boy:
I shall certainly look for you tomorrow morning at eight o'clock to have a piece of pie with me. That is real New England, you know.

Very cordially yours,
Oliver Wendell Holmes.

Edward was there at eight o'clock. Strictly speaking, he was there at seven-thirty, and found the author already at his desk in that room overlooking the Charles River, which he learned in after years to know better.

"Well," was the cheery greeting, "you couldn't wait until eight for your breakfast, could you? Neither could I when I was a boy. I used to have my breakfast at seven," and then telling the boy all about his boyhood, the cheery poet led him to the dining room, and for the first time he breakfasted away from home and ate pie—and that with "The Autocrat" at his own breakfast-table![11]

A cozier time no boy could have had. Just the two were there, and the smiling face that looked out over the plates and cups gave the boy courage to tell all that this trip was going to mean to him.

"And you have come on just to see us, have you?" chuckled the poet. "Now, tell me, what good do you think you will get out of it?"

He was told what the idea was: that every successful man had something to tell a boy that would be likely to help him, and that Edward wanted to see the men who had written the books that people enjoyed. Dr. Holmes could not conceal his amusement at this.

When breakfast was finished, Dr. Holmes said, "Do

[11] *The Autocrat of the Breakfast Table* (1858) is a series of essays that Holmes contributed to *Atlantic Monthly*. A critique of New England Calvinism, it contains fictional conversations among a group of boarders gathered around the table of an "autocrat."

you know that I am a full-fledged carpenter? No? Well, I am. Come into my carpenter-shop."

And he led the way into a front-basement room where was a complete carpenter's outfit.

"You know I am a doctor," he explained, "and this shop is my medicine. I believe that every man must have a hobby that is as different from his regular work as it is possible to be. It is not good for a man to work all the time at one thing. So this is my hobby. This is my change. I like to putter away at these things. Every day I try to come down here for an hour or so. It rests me because it gives my mind a complete change. For, whether you believe it or not," he added with his inimitable chuckle, "to make a poem and to make a chair are two very different things."

"Now," he continued, "if you think you can learn something from me, learn that and remember it when you are a man. Don't keep always at your business, whatever it may be. It makes no difference how much you like it. The more you like it, the more dangerous it is. When you grow up you will understand what I mean by an 'outlet'—a hobby, that is—in your life, and it must be so different from your regular work that it will take your thoughts into an entirely different direction. We doctors call it a safety valve, and it is. I would much rather," concluded the poet, "you would forget all that I have ever written than that you should forget what I tell you about having a safety-valve.

"And now do you know," smilingly said the poet, "about the Charles River here?" as they returned to his study and stood before the large bay window. "I love this river," he said. "Yes, I love it," he repeated, "love it in summer or in winter." And then he was quiet for a minute or so.

Edward asked him which of his poems were his favorites.

"Well," he said musingly, "I think 'The Chambered Nautilus' is my most finished piece of work, and I suppose it is my favorite.[12] But there are also 'The Voiceless,' 'My Aviary,' and 'Dorothy Q,' written to the portrait of my great-grandmother, which you see on the wall there. All these I have a liking for, and when I speak of the poems I like the best there are two others that ought to be included—'The Silent Melody' and 'The Last Leaf.' I think these are among my best."

"What is the history of 'The Chambered Nautilus'?" Edward asked.

"It has none," came the reply, "it wrote itself. So, too, did 'The One Hoss Shay.' That was one of those random conceptions that gallop through the brain, and that you catch by the bridle. I caught it and reined it. That is all."

Just then a maid brought in a parcel, and as Dr. Holmes opened it on his desk he smiled over at the boy and said:

"Well, I declare, if you haven't come just at the right time. See those little books? Aren't they wee?" and

---

[12]"The Chambered Nautilus," a poem by Oliver Wendell Holmes, Sr., uses a sea creature's enlargement of its shell as a source of human inspiration.

he handed the boy a set of three little books, six inches by four in size, beautifully bound in half levant.[13] They were his *Autocrat* in one volume, and his better-known poems in two volumes.[14]

"This is a little fancy of mine," he said. "My publishers, to please me, have gotten out this tiny wee set. And here," as he counted the little sets, "they have sent me six sets. Are they not exquisite little things?" and he fondled them with loving glee. "Lucky, too, for me that they should happen to come now, for I have been wondering what I could give you as a souvenir of your visit to me, and here it is, sure enough! My publishers must have guessed you were here and my mind at the same time. Now, if you would like it, you shall carry home one of these little sets, and I'll just write a piece from one of my poems and your name on the flyleaf of each volume. You say you like that little verse: " 'A few can touch the magic string.' Then I'll write those four lines in this volume." And he did.

[13]half levant: where the back of a book and part of the sides were bound with a type of leather and the remaining side areas were covered with another material.

[14]As Bok indicates, the set must have been strictly for Holmes's own use. No three-volume set of Holmes' *Autocrat* and poetry was published during the time-frame of his visit to Holmes, or at any other time. Possibly separate but uniform editions of *Autocrat* and selected poems were printed simultaneously, but the *National Union Catalog* and other standard reference works do not sustain even this hypothesis. (The editor is grateful for advice on this matter by Timothy Dodge and other staff members at Auburn University's Ralph Brown Draughon Library.)

As each little volume went under the poet's pen, Edward said, as his heart swelled in gratitude: "Dr. Holmes, you are a man of the rarest sort to be so good to a boy."

A few can touch the magic string,
And noisy Fame is proud to win them, —
Alas for those who never sing,
But die with all their music in them!

Oliver Wendell Holmes.

The pen stopped, the poet looked out on the Charles a moment, and then, turning to the boy with a little moisture in his eye, he said:

"No, my boy, I am not; but it does an old man's heart good to hear you say it. It means much to those on the downhill side to be well thought of by the young who are coming up."

As he wiped his gold pen, with its swan-quill holder, and laid it down, he said: "That's the pen with which I wrote 'Elsie Venner' and the *Autocrat* papers. I try to take care of it.

"You say you are going from me over to see Longfellow?" he continued, as he reached out once more for the pen. "Well, then, would you mind if I gave you a letter for him? I have something to send him."

Sly but kindly old gentleman! The "something" he had to send Longfellow was Edward himself, although the boy did not see through the subterfuge at that time.

"And now, if you are going, I'll walk along with you if you don't mind, for I'm going down to Park Street to thank my publishers for these little books, and that lies along your way to the Cambridge car."

As the two walked along Beacon Street, Dr. Holmes pointed out the residences where lived people of interest, and when they reached the Public Garden he said: "You must come over in the spring some time, and see the tulips and croci and hyacinths here. They are so beautiful.

"Now, here is your car," he said as he hailed a coming horse car. "Before you go back you must come and see me and tell me all the people you have seen, will you? I should like to hear about them. I may not have more books coming in, but I might have a very good-looking photograph of a very old-looking little man," he said as his eyes twinkled. "Give my love to Longfellow when you see him, and don't forget to give him my letter, you know. It is about a very important matter."

And when the boy had ridden a mile or so with his fare in his hand he held it out to the conductor, who grinned and said: "That's all right, Dr. Holmes paid me your fare, and I'm going to keep that nickel if I lose my job for it."

V

Going to the Theater with Longfellow

WHEN EDWARD BOK stood before the home of Longfellow, he realized that he was to see the man around whose head the boy's youthful reading had cast a sort of halo. And when he saw the head itself he had a feeling that he could see the halo. No kindlier pair of eyes ever looked at a boy, as, with a smile, "the white Mr. Longfellow," as Mr. Howells[1] had called him, held out his hand.

"I am very glad to see you, my boy," were his first words, and with them he won the boy. Edward smiled back at the poet, and immediately the two were friends.

"I have been taking a walk this beautiful morning," he said next, "and am a little late getting at my mail. Suppose you come in and sit at my desk with me, and we will see what the postman has brought. He brings me so many good things, you know.

"Now, here is a little girl," he said, as he sat down at the desk with the boy beside him, "who wants my autograph and a 'sentiment'. What sentiment, I wonder, shall I send her?"

---

[1]William Dean Howells, American novelist, was best known for *The Rise of Silas Lapham* (1885).

"Why not send her 'Let us, then, be up and doing'?"[2] suggested the boy. "That's what I should like if I were she."

"Should you, indeed?" said Longfellow. "That is a good suggestion. Now, suppose you recite it off to me, so that I shall not have to look it up in my books, and I will write as you recite. But slowly; you know I am an old man, and write slowly."

Edward thought it strange that Longfellow himself should not know his own great words without looking them up. But he recited the four lines, so familiar to every schoolboy, and when the poet had finished writing them, he said:

"Good! I see you have a memory. Now, suppose I copy these lines once more for the little girl, and give you this copy? Then you can say, you know, that you dictated my own poetry to me."

Of course Edward was delighted, and Longfellow gave him the sheet as it is here:

[2] From Henry Wadsworth Longfellow's "A Psalm of Life" (1839), 9th stanza.

Then, as the fine head bent down to copy the lines once more, Edward ventured to say to him: "I should think it would keep you busy if you did this for every one who asked you."

"Well," said the poet, "you see, I am not so busy a man as I was some years ago, and I shouldn't like to disappoint a little girl; should you?"

As he took up his letters again, he discovered five more requests for his autograph. At each one he reached into a drawer in his desk, took a card, and wrote his name on it.

"There are a good many of these every day," said Longfellow, "but I always like to do this little favor. It is so little to do, to write your name on a card; and if I didn't do it some boy or girl might be looking, day by day, for the postman and be disappointed. I only wish I could write my name better for them. You see how I break my letters? That's because I never took pains with my writing when I was a boy. I don't think I should get a high mark for penmanship if I were at school, do you?"

"I see you get letters from Europe," said the boy, as Longfellow opened an envelope with a foreign stamp on it.

"Yes, from all over the world," said the poet. Then, looking at the boy quickly, he said: "Do you collect postage stamps?"

Edward said he did.

"Well, I have some right here, then," and going to a drawer in a desk he took out a bundle of letters, and cut out the postage stamps and gave them to the boy.

"There's one from The Netherlands. There's where I was born," Edward ventured to say.

"In The Netherlands? Then you are a real Dutchman. Well! Well!" he said, laying down his pen. "Can you read Dutch?"

The boy said he could.

"Then," said the poet, "you are just the boy I am looking for." And going to a bookcase behind him he brought out a book, and handing it to the boy, he said, his eyes laughing: "Can you read that?"

It was an edition of Longfellow's poems in Dutch.

"Yes, indeed," said Edward. "These are your poems in Dutch."

"That's right," he said. "Now, this is delightful. I am so glad you came. I received this book last week, and although I have been in The Netherlands, I cannot speak or read Dutch. I wonder whether you would read a poem to me and let me hear how it sounds."

So Edward took "The Old Clock on the Stairs," and read it to him.

The poet's face beamed with delight. "That's beautiful," he said, and then quickly added: "I mean the language, not the poem.

"Now," he went on, "I'll tell you what we'll do: we'll strike a bargain. We Yankees are great for bargains, you know. If you will read me 'The Village Blacksmith' you can sit in that chair there made out of the wood of the old spreading chestnut tree, and I'll take you out and show you where the old shop stood. Is that a bargain?"

Edward assured him it was. He sat in the chair of wood and leather, and read to the poet several of his own poems in a language in which, when he wrote them, he never dreamed they would ever be printed. He was very quiet. Finally he said: "It seems so odd, so very odd, to hear something you know so well sound so strange."

"It's a great compliment, though, isn't it, sir?" asked the boy.

"Ye-es," said the poet slowly. "Yes, yes," he added quickly. "It is, my boy, a very great compliment.

"Ah," he said, rousing himself, as a maid appeared, "that means luncheon, or rather," he added, "it means dinner, for we have dinner in the old New England fashion, in the middle of the day. I am all alone today, and you must keep me company; will you? Then afterward we'll go and take a walk, and I'll show you Cambridge. It is such a beautiful old town, even more beautiful, I sometimes think, when the leaves are off the trees.

"Come," he said, "I'll take you upstairs, and you can wash your hands in the room where George Washington slept. And comb your hair, too, if you want to," he added, "only it isn't the same comb he used."

To the boyish mind it was an historic breaking of bread, that midday meal with Longfellow.

"Can you say grace in Dutch?" he asked, as they sat

down; and indeed the boy was able to fulfill the request.

"Well," the poet declared, "I never expected to hear that at my table. I like the sound of it."

Then while the boy told all that he knew about The Netherlands, the poet told the boy all about his poems. Edward said he liked "Hiawatha."

"So do I," he said. "But I think I like 'Evangeline' better. Still," he added, "neither one is as good as it should be. But those are the things you see afterward so much better than you do at the time."

It was a great event for Edward when, with the poet nodding and smiling to every boy and man he met, and lifting his hat to every woman and little girl, he walked through the fine old streets of Cambridge with Longfellow. At one point of the walk they came to a theatrical billboard announcing an attraction that evening at the Boston Theatre. Skillfully the old poet drew out from Edward that sometimes he went to the theater with his parents. As they returned to the gate of Craigie House,[3] Edward said he thought he would go back to Boston.

"And what have you on hand for this evening?" asked Longfellow.

Edward told him he was going to his hotel to think over the day's events. The poet laughed and said: "Now, listen to my plan. Boston is strange to you. Now

[3] A mansion in Cambridge, Massachusetts, given to Henry Wadsworth Longfellow and Frances Appleton in 1843 by Mrs. Longfellow's father upon the occasion of their wedding.

we're going to the theater this evening, and my plan is that you come in now, have a little supper with us, and then go with us to see the play. It is a funny play, and a good laugh will do you more good than to sit in a hotel all by yourself. Now, what do you think?"

Of course the boy thought as Longfellow did, and it was a very happy boy that evening who, in full view of the large audience in the immense theater, sat in that box. It was, as Longfellow had said, a play of laughter, and just who laughed louder, the poet or the boy, neither ever knew.

Between the acts there came into the box a man of courtly presence, dignified and gently courteous.

"Ah! Phillips," said the poet, "how are you? You must know my young friend here. This is Wendell Phillips,[4] my boy. Here is a young man who told me today that he was going to call on you and on Phillips Brooks[5] tomorrow. Now you know him before he comes to you."

"I shall be glad to see you, my boy," said Mr. Phillips. "And so you are going to see Phillips Brooks.

---

[4]Wendell Phillips was an American orator, abolitionist, and reformer. He advocated full civil rights for emancipated slaves, championed woman suffrage, urged the abolition of capital punishment, and fought for currency reform. He was among the most highly regarded public speakers of his time.

[5]Phillips Brooks, distinguished American preacher, became rector of Trinity Church, Boston, in 1868. His most enduring work is a poem, "O Little Town of Bethlehem," which he wrote in 1866. Set to music by Brooks's parish organist, Lewis Redner, it became one of the most beloved Christmas carols.

Let me tell you something about Brooks. He has a great many books in his library which are full of his marks and comments. Now, when you go to see him you ask him to let you see some of those books, and then, when he isn't looking, you put a couple of them in your pocket. They would make splendid souvenirs, and he has so many he would never miss them. You do it, and then when you come to see me tell me all about it." And he and Longfellow smiled broadly.

An hour later, when Longfellow dropped Edward at his hotel, he had not only a wonderful day to think over but another wonderful day to look forward to as well!

He had breakfasted with Oliver Wendell Holmes; dined, supped, and been to the theater with Longfellow; and tomorrow he was to spend with Phillips Brooks.

Boston was a great place, Edward Bok thought, as he fell asleep.

VI

Phillips Brooks's Books and Emerson's Mental Mist

NO ONE who called at Phillips Brooks's house was ever told that the master of the house was out when he was in. That was a firm rule laid down by Dr. Brooks: a maid was not to perjure herself for her master's comfort or convenience. Therefore, when Edward was told that Dr. Brooks was out, he knew he *was* out. The boy waited, and as he waited he had a chance to look around the library and into the books. The rector's faithful housekeeper said he might when he repeated what Wendell Phillips had told him of the interest that was to be found in her master's books. Edward did not tell her of Mr. Phillips's advice to "borrow" a couple of books. He reserved that bit of information for the rector of Trinity when he came in, an hour later.

"Oh! did he?" laughingly said Dr. Brooks. "That is nice advice for a man to give a boy. I am surprised at Wendell Phillips. He needs a little talk: a ministerial visit. And have you followed his shameless advice?" smilingly asked the huge man as he towered over the boy. "No? And to think of the opportunity you had, too. Well, I am glad you had such respect for my dumb friends. For they are my friends, each one of them," he continued, as he looked fondly at the filled shelves.

69

"Yes, I know them all, and love each for its own sake. Take this little volume," and he picked up a little book of Shakespeare's. "Why, we are the best of friends: we have traveled miles together—all over the world, as a matter of fact. It knows me in all my moods, and responds to each, no matter how irritable I am. Yes, it is pretty badly marked up now, for a fact, isn't it? Black; I never thought of that before that it doesn't make a book look any better to the eye. But it means more to me because of all that pencilling.

"Now, some folks dislike my use of my books in this way. They love their books so much that they think it nothing short of sacrilege to mark up a book. But to me that's like having a child so prettily dressed that you can't romp and play with it. What is the good of a book, I say, if it is too pretty for use? I like to have my books speak to me, and then I like to talk back to them.

"Take my Bible, here," he continued, as he took up an old and much-worn copy of the book. "I have a number of copies of the Great Book: one copy I preach from; another I minister from; but this is my own personal copy, and into it I talk and talk. See how I talk," and he opened the book and showed interleaved pages full of comments in his handwriting. "There's where St. Paul and I had an argument one day. Yes, it was a long argument, and I don't know now who won," he added smilingly. "But then, no one ever wins in an argument, anyway; do you think so?

"You see," went on the preacher, "I put into these

books what other men put into articles and essays for magazines and papers. I never write for publications. I always think of my church when something comes to me to say. There is always danger of a man spreading himself out thin if he attempts too much, you know."

Dr. Brooks must have caught the boy's eye, which, as he said this, naturally surveyed his great frame, for he regarded him in an amused way, and putting his hands on his girth, he said laughingly: "You are thinking I would have to do a great deal to spread myself out thin, aren't you?"

The boy confessed that he was, and the preacher laughed one of those deep laughs of his that were so infectious.

"But here I am talking about myself. Tell me something about *yourself*."

And when the boy told his object in coming to Boston, the rector of Trinity Church was immensely amused.

"Just to see us fellows! Well, and how do you like us so far?"

And in the most comfortable way this true gentleman went on until the boy mentioned that he must be keeping him from his work.

"Not at all; not at all," was the quick and hearty response. "Not a thing to do. I cleaned up all my mail before I had my breakfast this morning.

"These letters, you mean?" he said, as the boy pointed to some letters on his desk unopened. "Oh, yes! Well, they must have come in a later mail. Well, if it will make you feel any better I'll go through them, and you can go through my books if you like. I'll trust you," he added laughingly, as Wendell Phillips's advice occurred to him.

"You like books, you say?" he went on, as he opened his letters. "Well, then, you must come into my library here at any time you are in Boston and spend a morning reading anything I have that you like. Young men do that, you know, and I like to have them. What's the use of good friends if you don't share them? There's where the pleasure comes in."

He asked the boy then about his newspaper work: how much it paid him, and whether he felt it helped him in an educational way. The boy told him he thought it did; that it furnished good lessons in the study of human nature.

"Yes," he said, "I can believe that, so long as it is good journalism."

Edward told him that he sometimes wrote for the Sunday paper, and he asked the preacher what he thought of that.

"Well," he said, "that is not a crime."

The boy asked him if he, then, favored the Sunday paper more than did some other clergymen.

"There is always good in everything, I think," replied Phillips Brooks. "A thing must be pretty bad that hasn't some good in it." Then he stopped, and after a moment went on: "My idea is that the fate of Sunday newspapers rests very much with Sunday editors. There is a Sunday newspaper conceivable in

which we should all rejoice—all, that is, who do not
hold that a Sunday newspaper is always and *per se*
wrong. But some cause has, in many instances,
brought it about that the Sunday paper is below, and
not above, the standard of its weekly brethren. I mean
it is apt to be more gossipy, more personal, more sensational, more frivolous; less serious and thoughtful
and suggestive. Taking for granted the fact of special
leisure on the part of its readers, it is apt to appeal to
the lower and not to the higher art of them, which the
Sunday leisure has set free. Let the Sunday newspaper
be worthy of the day, and the day will not reject it. So
I say its fate is in the hands of the editor. He can give
it such a character as will make all good men its cham-
pions and friends, or he can preserve for it the suspicion and dislike in which it stands at present."

Edward's journalistic instinct here got into full
play; and although, as he assured his host, he had had
no such thought in coming, he asked whether Dr.
Brooks would object if he tried his reportorial wings
by experimenting as to whether he could report such
talk.

"I do not like the papers to talk about me," was the
answer; "but if it will help you, go ahead and practice
on me. You haven't stolen my books when you were
told to do so, and I don't think you'll steal my name."

The boy went back to his hotel and wrote an article much as this account is here written, which he sent
to Dr. Brooks. "Let me keep it by me," the doctor
wrote, "and I will return it to you presently."

And he did, with his comment on the Sunday newspaper, just as it is given here, and with this note:

If I must go into the newspapers at all — which I should always mostly prefer to avoid — no words could have been more kind than those of your article. You were very good to read it to me. I am ever

Sincerely Your friend

Phillips Brooks

As he let the boy out of his house, at the end of that first meeting, he said to him:

"And you're going from me now to see Emerson? I don't know," he added reflectively, "whether you will see him at his best. Still, you may. And even if you do not, to have seen him, even as you may see him, is better, in a way, than not to have seen him at all."

Edward did not know what Phillips Brooks meant. But he was, sadly, to find out the next day.[1]

A boy of sixteen was pretty sure of a welcome from Louisa Alcott, and his greeting from her was spontaneous and sincere.[2]

"Why, you good boy," she said, "to come all the way to Concord to see us," quite for all the world as if she were the one favored.

"Do tell me all about your visit," she continued.

Before the cozy fire they chatted. It was pleasant for the boy to sit there with that sweet-faced woman with those kindly eyes! After a while she said: "Now I shall put on my coat and hat, and we shall walk over to Emerson's house. I am almost afraid to promise that you will see him. He sees scarcely any one now. He is feeble, and—" She did not finish the sentence. "But we'll walk over there, at any rate."

She spoke mostly of her father as the two walked

[1]After Emerson's home in Concord was partly destroyed by fire, an event that had a profound effect on his mental state, his memory began to deteriorate and he gave up public lecturing. By 1874, his symptoms had become sufficiently noticeable to cause concern among friends. He became unable to call up terms like "chair" and "umbrella" and had to use circumlocutions instead. Biographers have suggested that he was a victim of anomic aphasia or senile dementia caused by cerebral arteriosclerosis.

[2]Louisa May Alcott, daughter of New England Transcendentalist Bronson Alcott, was raised in poverty by her improvident father. She published her first signed book, *Flower Fables,* in 1848 and became well known for *Hospital Sketches,* based on letters that she wrote in 1863 while nursing soldiers wounded in the Civil War. *Little Women,* published in 1868, made her famous.

along, and it was easy to see that his condition was now the one thought of her life. Presently, as they reached Emerson's house, Miss Emerson[3] welcomed them at the door. After a brief chat Miss Alcott told of the boy's hope. Miss Emerson shook her head.

"Father sees no one now," she said, "and I fear it might not be a pleasure if you did see him."

She had scarcely left the room when Miss Alcott rose and followed her, saying to the boy: "You shall see Mr. Emerson if it is at all possible."

In a few minutes Miss Alcott returned, her eyes moistened, and simply said: "Come."

The boy followed her through two rooms, and at the threshold of the third Miss Emerson stood, also with moistened eyes.

"Father," she said simply, and there, at his desk, sat Emerson—the man whose words had already won Edward Bok's boyish interest, and who was destined to impress himself upon his life more deeply than any other writer.

Slowly, at the daughter's spoken word, Emerson rose with a wonderful quiet dignity, extended his hand, and as the boy's hand rested in his, looked him full in the eyes.

No light of welcome came from those sad yet tender eyes. The boy closed upon the hand in his with a loving pressure, and for a single moment the eyelids rose, a different look came into those eyes, and Ed-

---

[3]Ellen Tucker Emerson served as her father's housekeeper.

ward felt a slight, perceptible response of the hand. But that was all!

Quietly he motioned the boy to a chair beside the desk. Edward sat down and was about to say something, when, instead of seating himself, Emerson walked away to the window and stood there softly whistling and looking out as if there were no one in the room. Edward's eyes had followed Emerson's every footstep, when the boy was aroused by hearing a suppressed sob, and as he looked around he saw that it came from Miss Emerson. Slowly she walked out of the room. The boy looked at Miss Alcott, and she put her finger to her mouth, indicating silence. He was nonplussed.

Edward looked toward Emerson standing in that window, and wondered what it all meant. Presently Emerson left the window and, crossing the room, came to his desk, bowing to the boy as he passed, and seated himself, not speaking a word and ignoring the presence of the two persons in the room.

Suddenly the boy heard Miss Alcott say: "Have you read this new book by Ruskin yet?"[4]

Slowly the great master of thought lifted his eyes from his desk, turned toward the speaker, rose with stately courtesy from his chair, and bowing to Miss

---

[4]John Ruskin was one of the nineteenth century's outstanding writers on art, architecture, and social criticism; he contended that great art must rest on strong foundations of beauty, morality, and truth.

Alcott, said with great deliberation: "Did you speak to me, madam?"

The boy was dumbfounded! Louisa Alcott, his Louisa! And he did not know her! Suddenly the whole sad truth flashed upon the boy. Tears sprang into Miss Alcott's eyes, and she walked to the other side of the room. The boy did not know what to say or do, so he sat silent. With a deliberate movement, Emerson resumed his seat, and slowly let his eyes roam over the boy sitting at the side of the desk.

"I thought, perhaps, Mr. Emerson," he said, "that you might be able to favor me with a letter from Carlyle?"[5]

At the mention of the name Carlyle his eyes lifted, and he asked: "Carlyle, did you say, sir, Carlyle?"

"Yes," said the boy, "Thomas Carlyle."

"Ye-es," Emerson answered slowly. "To be sure, Carlyle. Yes, he was here this morning. He will be here again tomorrow morning," he added gleefully, almost like a child.

Then suddenly: "You were saying—"

Edward repeated his request.

"Oh, I think so, I think so," said Emerson, to the boy's astonishment. "Let me see. Yes, here in this drawer I have many letters from Carlyle."

At these words Miss Alcott came from the other

---

[5]Emerson visited and corresponded with the Scottish writer Thomas Carlyle, whose anti-materialism, romanticism, and faith in the power of heroic individuals were congruent with many of Emerson's beliefs.

Edward Bok, twelve years old

Courtesy Rachel Bok Goldman

Illustration from articles describing Bok's boyhood
encounter with Ralph Waldo Emerson,
The Ladies' Home Journal, *March 1905*

part of the room, her wet eyes dancing with pleasure and her face wreathed in smiles.

"I think we can help this young man; do you not think so, Louisa?" said Emerson, smiling toward Miss Alcott. The whole atmosphere of the room had now changed. How different the expression of his eyes as now Emerson looked at the boy! "And you have come all the way from New York to ask me that!" he said smilingly as the boy told him of his trip. "Now, let us see," he said, as he delved in a drawer full of letters.

For a moment he groped among letters and papers, and then, softly closing the drawer, he began that ominous low whistle once more, looked inquiringly at each, and dropped his eyes straightaway to the papers before him on his desk. It was to be only for a few moments, then! Miss Alcott turned away.

The boy felt the interview could not last much longer. So, anxious to have some personal souvenir of the meeting, he said: "Mr. Emerson, will you be so good as to write your name in this book for me?" and he brought out an album he had in his pocket.

"Name?" he asked vaguely.

"Yes, please," said the boy, "your name: Ralph Waldo Emerson."

But the sound of the name brought no response from the eyes.

"Please write out the name you want," he said finally, "and I will copy it for you if I can."

It was hard for the boy to believe his own senses.

But picking up a pen he wrote: "Ralph Waldo Emerson, Concord, November 22, 1881."

Emerson looked at it, and said mournfully: "Thank you." Then he picked up the pen, and writing the single letter "R" stopped, followed his finger until it reached the "W" of Waldo, and studiously copied letter by letter! At the word "Concord" he seemed to hesitate, as if the task were too great, but finally he copied again, letter by letter, until the second "c" was reached. "Another 'o' " he said, and interpolated an extra letter in the name of the town which he had done so much to make famous the world over. When he had finished he handed back the book, in which there was written:

R. Waldo Emerson
Conorcord
November 22, 1881

The boy put the book into his pocket; and as he did so Emerson's eye caught the slip on his desk, in the boy's handwriting, and, with a smile of absolute enlightenment, he turned and said:

"You wish me to write my name? With pleasure. Have you a book with you?"

Overcome with astonishment, Edward mechanically handed him the album once more from his pocket. Quickly turning over the leaves, Emerson picked up the pen, and pushing aside the slip, wrote without a moment's hesitation:

Ralph Waldo Emerson
Concord

The boy was almost dazed at the instantaneous transformation in the man!

Miss Alcott now grasped this moment to say: "Well, we must be going!"

"So soon?" said Emerson, rising and smiling. Then turning to Miss Alcott he said: "It was very kind of you, Louisa, to run over this morning and bring your young friend."

Then turning to the boy he said: "Thank you so much for coming to see me. You must come over again while you are with the Alcotts. Good morning! Isn't it a beautiful day out?" he said, and as he shook the boy's hand there was a warm grasp in it, the fingers closed around those of the boy, and as Edward looked into those deep eyes they twinkled and smiled back.

The going was all so different from the coming. The boy was grateful that his last impression was of a moment when the eye kindled and the hand pulsated.

The two then walked back to the Alcott home in an almost unbroken silence. Once Edward ventured to remark: "You have no idea, Miss Alcott, how grateful I am to you."

"Well, my boy," she answered, "Phillips Brooks

may be right: that it is something to have seen him even so, than not to have seen him at all. But to us it is so *sad,* so very sad. The twilight is gently closing in."

And so it proved—just five months afterward.

Eventful day after eventful day followed Edward's Boston visit. The following morning he spent with Wendell Phillips, who presented him with letters from William Lloyd Garrison, Lucretia Mott,[6] and other famous persons; and then, he wrote a letter of introduction to Charles Francis Adams,[7] whom he enjoined to give Bok autograph letters from his two presidential forbears, John Adams and John Quincy Adams, sent Edward on his way rejoicing. Mr. Adams received the boy with equal graciousness and liberality. Wonderful letters from the two Adamses were his when he left.

And then, taking the train for New York, Edward Bok went home, sitting up all night in a day-coach for the double purpose of saving the cost of a sleeping berth and of having a chance to classify and clarify the events of the most wonderful week in his life!

---

[6]Like Emerson, William Lloyd Garrison and Lucretia Mott, who had played legendary roles in the antislavery movement, were in their dotage by the time Bok visited Massachusetts.

[7]Particularly given the context of the antislavery movement that is evident here, this reference is to the Charles Francis Adams who, as American ambassador to Great Britain during the Civil War, worked successfully to persuade the British government not to recognize the Confederacy. His son, of the same name, was a noted economist, historian, and expert on railroad finance and regulation.

VII

A Plunge into Wall Street

THE FATHER of Edward Bok passed away when Edward was eighteen years of age, and it was found that the amount of the small insurance left behind would barely cover the funeral expenses. Hence the two boys faced the problem of supporting the mother on their meager income. They determined to have but one goal: to put their mother back to that life of comfort to which she had been brought up and was formerly accustomed. But that was not possible on their income. It was evident that other employment must be taken on during the evenings.

The city editor of the *Brooklyn Eagle* had given Edward the assignment of covering the news of the theaters; he was to ascertain "coming attractions" and any other dramatic items of news interest. One Monday evening, when a multiplicity of events crowded the reportorial corps, Edward was delegated to "cover" the Grand Opera House, where Rose Coghlan[1] was to appear in a play that had already been seen in Brooklyn, and called, therefore, for no special dramatic criticism. Yet *The Eagle* wanted to cover it. It so happened that young Edward had made another

[1]Rose Coghlan was a British actress who gave frequent performances in America beginning in 1871.

appointment for that evening he considered more important; yet not wishing to disappoint his editor he accepted the assignment. He had seen Miss Coghlan in the play; so he kept his other engagement, and without approaching the theater he wrote a notice to the effect that Miss Coghlan acted her part, if anything, with greater power than on her previous Brooklyn visit, and so forth, and handed it in.

Unfortunately, however, Miss Coghlan had been taken ill just before the raising of the curtain, and, there being no understudy, no performance had been given and the audience dismissed. All this was duly commented upon by the New York morning newspapers. Edward read this bit of news on the ferry boat, but his notice was in the hands of the city editor.

On reaching home that evening he found a summons from the *Eagle,* and the next morning he received a rebuke, and was informed that his chances with the paper were over. The ready acknowledgement and evident regret of the crestfallen boy, however, appealed to the editor, and before the end of the week he called the boy to him and promised him another chance, provided the lesson had sunk in. It had, and it left a lasting impression.

One evening when Edward was attending a theatrical performance, he noticed the restlessness of the women in the audience between the acts. In those days it was, even more than at present, the custom for men to go out between acts, leaving the women alone.

Edward looked at the program in his hands. It was a large eleven-by-nine sheet, four pages, badly printed, with nothing in it save the cast, a few advertisements, and an announcement of some coming attraction. The boy mechanically folded the program, turned it long side up, and wondered whether a program of this smaller size, easier to handle, with an attractive cover and some reading matter, would not be profitable.

When he reached home he made up an eight-page "dummy," pasted an attractive picture on the cover, indicated the material to go inside, and on the next morning showed it to the manager of the theater. The program as issued was an item of considerable expense to management; Edward offered to supply his new program without cost, provided he was given the exclusive right, and the manager at once accepted the offer. Edward then sought a friend, Frederic L. Colver, who had a larger experience in publishing and advertising, with whom he formed a partnership. Deciding that immediately upon the issuance of their first program the idea was likely to be taken up by the other theaters, Edward proceeded to secure the exclusive rights to them all. The two young publishers solicited their advertisements on the way to and from business mornings and evenings, and shortly the first smaller-sized theater program, now in use in all theaters, appeared. The venture was successful from the start, returning a comfortable profit each week.

Edward's partner introduced him into a debating

society called the Philomathean Society, made up of young men connected with Plymouth Church, of which Henry Ward Beecher[2] was pastor. The debates took the form of a miniature congress, each member representing a state, and it is a curious coincidence that Edward drew, by lot, the representation of the Commonwealth of Pennsylvania. Edward became intensely interested in the society's doings, and it was not long before he was elected president.

The society derived its revenue from the dues of its members and from an annual concert given under its auspices in Plymouth Church. When the time for the concert under Edward's presidency came around, he decided that the occasion should be unique so as to insure a crowded house. He induced Mr. Beecher to preside; he got General Grant's promise to come and speak; he secured the gratuitous services of all of the first rank of concert singers of that day, with the result that the church could not accommodate the crowd attracted by such a program.

[2]Henry Ward Beecher became one of the most admired but nonetheless controversial ministers of the nineteenth century. He gained prominence in 1844 with *Seven Lectures to Young Men,* advocating the work ethic and the avoidance of dissipation. He accepted the pulpit of Brooklyn's Plymouth Congregational Church in 1847 and built a huge following. In 1874, he became involved in one of the greatest scandals of the late nineteenth century when one of his best friends, Theodore Tilton, sued him on grounds of committing adultery with his wife, leading to a trial that resulted in a hung jury. By the time of his association with Bok, Beecher had won back most of his public following and crowds of people jammed Plymouth Church to hear him preach.

Edward Bok, sixteen years old

Courtesy Rachel Bok Goldman

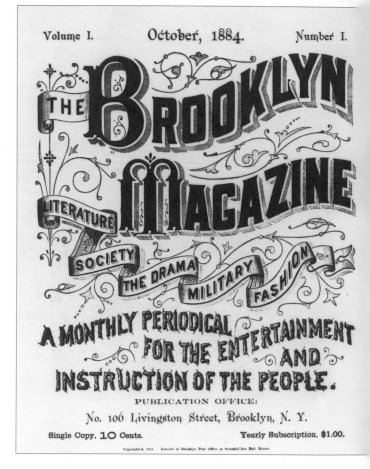

The Brooklyn Magazine, *established by Edward Bok and a partner,*
Frederic L. Colver, in 1884

It now entered into the minds of the two young theater-program publishers to extend their publishing interests by issuing an "organ" for their society, and the first issue of *The Philomathean Review* duly appeared with Mr. Colver as its publisher and Edward Bok as editor. Edward had now an opportunity to try his wings in an editorial capacity. The periodical was, of course, essentially an organ of the society; but gradually it took on a more general character, so that its circulation might extend over a larger portion of Brooklyn. With this extension came a further broadening of its contents, which now began to take on a literary character, and it was not long before its two projectors realized that the periodical had outgrown its name. It was decided—late in 1884—to change the name to *The Brooklyn Magazine*.

There was a periodical called *The Plymouth Pulpit*, which presented verbatim reports of the sermons of Mr. Beecher, and Edward got the idea of absorbing the *Pulpit* in the *Magazine*. But that required more capital than he and his partner could command. They consulted Mr. Beecher, who, attracted by the enterprise of the two boys, sent them with letters of introduction to a few of his most influential parishioners with the result that the pair soon had financial backing by some of the leading men in Brooklyn.

The young publishers could now go on. Understanding that Mr. Beecher's sermons might give a partial and denominational tone to the magazine, Edward arranged to publish also in its pages verbatim reports of the sermons of the Reverend T. DeWitt Talmage, whose reputation was then at its zenith.[3] The young editor now realized that he had a rather heavy cargo of sermons to carry each month; accordingly, in order that his magazine might not appear to be exclusively religious, he determined that its literary contents should be of a high order and equal in interest to the sermons. But this called for additional capital, and the capital furnished was not for that purpose.

It is here that Edward's autographic acquaintances stood him in good stead. He went in turn to each noted person he had met, explained his plight and stated his ambitions, with the result that very soon the magazine and the public were surprised at the distinction of the contributors to *The Brooklyn Magazine*. Each number contained a noteworthy list of them, and when an article by the president of the United States, then Rutherford B. Hayes, opened one of the numbers, the public was astonished, since up to that time the unwritten rule that a president's writings were confined to official pronouncements had scarcely been broken. William Dean Howells, General Grant, General Sherman, Phillips Brooks, Gen-

[3]Rev. T. DeWitt Talmage was a prominent American clergyman who became minister of Brooklyn's First Presbyterian Church in 1869. His sermons were published in approximately 3,500 newspapers, and he became wealthy as a lecturer and writer. He also wrote a regular monthly column, "Under My Study-Lamp," throughout the early 1890s in *The Ladies' Home Journal*.

eral Sheridan, Canon Farrar,[4] Cardinal Gibbons,[5] Marion Harland,[6] Margaret Sangster[7]—the most prominent men and women of the day, some of whom had never written for magazines—began to appear in the young editor's contents. Editors wondered how the publishers could afford it, whereas, in fact, not a single name represented an honorarium. Each contributor had come gratuitously to the aid of the editor.

At first, the circulation of the magazine permitted the boys to wrap the copies themselves; and then they, with two other boys, would carry as huge bundles as they could lift, put them late at night on the front platform of the street cars, and take them to the post office. Thus the boys absolutely knew the growth of their circulation by the weight of their bundles and the number of their front-platform trips each month.

[4]Frederic William Farrar, eminent British clergyman and Dean of Canterbury Cathedral, was also a prolific author.

[5]Cardinal James Gibbons was probably the most visible and powerful Catholic clergyman in America for almost half a century. He consistently espoused liberal doctrines on separation of church and state, workers' rights, and the incorporation of parochial schools into the public school system, and ignored directives from the Vatican that clashed with his democratic philosophy.

[6]Marion Harland was the pseudonym of Mary Virginia Hawes Terhune, who published a phenomenal number of novels and short stories, mostly about plantation life in the Old South. Her fiction condemned feminist agitation.

[7]Margaret Sangster, born Margaret Elizabeth Munson, sold her first story when she was seventeen. Obliged to write for a living when her husband died in 1870, she eventually became the editor of *Harper's Bazaar* in 1889. In ten years at its helm, she de-emphasized fiction and made it a "service" periodical aimed at female readers.

Soon a baker's handcart was leased for an evening and that was added to the capacity of the front platforms. Then one eventful month it was seen that a horse truck would have to be employed. Within three weeks, a double horse truck was necessary, and three trips had to be made.

By this time Edward Bok had become so intensely interested in the editorial problem, and his partner in the periodical publishing part, that they decided to sell out their theater program interests and devote themselves to the magazine and its rapidly increasing circulation. All of Edward's editorial work had naturally to be done outside of his business hours, in other words, in the evenings and on Sundays; and the young editor found himself fully occupied. He now revived the old idea of selecting a subject and having ten or twenty writers express their views on it. It was the old symposium idea, but it had not been presented in American journalism for a number of years. He conceived the topic "Should America Have a Westminster Abbey?" and induced some twenty of the foremost men and women of the day to discuss it. When the discussion was presented in the magazine, the form being new and the theme novel, Edward was careful to send advance sheets to the newspapers, which treated it at length in reviews and editorials with marked effect upon the circulation of the magazine.

All this time, while Edward Bok was an editor in his evenings he was, during the day, a stenographer and clerk of the Western Union Telegraph Company. The two occupations were hardly compatible, but each meant a source of revenue to the boy, and he felt he must hold on to both.

After his father passed away, the position of the boy's desk—next to the empty desk of his father—was a cause of constant depression to him. This was understood by the attorney for the company, a Mr. Clarence Cary, who sought the head of Edward's department, with the result that Edward was transferred to Mr. Cary's department as the attorney's private stenographer.

Edward had been much attracted to Mr. Cary, and the attorney believed in the boy, and decided to show his interest by pushing him along. He had heard of the dual role Edward was playing. He bought a copy of the magazine, and he was interested. Edward now worked with new zest for his employer and friend; while in every free moment he read law, feeling that, as almost all his forbears had been lawyers, he might perhaps be destined for the bar.

The control of the Western Union Telegraph Company had now passed into the hands of Jay Gould and his companions, and in the many legal matters arising therefrom, Edward saw much of "the little wizard of Wall Street."[8] One day, the financier had to dictate a

---

[8]Jason (Jay) Gould was one of the leading financial speculators of the period following the Civil War. His name was synonymous with financial chicanery. Historians have generally treated him harshly, but a distinguished scholar, Maury Klein, has written a more appreciative account of his career.

contract and, coming into Mr. Cary's office, decided to dictate it then and there. An hour afterward Edward delivered the copy of the contract to Mr. Gould, and the financier was so struck by its accuracy and by the legibility of the handwriting that afterward he almost daily "happened in" to dictate to Mr. Cary's stenographer. Mr. Gould's private stenographer was in his own office in lower Broadway; but on his way downtown in the morning, Mr. Gould invariably stopped at the Western Union Building, at 195 Broadway, and the habit resulted in the installation of a private office there. He borrowed Edward to do his stenography. The boy found himself taking not only letters from Mr. Gould's dictation, but, what interested him particularly, the financier's orders to buy and sell stock.

Edward watched the effects on the stock-market of these little notes which he wrote out and then shot through a pneumatic tube to Mr. Gould's brokers. Naturally, the results enthralled the boy, and he told Mr. Cary about his discoveries. This, in turn, interested Mr. Cary; Mr. Gould's dictations were frequently given in Mr. Cary's own office, where, as his desk was not ten feet from that of his stenographer, the attorney heard them, and began to buy and sell according to the magnate's decisions.

Edward had now become tremendously interested in the stock game that he saw constantly played by the great financier. Having a little money saved up, he concluded that he would follow in the wake of Mr.

Gould's orders. One day, he naively mentioned his desire to Mr. Gould, when the financier seemed in a particularly favorable frame of mind; but Edward did not succeed in drawing out the advice he hoped for. "At least," reasoned Edward, "he knew of my intentions; and if he considered it a violation of confidence he would have said as much."

Construing the financier's silence to mean at least not a prohibition, Edward went to his Sunday-school teacher, who was a member of a Wall Street brokerage firm, laid the facts before him, and asked him if he would buy for him some Western Union stock. Edward explained, however, that somehow he did not like the gambling idea of buying "on margin," and preferred to purchase the stock outright. He was shown that this would mean smaller profits; but the boy had in mind the loss of his father's fortune, brought about largely by "stock margins," and he did not intend to follow that example. So, prudently, under the brokerage of his Sunday-school teacher, and guided by the tips of no less a man than the controlling factor of stock market finance, Edward Bok took his first plunge in Wall Street!

Of course the boy's buying and selling tallied precisely with the rise and fall of Western Union stock. It could scarcely have been otherwise. Jay Gould had the cards all in his hands; and as he bought and sold, so Edward bought and sold. The trouble was, the combination did not end there, as Edward might have foreseen had he been older and wiser. For as Edward bought and sold, so did his Sunday-school teacher and all his customers who had seen the wonderful acumen of their broker in choosing exactly the right time to buy and sell Western Union. But Edward did not know this.

One day a rumor became current on the Street that an agreement had been reached by the Western Union Company and its bitter rival, the American Union Telegraph Company, whereby the former was to absorb the latter. Naturally, the report affected Western Union stock. But Mr. Gould denied it in toto; said the report was not true, no such consolidation was in view or had even been considered. Down tumbled the stock, of course.

But it so happened that Edward knew the rumor was true, because Mr. Gould, some time before, had personally given him the contract of consolidation to copy. The next day a rumor to the effect that the American Union was to absorb the Western Union appeared on the first page of every New York newspaper. Edward knew exactly whence this rumor emanated. He had heard it talked over. Again, Western Union stock dropped several points. Then he noticed that Mr. Gould became a heavy buyer. So became Edward—as heavy as he could. Jay Gould pooh-poohed the latest rumor. The boy awaited developments.

On Sunday afternoon, Edward's Sunday-school teacher asked the boy to walk home with him, and on reaching the house took him into the study and asked him whether he felt justified in putting all his savings in Western Union just at that time when the price was tumbling so fast and the market was so unsteady. Edward assured his teacher that he was right, although he explained that he could not discuss the basis of his assurance.

Edward thought his teacher looked worried, and after a little there came the revelation that he, seeing that Edward was buying to his limit, had likewise done so. But the broker had bought on margin and his margin had been wiped out by the decline in the stock caused by the rumors. He explained to Edward that he could recoup his losses, heavy though they were— in fact, he explained that nearly everything he possessed was involved—if Edward's basis was sure and the stock would recover.

Edward keenly felt the responsibility placed upon him. He could never clearly diagnose his feelings when he saw his teacher in this new light. The broker's "customers" had been hinted at, and the boy of eighteen wondered how far his responsibility went and how many persons were involved. But the deal came out all right, for when, three days afterward, the contract was made public, Western Union, of course, skyrocketed, Jay Gould sold out, and all the customers sold out!

How long a string it was Edward never discovered, but he determined there and then to end his Wall Street experience; his original amount had multiplied; he was content to let well enough alone, and from that day to this Edward Bok has kept out of Wall Street. He had seen enough of its manipulations; and, although on "the inside," he decided that the combination of his teacher and his customers was a responsibility too great for him to carry.

Furthermore, Edward decided to leave the Western Union. The longer he remained, the less he liked its atmosphere. And the closer his contact with Jay Gould, the more doubtful he became of the wisdom of such an association and perhaps its unconscious influence upon his own life in its formative period.

In fact, it was an experience with Mr. Gould that definitely fixed Edward's determination. The financier decided one Saturday to leave on a railroad inspection tour the following Monday. It was necessary that a meeting of one of his railroad interests should be held before his departure, and he fixed the meeting for Sunday at eleven-thirty at his residence on Fifth Avenue. He asked Edward to be there to take the notes of the meeting.

The meeting was protracted, and at one o'clock Mr. Gould suggested an adjournment for luncheon, the meeting to reconvene at two. Turning to Edward, the financier said: "You may go out to luncheon and return in an hour." So, on Sunday afternoon, with the Windsor Hotel on the opposite corner as the only visible place to get something to eat, but where he could not afford to go, Edward, with just fifteen cents in his pocket, was turned out to find a luncheon place.

He bought three apples for five cents—all that he could afford to spend, and even this meant that he must walk home from the ferry to his house in Brooklyn—and these he ate as he walked up and down Fifth Avenue until his hour was over. When the meeting ended at three o'clock, Mr. Gould said that, as he was leaving for the West early next morning, he would like Edward to write out his notes and have them at his house by eight o'clock. There were over forty notebook pages of minutes. The remainder of Edward's Sunday afternoon and evening was spent in transcribing the notes. By rising at half past five the next morning he reached Mr. Gould's house at a quarter to eight, handed him the minutes, and was dismissed without so much as a word of thanks or a nod of approval from the financier.

Edward felt that this exceeded the limit of fair treatment by employer of employee. He spoke of it to Mr. Cary, and asked whether he would object if he tried to get away from such influence and secure another position. His employer asked in which direction he would like to go, and Edward unhesitatingly suggested the publishing business. He talked it over from every angle with his employer, and Mr. Cary not only agreed with him that his decision was wise, but promised to find him a position such as he had in mind.

It was not long before Mr. Cary made good his word, and told Edward that his friend Henry Holt, the publisher, would like to give him a trial.[9]

[9]Henry Holt was one of the most creative figures in the history of American publishing. A partnership he helped establish became the first firm in America to publish books without printing

The day before he was to leave the Western Union Telegraph Company the fact of his resignation became known to Mr. Gould. The financier told the boy there was no reason for his leaving, and that he would personally see to it that a substantial increase was made in his salary. Edward explained that the salary, while of importance to him, did not influence him so much as securing a position in a business in which he felt he would be happier.

"And what business is that?" asked the financier.

"The publishing of books," replied the boy.

"You are making a great mistake," answered the little man, fixing his keen gray eyes on the boy. "Books are a luxury. The public spends its largest money on necessities: on what it can't do without. It must telegraph; it need not read. It can read in libraries. A promising boy such as you are, with his life before him, should choose the right sort of business, not the wrong one."

But, as facts proved, the "little wizard of Wall Street" was wrong in his prediction; Edward Bok was not choosing the wrong business.

Years afterward when Edward was cruising up the

—

or retailing them. It also pioneered in business ethics by paying for the right to publish books by popular European authors instead of pirating them. Holt successfully solicited manuscripts by a large number of eminent authors and poets, including Henry Adams, Robert Frost, Thomas Hardy, William James, Walter Lippman, John Stuart Mill, and H. G. Wells. He stimulated the creation of a market for quality literature by publishing outstanding books at low prices.

Hudson with a yachting party one Saturday afternoon, the sight of Jay Gould's mansion, upon approaching Irvington, awakened the desire of the women on board to see his wonderful orchid collection. Edward explained his previous association with the financier and offered to recall himself to him, if the party wished to take the chance of recognition. A note was written to Mr. Gould and sent ashore, and the answer came back that they were welcome to visit the orchid houses. Jay Gould, in person, received the party and, placing it under the personal conduct of his gardener, turned to Edward and, indicating a bench, said: "Come and sit down here with me."

"Well," said the financier, who was in his domestic mood, quite different from his Wall Street aspect, "I see in the papers that you seem to be making your way in the publishing business."

Edward expressed surprise that the Wall Street magnate had followed his work.

"I have because I always felt you had it in you to make a successful man. But not in that business," he added quickly. "You were born for the Street. You would have made a great success there, and that is what I had in mind for you. In the publishing business you will go just so far; in the Street you could have gone as far as you liked. There is room there; there is none in the publishing business. It's not too late now, for that matter," continued the "little wizard," fastening his steel eyes on the lad before him!

And Edward Bok has often speculated whither Jay

Gould might have led him. To many a young man, a suggestion from such a source would have seemed the one to heed and follow. But Edward Bok's instinct never failed him. He felt that his path lay far apart from that of Jay Gould—and the farther the better!

In 1882 Edward, with a feeling of distinct relief, left the employ of Western Union Telegraph Company and associated himself with the publishing business in which he had correctly divined that his future lay.

His chief regret on leaving his position was in severing the close relations, almost as of father and son, between Mr. Cary and himself. When Edward was left alone, with the passing away of his father, Clarence Cary had put his sheltering arm around the boy, and with the tremendous encouragement of the phrase that the boy never forgot, "I think you have it in you, Edward, to make a successful man," he took him under his wing. It was a turning point in Edward Bok's life as he felt at the time and as he saw more clearly afterward.

He remained in touch with his friend, however, keeping him advised of his progress in everything he did, not only at that time, but all through his later years. And it was given to Edward to feel the deep satisfaction of having Mr. Cary say, before he passed away, that the boy had more than justified the confidence reposed in him. Mr. Cary lived to see him well on his way, until, indeed, Edward had had the proud happiness of introducing to his benefactor the son who bore his name, Cary William Bok.

VIII

Starting a Newspaper Syndicate

EDWARD felt that his daytime hours, spent in a publishing atmosphere as a stenographer with Henry Holt and Company, were more in line with his editorial duties during the evenings. *The Brooklyn Magazine* was now earning a comfortable income for its two young proprietors, and their backers were entirely satisfied with the way it was being conducted. In fact, one of these backers, Mr. Rufus T. Bush,[1] associated with the Standard Oil Company, who became especially interested, thought he saw in the success of the two boys a possible opening for one of his sons, who was shortly to graduate from college. He talked to the publisher and editor about the idea, but the boys showed by their books that while there was a reasonable income for them, not wholly dependent on the magazine, there was no room for a third.

Mr. Bush now suggested that he buy the magazine for his son, alter its name, enlarge its scope, and make of it a national periodical. Arrangements were concluded, those who had financially backed the venture were paid, and the two boys received a satisfactory

[1]Presumably an owner of the Bush & Denslow Manufacturing Company, an oil-refining firm located in Brooklyn that belonged to the Standard Oil Trust.

amount for all their work in building up the magazine. Mr. Bush asked Edward to suggest a name for the new periodical, and in the following month of May 1887, *The Brooklyn Magazine* became *The American Magazine,* with its publication office in New York. But, though a great deal of money was spent on the new magazine, it did not succeed. Mr. Bush sold his interest in the periodical, which, once more changing its name, became *The Cosmopolitan Magazine.* Since then it has passed through the hands of several owners, but the name has remained the same. Before Mr. Bush sold *The American Magazine* he urged Edward to come back as its editor with promise of financial support; but the young man felt instinctively that his return would not be wise. The magazine had been *The Cosmopolitan* for only a short time when the new owners, Mr. Paul J. Slicht and Mr. E. D. Walker, also solicited the previous editor to accept reappointment. But Edward, feeling that his baby had been rechristened too often for him to father it again, declined the proposition. He had not heard the last of it, however, for, by a curious coincidence, its subsequent owner, entirely ignorant of Edward's previous association with the magazine, invited him to connect himself with it. Thus three times could Edward Bok have returned to the magazine for whose creation he was responsible.

Edward was now without editorial cares; but he had already, even before disposing of the magazine, embarked on another line of endeavor. In sending to a number of newspapers the advance sheets of a particularly striking "feature" in one of his numbers of *The Brooklyn Magazine,* it occurred to him that he was furnishing a good deal of valuable material to these papers without cost. It is true his magazine was receiving the advertising value of editorial comment; but the boy wondered whether the newspapers would not be willing to pay for the privilege of simultaneous publication. An inquiry or two proved that they would. Thus Edward stumbled upon the "syndicate" plan of furnishing the same article to a larger group of newspapers, one in each city, for simultaneous publication. He looked over the ground, and found that while his idea was certainly not a new one, since two "syndicate" agencies already existed, the field was by no means fully covered, and that the success of a third agency would depend entirely upon its ability to furnish the newspapers with material equally good or better than they received from the others. After following the material furnished by these agencies for two or three weeks, Edward decided that there was plenty of room for his new ideas.

He discussed the matter with his former magazine partner, Colver, and suggested that if they could induce Mr. Beecher to write a weekly comment about current events for the newspapers it would make an auspicious beginning. They decided to talk it over with the famous preacher. For to be a "Plymouth boy" that is, to go to the Plymouth Church Sunday school and to attend church there—was to know personally and become devoted to Henry Ward Beecher. And the two were synonymous. There was no distance between Mr. Beecher and his "Plymouth boys." Each understood the other. The tie was that of absolute comradeship.

"I don't believe in it, boys," said Mr. Beecher when Edward and his friend broached the syndicate letter to him. "No one yet ever made a cent out of my supposed literary work."

All the more reason, was the argument, why someone should.

Mr. Beecher smiled! How well he knew the youthful enthusiasm that rushes in, etc.

"Well, all right, boys! I like your pluck," he finally said. 'I'll help you if I can."

The boys agreed to pay Mr. Beecher a weekly sum of $250—which he knew was considerable for them.

When the first article had been written they took him their first check. He looked at it quizzically, and then at the boys. Then he said simply: "Thank you." He took a pin and pinned the check to his desk. There it remained, much to the curiosity of the two boys.

The following week he had written the second article and the boys gave him another check. He pinned that up over the other. "I like to look at them," was his only explanation, as he saw Edward's inquiring glance one morning.

The third check was treated the same way. When the boys handed him the fourth, one morning, as he was pinning it up over the others, he asked, "When do you get your money from the newspapers?"

He was told that the bills were going out that morning for the four letters constituting a month's service.

"I see," he remarked.

A fortnight passed, then one day Mr. Beecher asked: "Well, how are the checks coming in?"

"Very well," he was assured

"Suppose you let me see how much you've got in," he suggested, and the boys brought the accounts to him.

After looking at them he said: "That's very interesting. How much have you in the bank?"

He was told the balance, less the checks given to him.

"But I haven't turned them in yet," he explained.

"Anyhow, you have enough in the bank to meet the checks you have given me, and a profit besides, haven't you?"

He was assured they had.

Then, taking his bank book from a drawer, he unpinned the six checks on his desk, endorsed each thus:

For deposit Mechanics Bank

H. W. Beecher

wrote a deposit-slip, and, handing the book to Edward, said:

"Just hand that in at the bank as you go by, will you?"

Edward was very young then, and Mr. Beecher's methods of financiering seemed to him quite in line with current notions of the Plymouth pastor's lack of business knowledge. But as the years rolled on the incident appeared in a new light—a striking example of the great preacher's wonderful considerateness.

IX

The First "Woman's Page," "Literary Leaves," and Entering Scribner's

M R. BEECHER'S weekly newspaper "syndicate" letter was not only successful, it made liberal
money for the writer and for its two young publishers,
but it served to introduce Edward Bok's proposed
agency to the newspapers under the most favorable
conditions. With one stroke, the attention of newspaper editors had been attracted, and Edward concluded to take quick advantage of it. He organized the
Bok Syndicate Press, with offices in New York, and
his brother, William J. Bok, as partner and active manager. Edward's days were occupied, of course, with
his duties in the Holt publishing house, where he was
acquiring a first-hand knowledge of the business.

Edward's attention was now turned, for the first
time, to women and their reading habits. He became
interested in the fact that the American woman was
not a newspaper reader. He tried to find out the psychology of this, and finally reached the conclusion,
on looking over the newspapers, that the absence of
any distinctive material for women was a factor. He
talked the matter over with several prominent New
York editors, who frankly acknowledged that they
would like nothing better than to interest women and
make them readers of their papers. But they were

equally frank in confessing that they were ignorant both of what women wanted, and, even if they knew, of where such material was to be had. Edward at once saw that here was an open field. It was a productive field, since a newspaper would benefit enormously in its advertising if it could offer a feminine clientele.

There was a bright letter of New York gossip published in the *New York Star,* called "Bab's Babble." Edward had read it and saw the possibility of his syndicating this as a woman's letter from New York. He instinctively realized that women all over the country would read it. He then sought out the author, made arrangements with her and with former Governor Dorscheimer,[1] owner of the paper, and the letter was sent out to a group of papers. It was an instantaneous success, and a syndicate of ninety newspapers was quickly organized.

Edward followed this up by engaging Ella Wheeler Wilcox, then at the height of her career, to write a weekly letter on women's topics.[2] This he syndicated in conjunction with the other letter, and the editors invariably grouped the two letters. This naturally led to the idea of supplying an entire page of matter of in-

[1]Governor Dorscheimer: actually Lieutenant-Governor of New York from 1875–1880.

[2]Ella Wheeler Wilcox is best known for her poem, "Solitude," which contains the lines, "Laugh, and the world laughs with you; Weep, and you weep alone." She attained fame in 1883 when a publisher turned down a collection of her love poetry on the grounds that it was immoral. After its acceptance by another firm, it sold 60,000 copies in two years and established her reputation.

terest to women. The plan was proposed to a number of editors, who at once saw the possibilities in it and promised support. The young syndicator now laid under contribution all the famous women writers of the day. He chose the best of the men writers to write on women's topics and it was not long before the syndicate was supplying a page of women's material. The newspapers played up the innovation. Thus was introduced into the newspaper press of the United States the "Woman's Page."

The material supplied by the Bok Syndicate Press was of the best, the standard was kept high, writers were selected from among the popular authors of the day, and readability was the cardinal note. The women bought the newspapers containing the new page, the advertiser began to feel the presence of the new reader, and every newspaper that could not get the rights for the "Bok Page," as it came to be known, started a "Woman's Page" of its own. Naturally, the material obtained was inferior. No single newspaper could afford what the syndicate, with the expense divided among a hundred newspapers, could pay. Nor had the editors of these woman's pages either a standard or a policy. In desperation they engaged any person they could to "get a lot of woman's stuff." It was *stuff*, and of the trashiest kind. So that almost coincident with the birth of the idea began its abuse and disintegration; the result we now can see is the meaningless presentations that pass for "woman's pages" in the newspaper of today.

This is true even of the woman's material in the leading newspapers, and the reason is not difficult to find. The average editor has, as a rule, no time to study the changing conditions of women's interests; his time is and must be engrossed by the news and editorial pages. He usually delegates the Sunday "specials" to some editor who, again, has little time to study the ever-changing women's problems, particularly in these days, and he relies upon unintelligent advice, or he places his "woman's page" in the hands of some woman with the comfortable assurance that, being a woman, she ought to know what interests her sex.

But having given the subject little thought, he attaches minor importance to the woman's "stuff," regarding it rather in the light of something that he "must carry to catch the women"; and forthwith he either forgets it or refuses to give the editor of his woman's page even a reasonable allowance to spend on her material. The result is, of course, inevitable: pages of worthless material. There is, in fact, no part of the Sunday newspaper of today upon which so much good and now expensive white paper is wasted as upon the pages marked for the home, for women, and for children.

Edward Bok now became convinced, from his book-publishing association, that if the American women were not reading the newspapers, the American public, as a whole, was not reading the number of books that it should, considering the intelligence and wealth of the people, and the cheap prices at which books were sold. He concluded to see whether he could not induce the newspapers to give larger and more prominent space to the news of the book world.

Owing to his constant contact with authors, he was in a peculiarly fortunate position to know their plans in advance of execution, and he was beginning to learn the ins and outs of the book-publishing world. He canvassed the newspapers subscribing to his syndicate features, but found a disinclination to give space to literary news. To the average editor, purely literary features held less of an appeal than did the features for women. Fewer persons were interested in books, they declared; besides, the publishing houses were not so liberal advertisers as the department stores. The whole question rested on a commercial basis.

Edward believed he could convince editors of the public interest in a newsy, readable New York literary letter, and he prevailed upon the editor of the *New York Star* to allow him to supplement the book reviews of George Parsons Lathrop in that paper by a column of literary chat called "Literary Leaves." For a number of weeks he continued to write this department, and confine it to the New York paper, feeling that he needed the experience to acquire a readable style, and he wanted to be sure that he had opened a sufficient number of productive news channels to ensure a continuous flow of literary information.

Occasionally he sent to an editor here and there what he thought was a particularly newsy letter just "for his information, not for sale." The editor of the

Philadelphia Times was the first to discover that his paper wanted the letter, and the *Boston Journal* followed suit. Then the editor of the *Cincinnati Times-Star* discovered the letter in the *New York Star* and asked that it be supplied weekly with the letter. These newspapers then renamed the letter "Bok's Literary Leaves," and the feature began its successful career.

Edward had been in the employ of Henry Holt and Company as clerk and stenographer for two years when Mr. Cary sent for him and told him that there was an opening in the publishing house of Charles Scribner's Sons, if he wanted to make a change. Edward saw at once the larger opportunities possible in a house of the importance of the Scribners, and he immediately placed himself in communication with Mr. Charles Scribner,[3] with the result that in January 1884, he entered the employ of these publishers as stenographer to the two members of the firm and to Mr. Edward L. Burlingame,[4] literary advisor to the house. He was to receive a salary of eighteen dollars and thirty-three cents per week, which was then con-

[3]Charles Scribner founded a publishing company in New York City in 1846 with Isaac D. Baker. Choosing not to rely on reprinting British works, they successfully cultivated American authors. In 1850, when Baker died, Scribner continued the enterprise under his own name, built a distinguished list of theological works, and acquired Bangs & Co., a leading importer of British books. In 1870, he started a magazine, *Scribner's Monthly,* which ultimately became highly successful as *Scribner's Magazine.* His firm, continued by his descendants, continues to flourish today.

[4]Edward Livermore Burlingame was editor of *Scribner's Magazine* from 1886–1914.

sidered a fair wage for stenographic work. The type-writer had at that time not come into use. All letters were written in longhand. Once more his legible hand-writing had secured for him a position.

Edward Bok was now twenty-one years of age. He had already done a prodigious amount of work for a boy of his years. He was always busy. Every spare moment of his evenings was devoted either to writing his literary letter, to the arrangement or editing of articles for his newspaper syndicate, to the steady acquirement of autograph letters in which he still persisted, or to helping Mr. Beecher in his literary work.

Enterprise and energy the boy unquestionably possessed, but one need only think back even thus far in his life to see the continuous good fortune which had followed him in the friendships he had made and in the men with whom his life, at its most formative period, had come into close contact. If we are inclined to credit young Bok with an ever-willingness to work and a certain quality of initiative, the influences which played upon him must also be taken into account.

Take, for example, the peculiarly fortuitous circumstances under which he entered the Scribner publishing house. As stenographer to the two members of the firm, Bok was immediately brought into touch with the leading authors of the day, their works as they were discussed in the correspondence dictated to him, and the authors' terms upon which books were published. In fact, he was given as close an insight as it was possible for a young man to get into the inner workings of one of the large publishing houses in the United States, noted for the distinction of its authors and the broad scope of its books.

The Scribners had the foremost theological list of all the publishing houses; its educational list was exceptionally strong; its musical list excelled; its fiction represented the leading writers of the day; its general list was particularly noteworthy; and its foreign department, importing the leading books brought out in Great Britain and Europe, was an outstanding feature of the business. The correspondence dictated to Bok covered, naturally, all these fields, and a more remarkable opportunity for self-education was never offered a stenographer.

Mr. Burlingame was known in the publishing world for his singularly keen literary appreciation, and was accepted as one of the best judges of good fiction. Bok entered employ at Scribners as Mr. Burlingame was selecting the best short stories published within a decade for a set of books to be called Short Stories by American Authors. The correspondence for this series was dictated to Bok, and he decided to read after Mr. Burlingame and thus get an idea of the best fiction of the day. So whenever his chief wrote to an author asking for permission to include his story in the proposed series, Bok immediately hunted up the story and read it.

Later, when the house decided to start *Scribner's Magazine,* and Mr. Burlingame was selected to be its editor, all the preliminary correspondence was dictated to Bok, and he received a first-hand education in the setting up of the machinery necessary for the publication of a magazine. All this he eagerly absorbed.

He was again fortunate in that his desk was placed in the advertising department of the house; and here he found, as manager, an old-time Brooklyn friend with whom he had gone to school: Frank N. Doubleday,[5] today the senior partner of Doubleday, Page and Company. Bok had been attracted to advertising through his theater program and *Brooklyn Magazine* experience, and here was presented a chance to learn the art at first hand and according to the best traditions. So, whenever his stenographic work permitted, he assisted Mr. Doubleday in preparing and placing the advertisements of the books of the house.

Mr. Doubleday was just reviving the publication of

---

[5]Frank Nelson Doubleday began working for Charles Scribner's Sons in 1877. In 1897, he established a partnership with Samuel S. McClure, publisher of *McClure's Magazine*. In 1900, Doubleday withdrew and, with Walter Hines Page, founded Doubleday, Page and Company, which became a front-rank publishing house. Although Page left the business in 1913, Doubleday retained the corporate name until 1928 when he acquired the publishing firm established by George H. Doran and established Doubleday, Doran and Company. Doubleday pioneered in regarding publishing as a business, not merely as only a dignified literary avocation. He instituted modern accounting and auditing practices, emphasized the welfare of employees, built a chain of fifteen bookstores, and attracted an outstanding list of authors. He also competed with The Curtis Publishing Company by establishing periodicals including *World's Work* and *American Home*. Under Doubleday's son, Nelson, the firm became the largest publishing house in the United States.

a house-organ called *The Book Buyer,* and, given a chance to help in this, Bok felt he was getting back in the periodical field, especially since, under Mr. Doubleday's guidance, the little monthly soon developed into a literary magazine of very respectable size and generally bookish contents.

The house also issued another periodical, *The Presbyterian Review,* a quarterly under the editorship of a board of professors connected with Princeton and Union Theological Seminaries. This ponderous-looking magazine was not composed of what one might call "light reading," and as the price of a single copy was eighty cents and the advertisements it could reasonably expect were necessarily limited in number, the periodical was rather difficult to move. Thus the whole situation at the Scribners was adapted to give Edward an all-round training in the publishing business. It was an exceptional opportunity.

He worked early and late. An increase in his salary soon told him that he was satisfying his employers, and then, when the new *Scribner's Magazine* appeared and a little later Mr. Doubleday was delegated to take charge of the business end of it, Bok himself was placed in charge of the advertising department, with the publishing details of the two periodicals on his hands.

He suddenly found himself directing a stenographer instead of being a stenographer himself. Now his apprentice days were evidently over. He had, in addition, the charge of sending all the editorial copies of

Scribner's Magazine, *where Bok worked from 1884 to 1889*

Courtesy Library of Congress

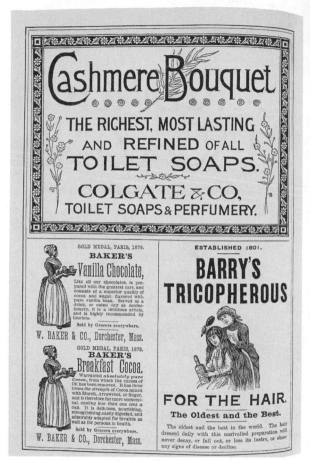

Advertisements in Scribner's Magazine *during Bok's tenure as advertising director*

Courtesy Library of Congress

the new books to the press for review, and of keeping a record of those reviews. This naturally brought to his desk the authors of the house who wished to see how the press received their works.

The study of the writers who were interested in following the press notices of their books, and those who were indifferent to them became a fascinating game to young Bok. He soon discovered that the greater the author, the less he seemed to care about his books once they were published. Bok noticed this, particularly, in the case of Robert Louis Stevenson,[6] whose work had attracted him, but, although he used the most subtle means to inveigle the author into the office to read the press notices, he never succeeded. Stevenson never seemed to have the slightest interest in what the press said of his books.

One day Mr. Burlingame asked Bok to take some proofs to Stevenson at his home. Thinking it might be the right moment to interest the author in the popular

[6]Robert Louis Stevenson made two extended visits to the United States. In 1879, as a struggling young writer, he traveled across the continent on an immigrant train to California. In 1887, now a world-famous author after the enormous success of *The Strange Case of Dr. Jekyll and Mr. Hyde* (1886), Stevenson returned to America trying to gain relief from tuberculosis. After arriving in New York City, Stevenson signed a contract with Charles Scribner's Sons under which he received $3,500 to write twelve monthly essays on any subjects he chose for *Scribner's Magazine*. He also gave Scribner's the American rights to all of his work. Stating that Burlingame sent him to make repeated visits to Stevenson "at his home" may indicate that Bok traveled to Saranac Lake, where Stevenson was living, to consult with the famous author.

acclaim that followed the publication of *Dr. Jekyll and Mr. Hyde,* Bok put a bunch of press notices in his pocket. He found the author in bed, smoking his inevitable cigarette.

As the proofs were to be brought back, Bok waited and thus had an opportunity for nearly two hours to see the author at work. No man ever went over his proofs more carefully than did Stevenson. His corrections were numerous. Sometimes for ten minutes at a time he would sit smoking and thinking over a single sentence, which, when he had satisfactorily shaped it in his mind, he would recast on the proof.

Stevenson was not a prepossessing figure at these times. With his sallow skin and his black disheveled hair, with finger nails that had been allowed to grow very long, with fingers discolored by tobacco—in short, with a general untidiness that was all his own, Stevenson, so Bok felt, was an author it was better to read than to see. And yet his kindliness and gentleness more than offset the unattractiveness of his physical appearance.

After one or two visits from Bok, having grown accustomed to him, Stevenson would discuss some sentence in an article or read some amended paragraph out loud and ask whether Bok thought it sounded better. To pass upon Stevenson as a stylist was of course hardly within Bok's mental reach, so he kept discreetly silent when Stevenson asked his opinion.

In fact, Bok reasoned it out that the novelist did not really expect an answer or an opinion, but was at such times thinking aloud. The mental process, however, was immensely interesting, particularly when Stevenson would ask Bok to hand him a book on words lying on an adjacent table. "So hard to find just the right word," Stevenson would say, and Bok got his first realization of the truth of the maxim: "Easy writing, hard reading; hard writing, easy reading."

On this particular occasion when Stevenson finished, Bok pulled out his clippings, told the author how his book was being received and was selling, what the house was doing to advertise it, explained the forthcoming play by Richard Mansfield,[7] and then offered the press notices.

Stevenson took the bundle and held it.

"That's very nice to tell me all you have," he said, "and I have been greatly interested. But you have really told me all about it, haven't you, so why should I read these notices? Hadn't I better get busy on another paper for Mr. Burlingame for the next magazine, else he'll be after me? You know how impatient these editors are." And he handed back the notices.

Bok saw it was of no use: Stevenson was interested in his work but, beyond a certain point, not in the world's reception of it. Bok's estimate of the author rose immeasurably.

His attitude was in such sharp contrast to that of

[7]Richard Mansfield established a brilliant acting career in Great Britain and the United States. In 1887, he played a dual role as Dr. Jekyll and Mr. Hyde in a dramatic adaptation of Stevenson's novel.

others who came almost daily into the office to see what the papers said, often causing discomfiture to the young advertising director by insisting on taking the notices with them. But Bok always countered this desire by reminding the author that, of course, in that case he could not get a quote from these desirable notices in his advertisements of the book. And, invariably, the notices were left behind!

It now fell to the lot of the young advertiser to arouse the interest of the public in what were to be some of the most widely read and best-known books of the day: Robert Louis Stevenson's *Dr. Jekyll and Mr. Hyde;* Frances Hodgson Burnett's *Little Lord Fauntleroy;* Andrew Carnegie's *Triumphant Democracy;* Frank R. Stockton's *The Lady, or the Tiger?* and his *Rudder Grange,* and a succession of other books.

When the stories of *Dr. Jekyll and Mr. Hyde* and *Little Lord Fauntleroy* were made into plays, Bok was given an opportunity for an entirely different kind of publicity.

Both plays were highly successful; they ran for weeks in succession. Each evening Bok had circulars of the books in every seat of the theater; he had a table filled with the books in the foyer of each theater; and he bombarded the newspapers with stories of Mr. Mansfield's method of making the quick change from one character to the other in the dual role of the Stevenson play and with anecdotes about the boy Tommy Russell in Mrs. Burnett's play. The sale of the books went merrily on, and kept pace with the success of the plays. And it all sharpened the initiative of the young advertiser and helped him developed his sense for publicity.

One day while waiting in the anteroom of a publishing house to see a member of the firm, he picked up a book and began to read it. Since he had to wait for nearly an hour, he had read a large part of the volume when he was at last admitted to the private office. When his business was finished, Bok then asked the publisher why this book was not selling.

"I don't know," replied the publisher. "We had great hopes for it, but somehow or other the public has not responded to it."

"Are you sure you are telling the public about it in the right way?" ventured Bok.

The Scribner advertising had by this time attracted the attention of the publishing world, and this publisher was entirely ready to listen to a suggestion from his youthful caller.

"I wish we published it," said Bok. "I think I could make it a go. It's all in the book."

"How would you advertise it?" asked the publisher.

Bok promised the publisher he would let him know. He carried with him a copy of the book, wrote some advertisements for it, prepared an attractive "broadside" of extracts, to which the book easily lent itself, wrote some literary notes about it, and sent the whole collection to the publisher.

Every particle of "copy" which Bok had prepared was used, the book began to sell, and within three months it was the most discussed book of the day. The book was Edward Bellamy's *Looking Backward.*[8]

[8]In 1888, Edward Bellamy created a sensation by publishing *Looking Backward, 2000–1887,* a utopian romance describing a future society that was based on cooperation that rewarded people according to their needs. More than 1,000,000 copies were sold, and Bellamy clubs sprang up all over the country. Bellamy contributed an article, "How I Wrote 'Looking Backward'," to *The Ladies' Home Journal,* April 1894.

X

The Chances for Success

EDWARD BOK does not now remember whether the mental picture had been given him, or whether he had conjured it up himself; but he certainly was possessed of the idea, as are so many young men entering business, that the path which led to success was very difficult: that it was overfilled with a jostling, bustling, panting crowd, each eager to reach the goal; and all ready to dispute every step that a young man should take; and that favoritism only could bring one to the top.

After Bok had been in the world of affairs, he wondered where were these choked avenues, these struggling masses, these competitors for every inch of vantage. Then he gradually discovered that they did not, in reality, exist.

In the first place, he found every avenue leading to success wide open and certainly not overpeopled. He was surprised how few there were who really stood in a young man's way. He found that favoritism was not the factor that he had been led to suppose. He realized it existed, but to these every one had pointed and about these every one had talked until, in the public mind, they had multiplied in number and assumed a proportion that the facts did not bear out.

Here and there a relative "played a favorite," but even with the push and influence behind him "the lucky one," as he was termed, did not seem to make progress, unless he had merit. It was not long before Bok discovered that the possession of sheer merit was the only real factor that actually counted in any of the places where he had been employed or in others which he had watched; that business was so constructed and conducted that nothing else, in the face of competition, could act as current coin. And the amazing part of it all to Bok was how little merit there was. Nothing astonished him more than the low average ability of those with whom he worked or came into contact.

He looked at the top, and instead of finding it overcrowded, he was surprised at the few who had reached there; the top fairly begged for more to climb its heights.

For every young man, earnest, eager to serve, and willing to do more than he was paid for, he found ten trying to solve the problem of how little they could actually do for the pay received.

It interested Bok to listen to the talk of his fellow workers during luncheon hours and at all other times outside of office hours. When the talk did turn on the business with which they were concerned, it consisted almost entirely of wages, and he soon found that, with scarcely an exception, every young man was terribly underpaid, and that his employer absolutely failed to appreciate his work. It was interesting, later, when Bok happened to get the angle of the employer, to discover that, invariably, these same lamenting young men were those who, from the employer's point of view, were either greatly overpaid or so entirely worthless as to be marked for early decapitation.

Bok felt that this constant thought of the wages earned or deserved was putting the cart before the horse; he had schooled himself into the belief that if he did his work well and accomplished more than was expected of him, the question of wages would take care of itself.

But, according to the talk on every side, it was he who had the cart before the horse. Bok had not only tried always to fill the particular job set for him, but had made it a rule at the same time to study the position just ahead, to see what it was like and what it demanded, and then, as the opportunity presented itself, do a part of that job in addition to his own. As a stenographer, he tried always to clear off the day's work before he closed his desk. This was not always possible, but he kept it before him as a rule to be followed rather than violated.

One morning Bok's employer happened to come to the office earlier than usual, to find the letters he had dictated late in the afternoon before lying on his desk ready to be signed.

"These are the letters I gave you late yesterday afternoon, are they not?" asked the employer.

"Yes, sir."

"Must have started early this morning, didn't you?"

"No, sir," answered Bok. "I wrote them out last evening before I left."

"Like to get your notes written out before they get stale?"

"Yes, sir."

"Good idea," said the employer.

"Yes, sir," answered Bok, "and I think it is even a better idea to get a day's work off before I take my apron off."

"Well said," answered the employer, and the following payday Bok found an increase in his weekly envelope.

It was only fair, however, to add here, parenthetically, that it is neither just nor considerate to a conscientious stenographer for an employer to delay his dictation until the end of the day's work, when, merely by judicious management of his affairs and time, he can give his dictation directly after opening his morning mail. There are two sides to every question; but sometimes the side of the stenographer is not kept in mind by the employer.

Bok found it a uniform rule among his fellow-workers to do exactly the opposite to his own idea; there was an astonishing unanimity in working by the clock; where the hour of closing was five o'clock the preparations began five minutes before, with the hat and overcoat over the back of the chair ready for the stroke of the hour. This concert of action was curiously universal, no "overtime" was ever to be thought of, and, as occasionally happened when the work did go over the hour, it was not, to use the very mildest term, done with care, neatness, or accuracy; it was, to use a current phrase, "slammed off." Every moment beyond five o'clock in which the worker was asked to do anything was by just so much an imposition on the part of the employer, and so far as it could be safely shown, this impression was gotten over to him.

There was an entire unwillingness to let business interfere with any anticipated pleasure or personal engagement. The office was all right between nine and five; one had to be there to earn a living; but, after five, it was not to be thought of for one moment. The elevators which ran on the stroke of five were never large enough to hold the throng which besieged them.

It soon became evident to Bok why scarcely five out of every hundred of the young men whom he knew made any business progress. They were not interested; it was a case of a day's work and a day's pay; it was not a question of how much one could do but how little one could get away with. The thought of how well one might do a given thing never seemed to occur to the average mind.

"Oh, what do you care?" was the favorite expression. "The boss won't notice it if you break your back over his work; you won't get any more pay."

And there the subject was dismissed, and thoroughly dismissed, too.

Eventually, then, Bok learned that the path that led to success was wide open: the competition was negligible. There was no jostling. In fact, travel on it was just a trifle lonely. One's fellow travelers were excellent company, but they were few! It was one of Edward Bok's greatest surprises, but it was also one of his greatest stimulants.

When others played, he worked, fully convinced that his playtime would come later. Where others shirked, he assumed. Where others lagged, he accelerated his pace. Where others were indifferent to things around them, he observed and put away the results for possible use later. He did not make of himself a packhorse; what he undertook he did from interest in it, and that made it a pleasure to him when to others it was a burden.

Obstacles, to Edward Bok, soon became merely difficulties to be overcome, and he trusted to his instinct to show him the best way to overcome them. He soon learned that the hardest kind of work was back of every success; that nothing in the world of business just happened, but that everything was brought about, and only in one way—by a willingness of spirit and a determination to carry through. He soon exploded for himself the misleading and comfortable theory of luck: the only lucky people he found were those who worked hard. To them, luck came in the shape of what they had earned.

And that became, for himself, the rule of Edward Bok's life.

XI

Baptism Under Fire

THE PERSONNEL of the Scribner house was very youthful from the members of the firm clear down the line. It was veritably a house of young men.

The story is told of a Boston publisher, sedate and fairly elderly, who came to the Scribner house to transact business with several of its departments. On one of his errands concerning itself with advertising, he was introduced to Bok, who was then twenty-four. Looking the youth over, he transacted his business as well as he felt it could be transacted with a manager of such tender years, and then sought the head of the educational department: this brought him to another young man of twenty-four.

With his yearnings for someone more advanced in years full upon him, the visitor now inquired for the business manager of the new magazine, only to find a man of twenty-six. His next introduction was to the head of the out-of-town business department, who was twenty-seven.

At this point the Boston man asked to see Mr. Scribner. This disclosed to him Mr. Arthur H. Scribner,[1] the junior partner, who owned to some twenty-eight

[1]Arthur Hawley Scribner entered his father's publishing firm in 1881. In 1889, he scored a coup by obtaining publication rights

summers. Mustering courage to ask faintly for Mr. Charles Scribner himself, he finally brought up in that gentleman's office only to meet a man just turning thirty-three!

"This *is* a young-looking crowd," said Mr. Scribner one day, looking over his young men. And his eye rested on Bok. "Particularly you, Bok. Doubleday looks his years better than you do, for at least he has a moustache." Then, contemplatively: "You raise a moustache, Bok, and I'll raise your salary."

This appealed to Bok very strongly, and within a month he pointed out the result to his employer. "Stand in the light here," said Mr. Scribner. "Well, yes," he concluded dubiously, "It's there—something at least. All right; I'll keep my part of the bargain."

He did. But the next day he was nonplussed to see that the moustache had disappeared from the lip of his youthful advertising manager. "Couldn't quite stand it, Mr. Scribner," was the explanation. "Besides, you didn't say I should keep it: you merely said to raise it."

But the increase did not follow the moustache. To Bok's great relief, it stuck!

This youthful personnel, while it made for *esprit de corps,* had also its disadvantages. One day as Bok was going out to lunch, he found a small-statured man, rather plainly dressed, wandering around the retail department, hoping for a salesman to wait on him.

----

to Henry M. Stanley's *In Darkest Africa,* a narrative of Stanley's search for David Livingstone.

The young salesman on duty, full of inexperience, had a ready smile and quick service ever ready for "carriage trade," as he called it. But this particular customer had come afoot, and this, together with his plainness of dress, did not impress the young salesman. His attention was called to this wandering customer, and it was suggested that he find out what was wanted. When Bok returned from lunch, the young salesman, who, with a beaming smile, had just most ceremoniously bowed the plainly dressed little customer out of the street door, said: "You certainly struck it rich that time when you suggested my waiting on that little man! Such an order! Been here ever since. Did you know who it was?"

"No," returned Bok. "Who was it?"

"Andrew Carnegie,"[2] beamed the salesman.

With so many young men of the same age, there was a natural sense of teamwork and a spirit of comradeship that made for successful cooperation. This spirit extended outside of business hours. At luncheon there was a Scribner table in a neighboring restaurant, and evenings saw the Scribner department heads mingling as friends. It was a group of young men who understood and liked each other, with the

[2]Andrew Carnegie was the symbol of the American success story. Starting as a bobbin boy in a textile factory and then a telegrapher, he ultimately amassed a fortune in steelmaking. In 1901, he sold out to J.P. Morgan for $480,000,000 in a deal resulting in the formation of United States Steel, the world's first billion-dollar corporation. Carnegie spent the rest of his life as a philanthropist.

natural result that business went easier and better because of it.

But Bok did not have much time for evening enjoyment, since his outside interests had grown and prospered and they kept him busy. His syndicate was regularly supplying over a hundred newspapers. His literary letter had become an established feature in thirty different newspapers.

Of course, his opportunities for making this letter interesting were unusual. Owing to his Scribner connection, however, he had taken his name from the letter and signed that of his brother. He had constantly to discriminate between the information that he could publish without violation of confidence and that which he felt he was not at liberty to print. This gave him excellent experience; for the most vital of all essentials in the journalist is the ability unerringly to decide what to print and what information to regard as confidential.

Of course, the best things that came to him he could not print. Whenever there was a question, he gave the benefit of the doubt to the confidential relation in which his position placed him with authors; and his Dutch caution, although it deprived him of many a toothsome morsel for his letter, soon became known to his confreres and was a large asset when, as an editor, he had to follow the golden rule of editorship that teaches one to keep the ears open but the mouth shut. This, the Alpha and Omega of all the commandments in the editorial creed, some editors only learned eventually through sorrowful experience.

He was now to receive his first public baptism of fire. He had published a symposium, through his newspaper syndicate, that discussed the question, "Should Clergymen Smoke?" He had induced all the prominent clergymen in the country to contribute their views, and so distinguished was the list that the article created widespread attention.

One of the contributors was the Reverend Richard S. Storrs, D.D.,[3] one of the most distinguished of Brooklyn's coterie of clergy of that day. A few days after the publication of the article, Bok was astounded to read in the *Brooklyn Eagle* a sensational article, with very large headlines, in which Dr. Storrs repudiated his contribution to the symposium, declared that he had never written or signed such a statement, and accused Edward Bok of forgery.

Coming from a man of Dr. Storrs's prominence, the accusation was, of course, a serious one. Bok realized this at once. He foresaw the damage it might work to the reputation of a young man trying to climb the ladder of success, and wondered why Dr. Storrs had seen fit to accuse him in this public manner instead of calling upon him for a personal explanation. He thought perhaps he might find such a letter from Dr. Storrs when he reached home, but instead he met a

[3]Reverend Richard S. Storrs, D.D., pastor of the Congregational Church of the Pilgrims in Brooklyn, New York, espoused a conservative theology that was at variance with the more radical, reformist, impassioned outlook of Henry Ward Beecher.

small corps of reporters from the Brooklyn and New York newspapers. He told them frankly that no one was more surprised at the accusation than he, but that the original contributions were in the New York office of the syndicate, and he could not corroborate his word until he had looked into the papers and found Dr. Storrs's contribution.

That evening Bok got at the papers in the case, and found out that, technically, Dr. Storrs was right: he had not written or signed such a statement. The compiler of the symposium, the editor of one of New York's leading evening papers whom Bok had employed, had found Dr. Storrs's declaration in favor of a clergyman's use of tobacco in an address made some time before, had extracted it, and incorporated it into the symposium. It was, therefore, Dr. Storrs's opinion on the subject but not written for the occasion for which it was used. Bok felt that his editor had led him into an indiscretion. Yet the sentiments were those of the writer whose name was attached to them, so that the act was not one of forgery. The editor explained that he had sent the extract to Dr. Storrs, who had not returned it, and he had taken silence to mean consent to the use of the material.

Bok decided to say nothing until he heard from Dr. Storrs personally, and so told the newspapers. But the clergyman did not stop his attack. Of course, the newspapers egged him on and extracted from him the further accusation that Bok's silence proved his guilt. Bok now took the case to Mr. Beecher for advice.

"Well, Edward, you are right and you are wrong," said Mr. Beecher. "And so is Storrs, of course. It is beneath him to do what he has done. Storrs and I are not good friends, as you know, and so I cannot go to him and ask him the reason of his disclaimer. Otherwise I would. Of course, he may have forgotten his remarks: that is always possible in a busy man's life. He may not have received the letter enclosing them. That is likewise possible. But I have a feeling that Storrs has some reason for wishing to repudiate his views on this subject just at this time. What it is I do not, of course, know, but his vehemence makes me think so. I think I should let him have his rein. Keep you quiet. It may damage you a little here and there, but in the end it won't harm you. In the main point, you are right. You are not a forger. The sentiments are his and he uttered them, and he should stand by them. He threatens to bring you into court, I see from today's paper. Wait until he does so."

Bok, chancing to meet Dr. Talmage, told him Mr. Beecher's advice, and he endorsed it. "Remember, boy," said Dr. Talmage, "silence is never so golden as when you are under fire. I know, for I have been there, as you know, more than once. Keep quiet; and always believe this: that there is a great deal of common sense abroad in the world, and a man is always safe in trusting it to do him justice."

They were not pleasant and easy days for Bok, for Dr. Storrs kept up the din for several days. Bok waited for the word to appear in court. But this never came, and the matter soon died down and out. And, although Bok met the clergyman several times afterward in the years that followed, no reference was ever made by him to the incident.

But Edward Bok had learned a valuable lesson of silence under fire—an experience that was to stand him in good stead when he was again publicly attacked.

XII

Last Years in New York

WITH *Scribner's Magazine* now in the periodical field, Bok would be asked on his trips to the publishing houses to have an eye open for advertisements for that periodical as well. Hence his education in the solicitation of advertisements became general, and gave him a sympathetic understanding of problems of the advertising solicitor, which was to stand him in good stead when, in his later experience, he was called upon to view the business problems of a magazine from the editor's position. His knowledge of the manufacture of the two magazines in his charge was likewise educative, as was the fascinating study of typography which always had, and has today, a wonderful attraction for him.

From his boyhood days (up to the present writing) Bok was a pronounced baseball "fan." There was a baseball team among the Scribner men of which Bok was a part. This team played, each Saturday afternoon, a team from another publishing house, and for two seasons it was unbeatable. Not only was this baseball aggregation close to the hearts of the Scribner employees, but, in an important game, the junior member of the firm played on it and the senior member was a spectator. Frank N. Doubleday played on first base;

William D. Moffat, later of Moffat, Yard & Company, and now editor of *The Mentor,* was behind the bat; Bok pitched; Ernest Dressel North, who is now an authority on rare editions of books, was in the field, as were also Ray Safford, now a director in Scribner corporation, and Owen W. Brewer, at present a prominent figure in Chicago's book world. It was a happy group, all closely banded together in their business interests and in their human relations as well.

Although the Scribners did not publish Mark Twain's books, the humorist was a frequent visitor to the retail store. Occasionally he would wander back to the publishing department located at the rear of the store, which was then at 743 Broadway.

Smoking was not permitted in the Scribner offices, and, of course, Mark Twain was always smoking. He generally smoked a granulated tobacco that he kept in a long check bag made of silk and rubber. When he sauntered to the back of the Scribner store, he would generally knock the residue from the bowl of the pipe, take out the stem, place it in his vest pocket, like a pencil, and drop the bowl into the bag containing the granulated tobacco. When he wanted to smoke again (which was usually five minutes later), he would fish out the bowl, now automatically filled with tobacco, insert the stem, and strike a light. One afternoon as he wandered into Bok's office, he was just putting his pipe away. The pipe, of the corncob variety, was very aged and black. Bok asked him whether it was the only pipe he had.

"Oh, no," Twain answered, "I have several. But they're all like this. I never smoke a new corncob pipe. A new pipe irritates the throat. No corncob pipe is fit for anything until it has been used at least a fortnight."

"How do you break in a pipe, then?" asked Bok.

"That's the trick," answered Mark Twain. "I get a cheap man—a man who doesn't amount to much, anyhow: who would be as well, or better, dead—and pay him a dollar to break in a new pipe for me. I get him to smoke the pipe for a couple of weeks, then put in a new stem, and continue operations as long as the pipe holds together."

The Scribner house, in its foreign-book department, had imported some copies of Bourrienne's *Life of Napoleon*,[1] and a set had found its way to Bok's desk for advertising purposes. He took the books home to glance them over, found himself interested, and sat up half the night to read them. Then he took the set to the editor of the *New York Star,* and suggested that such a book warranted a special review, and offered to leave the work for the literary editor.

"You have read the books?" asked the editor.

"Every word," returned Bok.

[1] Louis-Antoine de Bourrienne was at one time private secretary to Napoleon Bonaparte. After Napoleon's abdication in 1814 and exile to Elba, Bourrienne became briefly minister of post and minister of state but fled to Brussels to escape creditors and attempted to recoup his finances by writing a ten-volume biography of Napoleon, eight volumes of which may have been ghostwritten by Maxime de Villemarest. An English-language translation of this work was published by Scribner's, in four volumes.

"Then, why don't you write the review?" suggested the editor.

This was a new thought to Bok. "Never wrote a review," he said.

"Try it," answered the editor. "Write a column."

"A column wouldn't scratch the surface of this book," suggested the embryo reviewer.

"Well, give it what it is worth," returned the editor.

Bok did. He wrote a page of the paper.

"Too much, too much," said the editor. "Heavens, man, we've got to get some news into this paper."

"Very well," returned the reviewer. "Read it, and cut it where you like. That's the way I see the book."

And next Sunday the review appeared, word for word, as Bok had written it. His first review had successfully passed!

But Bok was really happiest in that part of his work which concerned itself with the writing of advertisements. The science of advertisement writing, which meant to him the capacity to say much in little space, appealed strongly. He found himself more honestly attracted to this than to the writing of his literary letter, his editorials, or his book reviewing. He determined to follow where his bent led; he studied the mechanics of unusual advertisements wherever he saw them; he eagerly sought a knowledge of typography and its best handling in an advertisement, and of the value and relation of illustrations to text. He perceived that his work seemed to give satisfaction to his employers, since they placed more of it in his hands to do.

To publishers whose advertisements he secured for the periodicals in his charge, he made suggestions for the improvement of their announcements, and found his suggestions accepted. He early saw the value of white space as one of the most effective factors in advertising; but this was a difficult argument, he soon found, to convey successfully to others. White space in an advertisement was to the average publisher something to fill up; Bok saw in it something to cherish for its effectiveness. But he never got very far with his idea: he could not convince (perhaps because he failed to express his ideas convincingly) his advertisers of what he felt and believed so strongly.

An occasion came in which he was permitted to prove his contention. The Scribners had published Andrew Carnegie's volume, *Triumphant Democracy,* and the author desired that some special advertising should be done in addition to that allowed by the appropriation made by the house.[2] To Bok's grateful ears came the injunction from the steel magnate: "Use plenty of white space." In conjunction with Mr. Doubleday, Bok prepared and issued this extra advertising, and for once, at least, the wisdom of using white space was demonstrated. But it was only a flash in the pan. Publishers were unwilling to pay for "unused space,"

[2]In the book, published in 1886, Carnegie lavished praise on the United States and its institutions and attacked the British form of government as outdated and self-defeating. The book produced a sensation, went through multiple printings on both sides of the Atlantic, and was translated into French and German.

as they termed it. Each book was a separate unit, others argued: it was not like advertising one article continuously in which money could be invested; and only a limited amount could be spent on a book which ran its course, even at its best, in a very short time.

That there is a tremendous unsupplied book demand in this country there is no doubt: the wider distribution and easier access given to periodicals prove this point. Now and then there has been tried an unsupported or not well-thought-out plan for bringing books to a public not now reading them, but there seems little or no understanding of the fact that there lies an uncultivated field of tremendous promise to the publisher who will strike out on a new line and market his books, so that the public will not have to ferret out a book-store or wind through the maze of a department store. The American reading public is not the book-reading public that it should be or could be made to be; but the habit must be made easy for it to acquire. Books must be placed where the public can readily get at them. It will not, of its own volition, seek them.

In the meanwhile, Bok's literary letter had prospered until it was now published in some forty-five newspapers. One of these was the *Philadelphia Times.* In that paper, each week, the letter had been read by Mr. Cyrus H. K. Curtis,[3] the owner and publisher of *The Ladies' Home Journal.* Mr. Curtis had

[3]Cyrus Hermann Kotzschmar Curtis, born in Portland, Maine, started with three cents, sold newspapers, bought his own small hand press, made visiting cards, and printed a four-page maga-

decided that he needed an editor for his magazine, in order to relieve his wife,[4] who was then editing it, and he fixed upon the writer of "Literary Leaves" as his man. He came to New York, consulted Will Carleton,[5] the poet, and found that while the letter was signed by William J. Bok, it was actually written by his brother who was with Scribner's. So he sought Bok there.

The publishing house had been advertising in the

---

zine, which made its debut in 1865. After his plant was destroyed in a fire, he moved to Boston and started a newspaper, which he later moved to New York City. In 1876, he discovered that printing costs were lower in Philadelphia and resettled there, but his paper failed. In 1879, he borrowed $2,000 and started a four-page weekly, *The Tribune and Farmer.* It had a section, "Women at Home," that became a full-fledged journal in itself, appearing as an eight-page women's magazine, *The Ladies' Home Journal,* in December 1883. As its popularity grew under his wife's editorship, its circulation skyrocketed to 200,000 by 1889, at which point Mrs. Curtis stepped down and Curtis lured Bok away from Scribner's to become editor in her place. Curtis ultimately made a vast fortune from *The Ladies' Home Journal* and two other magazines, *The Saturday Evening Post,* which he acquired in 1897, and *Country Gentleman,* which he bought in 1911.

[4]In 1873, while still struggling in Boston, Cyrus Curtis married Louisa Knapp, who was private secretary of a prominent physician. Their daughter, Mary Louise Curtis, future wife of Edward W. Bok, was born in Boston on 6 August 1876. After the family moved to Philadelphia, Mrs. Curtis ably edited *The Ladies' Home Journal* from 1883 to 1889, when she decided to devote full time to domestic responsibilities, creating the vacancy that Bok was hired to fill.

[5]Will Carleton was a minor American poet who published several collections of verse. He contributed a long poem, "Captain Young's Thanksgiving," to *The Ladies' Home Journal,* in the November 1893 issue.

Philadelphia magazine, so that the visit of Mr. Curtis was not an occasion for surprise. Mr. Curtis told Bok he had read his literary letter in the *Philadelphia Times,* and suggested that perhaps he might write a similar department for *The Ladies' Home Journal.* Bok saw no reason why he should not, and promised to send over a trial installment. The Philadelphia publisher then went on and explained editorial conditions in his magazine. He recognized the ethics of the occasion by not offering Bok another position while he was already occupying one, asked him if he knew the man for the place.

"Are you talking at me or through me?" asked Bok.

"Both," replied Mr. Curtis.

This was in April of 1889.

Bok promised Mr. Curtis he would look over the field, and meanwhile he sent over to Philadelphia the promised trial "literary gossip" installment. It pleased Mr. Curtis, who suggested a monthly department, to which Bok consented. He also turned over in his mind the wisdom of interrupting his line of progress with Scribners, and began to contemplate the possibilities in Philadelphia.

He gathered a collection of domestic magazines then published, and looked them over to see what was already in the field. Then he began to study himself, his capacity for the work, and the possibility of his finding it congenial. He realized that the work was absolutely foreign to his Scribner work: that it meant a radical departure. But his work with his newspaper syndicate occurred to him, and he studied it with a view of adapting it to the Philadelphia magazine.

His next step was to take into his confidence two or three friends whose judgment he trusted and discuss the possible change. Without exception, they advised against it. The periodical had no standing, they argued; Bok would be out of sympathy with its general atmosphere after his Scribner environment; he was now in the direct line of progress in New York publishing houses; and, to cap the climax, they each argued in turn, he would be buried in Philadelphia: New York was the center, etc., etc.

More than any other single argument, this last point destroyed Bok's faith in the judgment of his friends. He had had experience enough to realize that a man could not be buried in any city, provided he had the ability to stand out from his fellow men. It all depended on whether the cream was there: it was up to the man. Had he within him that peculiar, subtle something that, for the want of a better phrase, we call the editorial instinct?

A business trip for the Scribners now calling him West, Bok decided to stop at Philadelphia, have a talk with Mr. Curtis, and look over his business plant. He did this, and found Mr. Curtis even more desirous than before to have him consider the position. Bok's instinct was strongly in favor of an acceptance.

On his way back from the West, he stopped in Philadelphia again to consult his friend, George W. Childs; and here he found the only person who was ready to encourage him to make the proposed change.

Bok now laid the matter before his mother, in whose feminine instinct he had supreme confidence. With her, he met with instant discouragement. But in subsequent talks he found that her opposition was based not upon the possibilities inherent in the position, but on a mother's natural disinclination to be separated from one of her sons.

Bok now consulted his business associates, and, to a man, they discouraged the step, but almost invariably upon the argument that it was suicidal to leave New York. He had now a glimpse of the truth that there is no man so provincially narrow as the untravelled New Yorker who believes in his heart that the sun rises in the East River and sets in the North River.[6]

He realized more keenly than ever before that the decision rested with him alone. On 1 September 1889, Bok wrote to Mr. Curtis, accepting the position in Philadelphia; and on 13 October following he left the Scribners, where he had been so fortunate and so happy, and, after a week's vacation, followed where his instinct so strongly led, but where his reason wavered.

On 20 October 1889, Edward Bok became the editor of *The Ladies' Home Journal.*

---

[6]North River: the name by which the Hudson River is known at its southern end.

XIII

Successful Editorship

THERE IS a popular notion that the editor of a woman's magazine should be a woman. At first thought, perhaps, this sounds logical. But it is a curious fact that by far the larger number of periodicals for women, the world over, are edited by men; and where, as in some cases, a woman is the proclaimed editor, the direction of the editorial policy is generally in the hands of a man, or group of men, in the background. Why this is so has never been explained any more than why the majority of women's dressmakers are men; why music, with its larger appeal to women, has been and is still being composed, largely, by men, and why its greatest instrumental performers are likewise men; and why the church, with its larger membership of women, still has, as it always has had, men for its greatest preachers.

In fact, we may well ponder whether the full editorial authority and direction of a modern magazine, either essentially feminine in its appeal or not, can safely be entrusted to a woman when one considers how largely executive is the nature of such a position, and how thoroughly sensitive the modern editor must be to the 101 practical business matters which today enter into and form so large a part of the editorial duties. We

may question whether women have as yet had sufficient experience in the world of business successfully
to cope with the material questions of a pivotal editorial position. Then, again, it is absolutely essential in
the conduct of a magazine with a feminine or home
appeal to have on the editorial staff women who are
experts in their line; and the truth is that women work
infinitely better under the direction of a man than of a
woman.

It would seem from the present outlook that, for
some time, at least, the so-called woman's magazine of
large purpose and wide vision is very likely to be
edited by a man. It is a question, however, whether
the day of the woman's magazine, as we have known
it, is not passing. Already the day has gone for the
woman's magazine built on the old lines which now
seem so grotesque and feeble in the light of modern
growth. The interests of women and of men are being
brought closer with the years, and it will not be long
before they will entirely merge. This means a constantly diminishing necessity for the distinctly feminine magazine.

Naturally, there will always be a field in the essentially feminine pursuits which have no place in the life
of a man, but these are rapidly being cared for by
books, gratuitously distributed, issued by the manufacturers of distinctly feminine and domestic wares;
for such publications the best talent is employed, and
the results are placed within easy access of women, by
means of newspaper advertisement, the store-counter,

or the mails. These will sooner or later—and much sooner than later—supplant the practical portions of the woman's magazine, leaving only the general contents, which are equally interesting to men and to women. Hence the field for the magazine with the essentially feminine appeal is contracting rather than broadening, and it is likely to contract much more rapidly in the future.

The field was altogether different when Edward Bok entered it in 1889. It was not only wide open, but fairly crying out to be filled. The day of *Godey's Lady's Book*[1] had passed; *Peterson's Magazine*[2] was breathing its last; and the home or women's magazines that had attempted to take their place were sorry affairs. It was this consciousness of a void ready to be filled that made the Philadelphia experiment so attractive to the embryo editor. He looked over the field and reasoned that if such magazines as did exist could be fairly successful, if women were ready to buy such, how much

[1] Founded in 1830 in Philadelphia by Louis Antoine Godey, and co-edited—edited (with Godey) from 1837–1877 by Sarah Josepha Hale, *Godey's Lady's Book* was the most important of early women's magazines in the United States. It contained stories and poems by famous authors and hand-colored engravings of fashionable costumes. It reached a circulation of 150,000 in the late 1850s and remained in publication until 1898.

[2] *Peterson's Magazine* was the second in importance of early American women's magazines. Founded in 1842 in Philadelphia by Charles J. Peterson, it was co-edited from 1842–1853 by Ann Sophia Stephens, who contributed many serial stories to it over a forty-year period. During the Civil War, *Peterson's* outstripped *Godey's Lady's Book* in circulation. It ceased publication in 1898.

greater response would there be to a magazine of higher standards, of larger initiative—a magazine that would be an authoritative clearing-house for all the problems confronting women in the home, that brought itself closely into contact with those problems and tried to solve them in an entertaining and efficient way; and yet a magazine of uplift and inspiration.

The method of editorial expression in the magazines of 1889 was also distinctly vague and prohibitively impersonal. The public knew the name of scarcely a single editor of a magazine: there was no personality that stood out in the mind: the accepted editorial expression was the indefinite "we"; no one ventured to use the first person singular and talk intimately to the reader. Edward Bok's biographical reading had taught him that the American public loved a personality: that it was always ready to recognize and follow a leader, provided, of course, that the qualities of leadership were demonstrated. He felt the time had come—the reference here and elsewhere is always to the realm of popular magazine literature appealing to a very wide audience—for the editor of some magazine to project his personality through the printed page and to convince the public that he was not an oracle removed from the people, but a real human being who could talk and not merely write on paper.

He saw, too, that the average popular magazine of 1889 failed of large success because it wrote down to the public—a grievous mistake that so many editors have made and still make. No one wants to be told, either directly or indirectly, that he knows less than he does, or even that he knows as little as he does: every one is benefited by the opposite implication, and the public will always follow the leader who comprehends this bit of psychology. There is always a happy medium between shooting over the public's head and shooting too far under it.

It is the rare editor who rightly gauges his public psychology. Perhaps that is why, in the enormous growth of the modern magazine, there have been produced so few successful editors. The average editor is obsessed with the idea of "giving the public what it wants," whereas, in fact, the public, while it knows what it wants when it sees it, cannot clearly express its wants, and never wants the thing that it does ask for, although it thinks it does at the time.

The editor has, therefore, no means of finding it out aforehand by putting his ear to the ground. Only by the simplest rules of psychology can he edit rightly so that he may lead, and to the average editor of today, it is to be feared, psychology is a closed book. His mind is all too often focused on the circulation and advertising, and all too little on the intangibles that will bring to his periodical the essential results.

The editor is the pivot of a magazine. On him everything turns. If his gauge of the public is correct, readers will come: they cannot help coming to the man who has something to say himself, or who presents writers who have. And if the reader comes, the advertiser must come. He must go where his largest market is: where the buyers are. The advertiser, instead of being the most difficult factor in a magazine proposition, as is so often mistakenly thought, is, in reality, the simplest. He has no choice but to advertise in the successful periodical. He must come along. The editor need never worry about him. If the advertiser shuns the periodical's pages, the fault is rarely that of the advertiser: the editor can generally look for the reason nearer home.

One of Edward Bok's first acts as editor was to offer a series of prizes for the best answers to three questions he put to his readers: what in the magazine did they like least and why; what did they like best and why; and what omitted feature or department would they like to see installed? Thousands of answers came, and these the editor personally read carefully and classified. Then he gave his readers' suggestions back to them in articles and departments, but never on the level suggested by them. He gave them the subjects they asked for, but invariably on a slightly higher plane; and each year he raised the standard a notch. He always kept "a huckleberry or two" ahead of his readers. His psychology was simple: come down to the level which the public sets and it will leave you at the moment you do it. It always expects of its leaders that they shall keep a notch above or a step ahead. The American public always wants something a little better than it asks for, and the successful man, in catering to it, is he who follows this golden rule.

XIV

First Years as a Woman's Editor

EDWARD BOK has often been referred to as the one "who made *The Ladies' Home Journal* out of nothing," who "built it from the ground up," or, in similar terms, implying that when he became its editor in 1889 the magazine was practically nonexistent. This is far from the fact. The magazine was begun in 1883, and had been edited by Mrs. Cyrus H. K. Curtis, for six years, under her maiden name of Louisa Knapp, before Bok undertook its editorship. Mrs. Curtis had laid a solid foundation of principle and policy for the magazine: it had achieved a circulation of 440,000 copies a month when she transferred the editorship. It had already acquired such a standing in the periodical world as to attract the advertisements of Charles Scribner's Sons, which Mr. Doubleday and later Bok himself, gave to the Philadelphia magazine— advertising which was never given lightly or without the most careful investigation of the worth of the circulation of a periodical.

What every magazine publisher knows as the most troublous years in the establishment of a periodical, the first half dozen years of its existence, had already been weathered by the editor and publisher. The wife as editor and the husband as publisher had combined to lay a solid basis upon which Bok had only to build: his task was simply to rear a structure upon the foundation already laid. It is to the vision and to the genius of the first editor of *The Ladies' Home Journal* that the unprecedented success of the magazine is primarily due. It was the purpose and the policy of making a magazine of authoritative service which would visualize for womanhood its highest domestic estate, that had won success for the periodical from its inception. It is difficult to believe, in the multiplicity of similar magazines today, that such a purpose was new; that *The Ladies' Home Journal* was a pathfinder; but the convincing proof is found in the fact that all the later magazines of this class have followed in the wake of the periodical conceived by Mrs. Curtis, and have ever since been its imitators.

When Edward Bok succeeded Mrs. Curtis, he immediately encountered another popular misconception of a woman's magazine—the conviction that if a man is the editor of a periodical with a distinctly feminine appeal, he must, as the term goes, "understand women." If Bok had believed this to be true, he would never have assumed the position. How deeply rooted is this belief was brought home to him on every hand when his decision to accept the Philadelphia position was announced. His mother, knowing her son better than did anyone else, looked at him with amazement. She could not believe that he was serious in his decision to cater to women's needs when he knew so very little about them. His friends, too, were intensely amused and took no pains to hide their amusement from him. They knew him to be the very opposite of "a lady's man," and when they were not convulsed with hilarity they were incredulous and marveled.

No man, perhaps, could have been chosen for the position at hand who had a less intimate knowledge of women. Bok had no sister, no women confidantes: he had lived with and for his mother. She was the only woman he really knew or who really knew him. His boyhood days had been too full of poverty and struggle to permit him to mingle with the opposite sex. And it is a curious fact that Edward Bok's instinctive attitude toward women was that of avoidance. He did not dislike women, but it could not be said that he liked them. They had never really interested him. Of women, therefore, he knew little; of their needs less. Nor had he the slightest desire, even as an editor, to know them better or to seek to understand them. Even at that age, he knew that, as a man, he could not, no matter what effort he might make, and he let it go at that.

What he saw in the position was not the need to know women; he could employ women for that purpose. He perceived clearly that the editor of a magazine was largely an executive: his was principally the work of direction; of studying currents and movements, watching their formation, their tendency, their efficacy if advocated or translated into actuality; and then selecting from the horizon those that were for the very best interests of the home. For a home was something Edward Bok did understand. He always lived in one; had struggled to keep it together, and he knew every inch of the hard road that makes for domestic permanence amid adverse financial conditions. At the home he aimed rather than at the woman in it.

It was upon his instinct that he intended to rely rather than upon any knowledge of woman. His first act in the editorial chair of *The Ladies' Home Journal* showed him to be right in this diagnosis of himself, for the incident proved not only how correct was his instinct, but how woefully lacking he was in any knowledge of the feminine nature.

He had divined the fact that in thousands of cases the American mother was not the confidante of her daughter, and reasoned if an inviting human personality could be created on the printed page that would supply this lamentable lack of American family life, girls would flock to such a figure. But all depended on the confidence which the written word could inspire. He tried several writers, but in each case the particular touch that he sought for was lacking. It seemed so simple to him, and yet he could not translate it to others. Then, in desperation, he wrote an installment of such a department as he had in mind himself, intending to show it to a writer he had in view, thus giving her a visual demonstration. He took it to the office the next morning, intending to have it copied but the manuscript accidentally attached itself to another intended for the composing room. It was not until the superintendent of the composing room during the day said to him, "I didn't know Miss Ashmead wrote," that Bok knew where his manuscript had gone.

"Miss Ashmead?" asked the puzzled editor.

"Yes, Miss Ashmead in your department," was the answer.

The whereabouts of the manuscript was then disclosed, and the editor called for its return. He had called the department "Side Talks with Girls" by Ruth Ashmead.

"My girls all hope this is going into the magazine," said the superintendent when he returned the manuscript.

"Why?" asked the editor.

"Well, they say it's the best stuff for girls they have ever read. They'd love to know Miss Ashmead better."

Here was exactly what the editor wanted, but he was the author! He changed the name to Ruth Ashmore and decided to let the manuscript go into the magazine. He reasoned that he would then have a month in which to see the writer he had in mind, and he would show her the proof. But the month filled itself with other duties. Before the editor was aware of it, the composition room wanted "copy" for the second installment of "Side Talks with Girls." Once more the editor furnished the copy!

Within two weeks after the second article had been written, the magazine containing the first installment of the new department appeared, and the next day 200 letters were received for "Ruth Ashmore," with the mail clerk asking where they should be sent.

"Leave them with me, please," replied the editor. On the following day the mail clerk handed him 500 more.

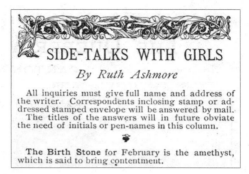

SIDE-TALKS WITH GIRLS

By Ruth Ashmore

All inquiries must give full name and address of the writer. Correspondents inclosing stamp or addressed stamped envelope will be answered by mail. The titles of the answers will in future obviate the need of initials or pen-names in this column.

The Birth Stone for February is the amethyst, which is said to bring contentment.

The editor now took two letters from the top and opened them. He never opened the third! That evening he took the bundle home, and told his mother of his predicament. She read the letters and looked at her son. "You have no right to read these," she said. The son readily agreed.

His instinct had correctly interpreted the need, but he never dreamed how far the feminine nature would reveal itself on paper.

The next morning the editor, with his letters, took the train for New York and sought out his friend, Mrs. Isabel A. Mallon,[1] the "Bab" of his popular syndicate letter.

[1]Isabel Allderdice Mallon, a journalist, wrote a regular column on women's fashions for the *Ladies' Home Journal* in the 1890s.

Early cover of The Ladies' Home Journal, *August 1891*

Peterson's Magazine, *which covered subjects
of interest to women through the late 1800s*

Godey's Lady's Book, *a leader in women's
periodicals during the nineteenth century*

Ladies' Home Journal
covers from the 1890s

Ladies' Home Journal
*covers from the early
twentieth century*

Cover illustration by Frank S. Guild, April 1903

Cover illustrations by (from top):
Lester Ralph, June 1915; Harrison Fisher,
August 1914; Emlen McConnell,
September 1914

Cover illustration by Francis Miller, May 1915

*Cover art that featured Bok's campaign to protect
migratory and other bird life, February 1917*

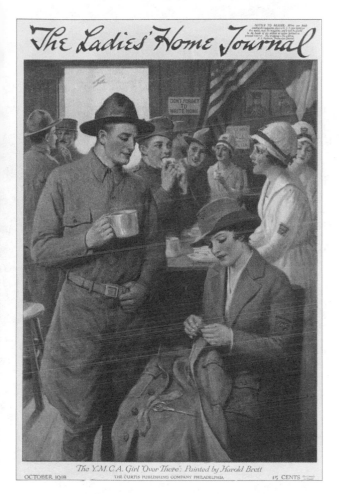

The Y.M.C.A. Girl "Over There": Painted by Harold Brett

OCTOBER 1918   THE CURTIS PUBLISHING COMPANY PHILADELPHIA   15 CENTS

Cover illustration by Harold Brett, October 1918

From a Photograph by Paul Thompson

THE BEST·DRESSED WOMEN IN THE WORLD

THEIR faces alight with the exaltation of their mission, bearing on their brows the holy insignia of their tender mercy, these marching women of the New York Red Cross sent into the hearts of those who watched them reverently a thrill that they had never felt before.

Part of the magazine's editorial coverage of World War I, July 1918

Curtis Building exterior, Philadelphia, Pennsylvania

Courtesy The Atwater Kent Museum/Philadelphia History Museum

Curtis Building production facilities

Courtesy The Atwater Kent Museum/Philadelphia History Museum

176

Edward Bok's office in the Curtis Building

The Ladies' Home Journal *fashion coverage, September 1914*

178

The Ladies' Home Journal *series on fine art, January 1917*

Saturday Evening Post cover illustration by Thomas Penfield, 14 August 1909

Courtesy The Curtis Publishing Company

"Have you read this department?" he asked, pointing to the page in the magazine.

"I have," answered Mrs. Mallon. "Very well done, too, it is. Who is 'Ruth Ashmore'?"

"You are," answered Edward Bok. And while it took considerable persuasion, from that time on Mrs. Mallon became Ruth Ashmore, the most ridiculed writer in the magazine world, and yet the most helpful editor that ever conducted a department in periodical literature. For sixteen years she conducted the department, until she passed away, her last act being to dictate a letter to a correspondent. In those sixteen years she had received 158,000 letters: she kept three stenographers busy, and the number of girls who today bless the name of Ruth Ashmore is legion.

But the newspaper humorists who insisted that Ruth Ashmore was none other than Edward Bok never knew the partial truth of their joke!

The editor soon supplemented this department with one dealing with the spiritual needs of the mature woman. "The King's Daughters" was then an organization at the summit of its usefulness, with Margaret Bottome its president.[2] Edward Bok had heard Mrs. Bottome speak, had met her personally, and decided that she was the editor for the department he had in mind.

[2]Margaret Bottome, an associate editor of *The Ladies' Home Journal,* lectured about biblical subjects and wrote essays for religious publications. She helped found the International Order of King's Daughters, of which she was president at the time of her death in 1906.

"I want it written in an intimate way as if there were only two persons in the world, you and the person reading. I want heart to speak to heart. We will make that the title," said the editor, and unconsciously he thus created the title that has since become familiar wherever English is spoken: "Heart to Heart Talks." The title gave the department an instantaneous hearing; the material in it carried out its spirit, and soon Mrs. Bottome's department rivaled, in popularity, the page by Ruth Ashmore.

Margaret Bottome

These two departments more than anything else, and the irresistible picture of a man editing a woman's magazine, brought forth an era of newspaper paragraphing and a flood of so called "humorous" refer-

ences to the magazine and editor. It became the vogue
to poke fun at both. The humorous papers took it up,
the cartoonists helped it along, and actors introduced
the name of the magazine on the stage in plays and
skits. Never did a periodical receive such an amount
of gratuitous advertising. Much of the wit was absolutely without malice: some of it was written by Edward Bok's best friends, who volunteered to let up
would he but raise a finger.

But he did not raise the finger. No one enjoyed the
"paragraphs" more heartily when the wit was good. In
that case, if the writer was unknown to him, he sought
him out and induced him to write for him. In this way
George Fitch[3] was found on the Peoria, Illinois, *Transcript* and introduced to his larger public in the magazine and book world through *The Ladies' Home
Journal,* whose editor he believed he had "most un-
mercifully roasted." But he had done it so cleverly that
the editor at once saw his possibilities.

When all his friends begged Bok to begin proceedings against the *New York Evening Sun* because of
the libelous articles written about him by "The
Woman About Town,"[4] the editor admired the style
rather than the contents, made her acquaintance, and

[3]George Fitch, journalist, author, and humorist, wrote highly
successful stories about student life at "Old Siwash," a fictional institution based on his alma mater, Knox College, at Galesburg,
Illinois.

[4]The editor has been unable to discover the identity of this
person.

secured her as a regular writer: she contributed to the magazine some of the best things published in its pages. But she did not abate her opinions of Bok and his magazine in her articles in the newspaper, and Bok did not ask it of her. He felt she had a right to her opinions—those he was not buying. But he was eager to buy her direct style in treating subjects he knew no other woman could so effectively handle.

And with his own limited knowledge of the sex, he needed, and none knew it better than he did, the ablest women he could obtain to help him realize his ideals. Their personal opinions of him did not matter so long as he could command their best work. Sooner or later, when his purposes were better understood, they might alter those opinions. For that he could afford to wait. But he could not wait to get their work.

By this time the editor had come to see that the power of a magazine might lie more securely behind the printed page than in it. He had begun to accustom his readers to writing to his editors upon all conceivable problems.

This he decided to encourage. He employed an expert in each line of feminine endeavor, knowing the most scrupulous attention should be given to her correspondence: that every letter, no matter how inconsequential, should be answered quickly, fully, and courteously, with the questioner always encouraged to come again if any problem of whatever nature came to her. He told his editors that ignorance on any question was a misfortune, not a crime; and he wished their correspondence treated in the most courteous and helpful spirit.

Step by step, the editor built up this service behind the magazine until he had a staff of thirty-five editors on the monthly payroll; in each issue, he proclaimed the willingness of the editors to answer immediately any questions by mail, he encouraged and cajoled his readers to form the habit of looking upon his magazine as a great clearing house of information. Before long, the letters streamed in by the tens of thousands during a year. The editor still encouraged, and the total ran into the hundreds of thousands, until during the last year, before the service was finally stopped by the Great War of 1917–18, the yearly correspondence totaled nearly a million letters.

The lack of opportunity for an education in Bok's own life led him to cast about for some plan whereby an education might be obtained without expense by anyone who desired. He finally hit upon the simple plan of substituting free scholarships for the premiums frequently offered by periodicals for subscriptions secured. Free musical education at the leading conservatories was first offered to any girl who would secure a certain number of subscriptions to *The Ladies' Home Journal,* the complete offer being a year's free tuition, with free room, free board, free piano in her own room, and all travelling expenses paid. The plan was an immediate success: the solicitation of a subscription by a girl desirous of educating herself made an irresistible appeal.

This plan was soon extended, so as to include all the girls' colleges, and finally all the men's colleges, so that a free education might be possible at any educational institution. So comprehensive it became that to the close of 1919, 1,455 free scholarships had been awarded. The plan has now been in operation long enough to have produced some of the leading singers and instrumental artists of the day, whose names are familiar to all, as well as instructors in colleges and scores of teachers; and to have sent several score of men into conspicuous positions in the business and professional world.

The editor's correspondence was revealing, among other deficiencies, the widespread unpreparedness of the average American girl for motherhood, and her desperate ignorance when a new life was given her. On the theory that with the realization of a vital need there is always the person to meet it, Bok consulted the authorities of the Babies' Hospital of New York, and found Dr. Emmet Holt's house physician, Dr. Emelyn L. Coolidge. To the authorities in the world of babies, Bok's discovery was, of course, a known and serious fact.[5]

---

[5]During the period to which Bok refers, pediatrics, like other types of medical practice, was emerging as a field of specialization. One of the developments associated with the rise of pediatrics was an "infant hygiene movement" that stressed the importance of mothers seeking out the guidance of physicians in the preventative care of their babies. The regular columns launched by Bok in the *Journal* were highly consistent with this trend.

Dr. Coolidge proposed that the magazine create a department of questions and answers devoted to the problems of young mothers. This was done. From the publication of the first issue, the questions began to come in. Within five years the department had grown to such proportions that Dr. Coolidge proposed a plan whereby mothers might be instructed, by mail, in the rearing of babies—in their general care, their feeding, and the complete hygiene of the nursery.

Bok had already learned, in his editorial experience, carefully to weigh a woman's instinct against a man's judgment, but the idea of raising babies by mail floored him. He reasoned, however, that a woman, and more particularly one who had been in a babies' hospital for years, knew more about babies than he could possibly know. He consulted baby specialists in New York and Philadelphia, and, with one accord, they declared the plan not only absolutely impracticable but positively dangerous. Bok's confidence in woman's instinct, however, persisted, and he asked Dr. Coolidge to map out a plan.

This called for the services of two physicians: Miss Marianna Wheeler,[6] for many years superintendent of the Babies' Hospital, was to look after the prospec-

[6]Marianna Wheeler, writer, educator, and administrator, took charge of Babies' Hospital, New York City, and remained at that institution until she resigned early in 1906 to organize a school for Nursery Maids. She was the author of *The Baby, His Care and Training* (1900), *Plain Hints for Busy Mothers* (1902), and *A Babe in the House* (1908).

tive mother before the baby's birth; and Dr. Coolidge, when the baby was born, would immediately send to the young mother a printed list of comprehensive questions, which, when answered, would be immediately followed by a full set of directions as to the care of the child, including carefully prepared food formulae. At the end of the first month, another set of questions was to be forwarded for answer by the mother, and this monthly service was to be continued until the child reached the age of two years. The contact with the mother would then become intermittent, dependent upon the condition of mother and child. All the directions and formulae were to be used only under the direction of the mother's physician, so that the fullest cooperation might be established between the physician on the case and the advisory department of the magazine.

Despite advice to the contrary, Bok decided, after consulting a number of mothers, to establish the system. It was understood that the greatest care was to be exercised: the most expert advice, if needed, was to be sought and given, and the thousands of cases at the Babies' Hospital were to be laid under contribution.

There was then begun a magazine department which was to be classed among the most clear-cut pieces of successful work achieved by *The Ladies' Home Journal.*

Step by step, the new department was welcomed eagerly by thousands of young mothers. It was not long before the warmest commendation from physicians

The Young Mothers' Home Club

By Emelyn Lincoln Coolidge, M.D.

Of The Babies' Hospital, New York

Club Motto: "An Ounce of Prevention is Better than a Pound of Cure"

THIS year we are going to have a "Mothers Club," to which I think no one can possibly object, for it will not take the mother out of her home nor away from her children, and she may devote just as much or as little time to it as she pleases. Every month we shall have a short talk or lecture first, then we will devote a few moments to hearing the opinions of the mothers themselves. I should like to have them tell me of anything they may have invented to make the care of the baby or nurse easier; of any particular plan they may have followed in managing an unruly child. Many of their children have said or done anything especially "cute," I shall be delighted to hear about it; and I should also like to have them discuss subjects like y to interest other mothers, as, for instance, "Is it best to give a child a regular allowance?" "S all we use corporal or other means of punishment for the children?" "Shal ‧ evening society at home be allowed?" etc. Of course, everything that is written cannot be printed, for we can only have just so much space in THE JOURNAL, but subjects likely to interest the greatest number of readers will be chosen

EVERY one has seen grown people with ugly ears that stand away out from their heads; the children of such people are very likely to inherit similar ears, and a great deal may be done to remedy, if not entirely cure, this defect. Every time the baby is laid down the mother should gently press the little ear, on whichever side he may be lying, down flat, close against his head, and after a little while he should be turned over and made to lie on the other ear. If the trouble is only slight this care may be all that is necessary to make the ears lie permanently flat, but if they stand out any considerable distance it will be best to have the baby wear an ear-cap which is especially made for this purpose. There are two kinds of these car-

the child grows older he should be taught to make a careful toilette of his nose every morning when he is dressing, blowing it well and clearing out all secretions that may have collected during the night. If this is done at a regular time each morning, the child will not form that very ugly habit of picking at the nose during the day, which will often tend to make a flat or badly-shaped nose very much worse.

A BABY who inherits a turned-up nose is usually considered "cute" and "saucy," but later in life it is not thought quite so pretty and may spoil an otherwise perfect face. While it is never a good plan to put a clothespin on the poor child's nose, as Miss Alcott's Amy once did, the mother should make some attempt to give the little nose a better shape by gently pulling and stroking it between her fingers two or three times a day. As

ANOTHER thing which babies often inherit from father or mother is a tendency to use the left hand in place of the right. When the mother knows this trouble has been in the family she should be on the watch for it in her children from the very first, for if

all over the country was received. Promptness of response and thoroughness of diagnosis were of course the keynotes of the service: where the cases were urgent, the special delivery post and, later, the night letter telegraph service was used.

The plan is now in its eleventh year of successful operation. Some idea of the enormous extent of its service can be gathered from the amazing figures that, at the close of the tenth year, show over 40,000 prospective mothers have been advised, while the number of babies actually "raised" by Dr. Coolidge approaches 80,000. Fully 95 of every 100 of these babies registered have remained under the monthly letter care of Dr. Coolidge until their first year, when the mothers receive a diet list which has proved so effective for future guidance that many mothers cease to report regularly. Eighty-five out of every 100 babies have remained in the registry until their graduation at the age of two. Over eight sets of library drawers are required for the records of the babies always under the supervision of the registry.

Scores of physicians who vigorously opposed the work at the start have amended their opinions and now not only give their enthusiastic endorsement, but have adopted Dr. Coolidge's food formulae for their private and hospital cases.

It was this comprehensive personal service, built up back of the magazine from the start, that gave the periodical so firm and unique a hold on its clientele. It was not the printed word that was its chief power;

scores of editors who have tried to study the appeal of the magazine from the printed page, have remained baffled at the remarkable confidence elicited from its readers. Bok went through three financial panics with the magazine, and while other periodicals severely suffered from diminished circulation at such times, *The Ladies' Home Journal* always held its own. Thousands of women had been directly helped by the magazine; it had not remained an inanimate printed thing but had become a vital need in the personal lives of its readers.

So intimate had become this relation, so efficient was the service rendered, that its readers could not be pried loose from it; where women were willing and ready, when the domestic pinch came, to let go of other reading matter, they explained to their husbands or fathers that *The Ladies' Home Journal* was a necessity—they did not feel that they could do without it. The very quality for which the magazine had been held up to ridicule by the unknowing and unthinking had become, with hundreds of thousands of women, its source of power and the bulwark of its success.

Bok was beginning to realize the vision which had lured him from New York: that putting into the field of American magazines a periodical that should become such a clearing house as virtually to make it an institution.

He felt that, for the present at least, he had sufficiently established the personal contact with his readers that he desired through the introduction of the more intimate departments, and he then decided to devote his efforts to the literary features of the magazine.

XV

Eugene Field's Practical Jokes

EUGENE FIELD[1] was one of Edward Bok's close friends and also his despair, as was likely to be the case with those who were intimate with the Western poet. One day Field said to Bok: "I am going to make you the most widely paragraphed man in America." The editor passed the remark over, but he was to recall it often as his friend set out to make his boast good.

The fact that Bok was unmarried and the editor of a woman's magazine appealed strongly to Field's sense of humor. He knew the editor's opposition to patent medicines, and so he decided to join the two facts in a paragraph, put on the wire at Chicago, to the effect that the editor was engaged to be married to Miss Lavinia Pinkham, the granddaughter of Mrs. Lydia Pinkham, of patent-medicine fame.[2] The paragraph carefully described Miss Pinkham, the school

[1]Eugene Field, humorist, journalist, and poet, wrote a popular daily column, "Sharps and Flats," interspersing prose and poetry, that had a twenty-year run in the Chicago *Daily News*. Many of his poems, including "Little Boy Blue," "Wynken, Blynken, and Nod," and "The Gingham Dog and the Calico Cat," celebrated childhood.

[2]Lydia Estes Pinkham began marketing a home remedy, consisting mainly of *Aletris farinosa* (unicorn root) and *Asclepius tuberosa* (pleurisy root), in 1875. The product contained about 18 percent alcohol and was advertised as beneficial for female re-

where she had been educated, her talents, her wealth, etc. Field was wise enough to put the paragraph not in his own column in the *Chicago News,* lest it be considered in the light of one of his practical jokes, but on the news page of the paper, and he had it put on the Associated Press Wire.

He followed this up a few days later with a paragraph announcing Bok's arrival at a Boston hotel. Then came a paragraph saying that Miss Pinkham was sailing for Paris to buy her trousseau. The paragraphs were worded in the most matter-of-fact manner, and completely fooled the newspapers, even those of Boston. Field was delighted at the success of his joke, and the fact that Bok was in despair over the letters that poured in upon him added to Field's delight.

He now asked Bok to come to Chicago. "I want you to know some of my cronies," he wrote. "Julia [his wife] is away, so we will shift for ourselves." Bok arrived in Chicago one Sunday afternoon, and was to dine at Field's house that evening. He found a jolly company: James Whitcomb Riley,[3] Sol Smith Russell

---

productive disorders. As Bok indicates, the joke Field was playing, linking Bok romantically with Lavinia Pinkham, was calculated to be particularly embarrassing to Bok because of his editorial crusade against patent medicines.

[3]James Whitcomb Riley, the "Hoosier Poet," followed the advice of his favorite poet, Longfellow, by writing in simple words about familiar, everyday things, usually in carefully cultivated local dialect. A talented actor who was skilled in declamation, Riley was a favorite on the Chautauqua lecture circuit, as well.

the actor, Opie Read,[4] and a number of Chicago's literary men.

When seven o'clock came, someone suggested to Field that something to eat might not be amiss.

"Shortly," answered the poet. "Wife is out; cook is new, and dinner will be a little late. Be patient." But at eight o'clock there was still no dinner. Riley began to grow suspicious and slipped downstairs. He found no one in the kitchen and the range cold. He came back and reported. "Nonsense," said Field. "It can't be." All went downstairs to find out the truth. "Let's get supper ourselves," suggested Russell. Then it was discovered that not a morsel of food was to be found in the refrigerator, closet, or cellar. "That's a joke on us," said Field. "Julia has left us without a crumb to eat."

It was then nine o'clock. Riley and Bok held a council of war and decided to slip out and buy some food, only to find out that the front, basement, and back doors were locked and the keys missing! Field was indeed very sober. "Thorough woman, that wife of mine," he commented. But his friends knew better.

Finally, the Hoosier poet and the Philadelphia editor crawled through one of the basement windows and started on a foraging expedition. Of course, Field lived in a residential section where there were few stores, and on Sunday these were closed. There was

[4]Opie Read was one of America's most beloved humorists. He wrote more than fifty books, many of them becoming best-sellers, and lectured on the Chautauqua circuit.

nothing to do but to board a downtown car. Finally they found a delicatessen shop open, and the two hungry men amazed the proprietor by nearly buying out his stock.

It was after ten o'clock when Riley and Bok got back to the house with their load of provisions to find every door locked, every curtain drawn, and the bolt sprung on every window. Only the cellar grating remained, and through this the two dropped their bundles and themselves, and appeared in the dining room, dirty and disheveled, to find the party at table enjoying a supper which Field had carefully hidden and brought out when they had left the house.

Riley, cold and hungry, and before this time the victim of Field's practical jokes, was not in a merry humor and began to recite paraphrases of Field's poems. This started Sol Smith Russell, who mimicked both Field and Riley. The fun grew fast and furious, the entire company now took part, Mrs. Field's dresses were laid under contribution, and Field, Russell, and Riley gave an impromptu play. And it was upon this scene that Mrs. Field, after a continuous ringing of the doorbell and nearly battering down the door, appeared at seven o'clock the next morning!

The success of Field's paragraph engaging Bok to Miss Pinkham stimulated the poet to greater effort. Bok had gone to Europe; Field, having found out the date of his probable return, just about when the steamer was due, printed an interview with the editor "at quarantine" which sounded so plausible that even

James Whitcomb Riley   *Eugene Field*

Courtesy Library of Congress

Bok as a young editor working in the original Curtis offices

Courtesy Rachel Bok Goldman

198

the men in Bok's office in Philadelphia were fooled and prepared for his arrival. The interview recounted in detail the changes in women's fashions in Paris, and so plausible had Field made it, based upon information obtained at Marshall Field's, that even the fashion papers copied it.

All this delighted Field beyond measure. Bok begged him to desist; but Field answered by printing an item to the effect that there was the highest authority for denying "the reports industriously circulated some time ago to the effect Mr. Bok was engaged to be married to a New England young lady, whereas, as a matter of fact, it is no violation of friendly confidence that makes it possible to announce that the Philadelphia editor is engaged to Mrs. Frank Leslie, of New York."[5]

It so happened that Field put this new paragraph on the wire just about the time that Bok's actual engagement was announced. Field was now deeply contrite, and he sincerely promised Bok and his fiancée[6]

[5]Miriam Florence (Folline) Leslie, better known as Mrs. Frank Leslie, had a flamboyant career in journalism after publisher Frank Leslie (born Henry Carter) added her to his staff in 1863. She became best known for building *Frank Leslie's Popular Monthly* into a mass circulation magazine. She bequeathed a $2 million fortune to the woman's suffrage movement.

[6]his fiancée: Mary Louise Curtis, daughter and only child of Cyrus H. K. Curtis and Louisa Knapp Curtis, became the wife of Edward W. Bok. She also was the chief beneficiary of her father's estate, which was conservatively estimated at $18 million to $20 million, including estates in Wyncote, Pennsylvania, and Camden and Rockport, Maine; Curtis's yacht, the *Lyndonia;* and "net in-

to reform. "I'm through, you mooning, spooning calf, you," he wrote Bok, and his friend believed him, only to receive a telegram the next day from Mrs. Field warning him that "Gene is planning a series of telephonic conversations with you and Miss Curtis at college that I think should not be printed." Bok knew it was of no use trying to curb Field's industry, and so he wired the editor of the *Chicago News* for his cooperation. Field, now checked, asked Bok and his fiancée and the parents of both to come to Chicago and to be his guests for the World's Fair, and "let me make amends."

It was a happy visit. Field was all kindness, and, of course, the entire party was charmed by his personality. But the boy in him could not be repressed. He had kept it down all through the visit. "No, not a joke— cross my heart," he would say, and then he invited the party to lunch with him on their way to the train when they were leaving for home. "But we shall be in our traveling clothes, not dressed for luncheon," protested the women. It was an unfortunate protest, for it gave Field an idea! "Oh," he assured them, "just a good-bye luncheon at the club: just you folks and Julia and me." They believed him, only to find upon their arrival at

come for life of her father's stock in The Curtis Publishing Company and the Curtis-Martin Newspapers." Wood's history of The Curtis Publishing Company states that she was "principal stockholder, director, and a vice president" of the firm. After Bok's death in 1930, she married concert violinist Efrem Zimbalist. She died on 4 January 1970 at the age of ninety-three.

the club an assembly of over sixty guests at one of the most elaborate luncheons ever served in Chicago, with each woman guest carefully enjoined by Field, in his invitation, to "put on her prettiest and most elaborate costume in order to dress up the table!"

One day Bok received a wire from Field: "City of New Orleans purposing give me largest public reception on sixth ever given an author. Event of unusual quality. Mayor and city officials peculiarly desirous of having you introduce me to vast audience they propose to have. Hate to ask you to travel so far, but would be great favor to me. Wire answer." Bok wired back his willingness to travel to New Orleans and oblige his friend. It occurred to Bok, however, to write to a friend in New Orleans and ask the particulars. Of course, there was never any thought of Field going to New Orleans or of any reception. Bok waited for further advice, and a long letter followed from Field that gave him a glowing picture of the reception planned. Bok sent a message to his New Orleans friend to be telegraphed from New Orleans on the sixth: "Find whole thing to be a fake. Nice job to put over on me. Bok." Field was overjoyed at the apparent success of his joke and gleefully told his Chicago friends all about it—until he found out that the joke had been on him. "Durned dirty, I call it," he wrote Bok.

It was a lively friendship that Eugene Field gave to Edward Bok, full of anxieties and of continuous forebodings, but it was worth all that it cost in mental perturbation. No rarer friend ever lived: in his serious moments he gave one a quality of unforgettable friendship that remains a precious memory. But his desire for practical jokes was uncontrollable: it meant being constantly on one's guard, and even then the pranks could not always be thwarted!

XVI

Building Up a Magazine

THE NEWSPAPER paragraphers were now having a delightful time with Edward Bok and his woman's magazine, and he was having a delightful time with them. The editor's publicity sense made him realize how valuable for his purposes was all this free advertising. The paragraphers believed, in their hearts, that they were annoying the young editor; they tried to draw his fire through their articles. But he kept quiet, put his tongue in cheek, and determined to give them some choice morsels for their wit.

He conceived the idea of making familiar to the public the women who were in back of the successful men of the day. He felt sure that his readers wanted to know about these women. But to attract his newspaper friends he labeled the series, "Unknown Wives of Well-Known Men" and "Clever Daughters of Clever Men."

The alliterative titles at once attracted the paragraphers; they fell upon them like hungry trout, and a perfect fusillade of paragraphs began. This is exactly what the editor wanted, and he followed these two series immediately by inducing the daughter of Charles Dickens to write of "My Father as I Knew Him," and Mrs. Henry Ward Beecher, of "Mr. Beecher as I Knew

Him." Bok now felt that he had given the newspapers enough ammunition to last for some time, and he turned his attention to building up a more permanent basis for his magazine.

The two authors of that day who commanded more attention than any others were William Dean Howells and Rudyard Kipling.[1] Bok knew that these two would give to his magazine the literary quality that it needed, and so he laid them both under contribution. He bought Mr. Howell's new novel, *The Coast of Bohemia,*[2] and arranged that Kipling's new novelette upon which he was working should come to the magazine. Neither the public nor the magazine editors had

---

[1]Joseph Rudyard Kipling helped create a literary genre based on the European encounter with exotic cultures in the heyday of late nineteenth-century imperialism. Born in Bombay, India, he was educated in England. Returning to India, he became a journalist and wrote more than seventy widely admired short stories on Anglo-Indian society. His many poems (including "Mandalay," "Danny Deever," and "Gunga Din"), stories *(The Jungle Book* and *The Second Jungle Book)*, and a novella, *Captains Courageous,* made him rich. In 1901, after going to South Africa and reporting the Boer War, he published *Kim,* an evocative portrayal of life in India, followed by children's classics including *Just So Stories* (1902) and *Puck of Pook's Hill* (1906). In 1907, he became the first English writer to win the Nobel Prize for Literature. His popularity ultimately waned because of his identification with imperialism, elitism, and racism.

[2]*The Coast of Bohemia* was published in 1893. The book was run serially, in twelve installments, in *The Ladies' Home Journal* from December 1892 to November 1893. Howells was also the subject of an extended article, "Mr. Howells At Close Range," by H. H. Boyesen, which appeared in *The Ladies' Home Journal* in November 1893.

expected Bok to break out along these more permanent lines, and magazine publishers began to realize
that a new competitor had sprung up in Philadelphia.
Bok knew they would feel this; so before he announced Mr. Howell's new novel, he contracted with
the novelist to follow this with his autobiography. This
surprised the editors of the older magazines, for they
realized that the Philadelphia editor had completely
tied up the leading novelist of the day for his next two
years' output.

Meanwhile, in order that the newspapers might be
well supplied with barbs for their shafts, he published
an entire number of his magazine written by famous
daughters of famous men. This unique issue presented contributions by the daughters of Charles
Dickens, Nathaniel Hawthorne, President Harrison,[3]
Horace Greeley, William M. Thackeray, William Dean
Howells, General Sherman, Jefferson Davis, Mr. Gladstone,[4] and a score of others. This issue simply filled
the paragraphers with glee. Then once more Bok
turned to material calculated to cement the foundation
for a more permanent structure.

[3]Benjamin Harrison was the twenty-third president of the
United States. He served one term (1889–1893). His administration was noted for the Sherman Anti-Trust Act and the ultra-pro-
tectionist McKinley Tariff Act, both passed in 1890.

[4]A reference to William Ewart Gladstone who was four times
prime minister of Great Britain. First elected to Parliament in 1832,
he served in that body for sixty years. Though conservative in his
early career, he became steadily more liberal and fought for such
things as free trade, expanded voting rights, and Irish home rule.

He noted, early in its progress, the gathering strength of the drift toward woman suffrage, and realized that the American woman was not prepared, in her knowledge of her country, to exercise the privilege of the ballot. Bok determined to supply the deficiency to his readers, and concluded to put under contract the president of the United States, Benjamin Harrison, the moment he left office, to write a series of articles explaining the United States. No man knew this subject better than the president; none could write better; and none would attract such general attention to his magazine, reasoned Bok. He sought the president, talked it over with him, and found him favorable to the idea. President Harrison entered into an agreement with the editor to begin to write the articles immediately upon his retirement from office. And the day after Inauguration Day every newspaper contained an Associated Press dispatch announcing the former president's contract with *The Ladies' Home Journal.* Shortly afterward, Benjamin Harrison's articles on "This Country of Ours" successfully appeared in the magazine.

The material that the editor was publishing and the authors he was laying under contribution began to have marked effect upon the circulation of the magazine, and it was not long before the original figures were doubled; an edition—enormous for that day—of 750,000 copies was printed and sold each month, the magical figure of a million was in sight, and the periodical was rapidly taking its place as one of the largest successes of the day.

Mr. Curtis's single proprietorship of the magazine had been changed into a corporation called The Curtis Publishing Company, with a capital of $500,000, with Mr. Curtis as president and Bok as the vice president.

THE LADIES' HOME JOURNAL

INCORPORATING THE HOME JOURNAL
Registered in the United States Patent Office

PUBLISHED ON THE TWENTIETH OF EACH
MONTH PRECEDING DATE OF ISSUANCE BY
THE CURTIS PUB-
LISHING COMPANY
INDEPENDENCE SQUARE
PHILADELPHIA, PENNSYLVANIA

CYRUS H·K·CURTIS
PRESIDENT
EDWARD W·BOK
VICE-PRESIDENT AND EDITOR
C·H·LUDINGTON
SECRETARY AND TREASURER

EDITED BY EDWARD W·BOK
KARL EDWIN HARRIMAN, MANAGING EDITOR

Copyright, 1914 (Trade-mark registered) by The Curtis Publishing Company, in the United States and Great Britain. Entered at Stationers' Hall, London, England. All rights reserved. Entered as second-class matter May 6, 1911, at the Post Office at Philadelphia, Pennsylvania, under the Act of March 3, 1879.

The magazine had by no means an easy road to travel financially. The doubling of the subscription price to one dollar per year had materially checked the income for the time being; the huge advertising bills, sometimes exceeding $300,000 a year, were difficult to pay; large credit had to be obtained, and the banks were carrying a considerable quantity of Mr. Curtis's notes. But Mr. Curtis never wavered in his faith in his proposition and his editor. In the first he invested all he had and could borrow, and to the latter he gave his undivided support. The two men worked together rather as father and son—as, curiously enough, they were to be later—than as employer and employee. To Bok, the daily experience of seeing Mr.

Curtis finance his proposition in sums that made the publishing world of that day gasp with skeptical astonishment was a wonderful opportunity, of which the editor took full advantage so as to learn the intricacies of a world which up to that time he had known only in a limited way.

What attracted Bok immensely to Mr. Curtis's methods was their perfect simplicity and directness. He believed absolutely in the final outcome of his proposition: where others saw mist and failure ahead, he saw clear weather and the port of success. Never did he waver: never did he deflect from his course. He knew no path save the direct one that led straight to success, and, through his eyes, he made Bok see it with equal clarity until Bok wondered why others could not see it. But they could not. Cyrus Curtis would never be able, they said, to come out from under the load he had piled up. Where they differed from Mr. Curtis was in their lack of vision: they could not see what he saw!

It has been said that Mr. Curtis banished patent medicine advertisements from his magazine only when he could afford to do so. That is not true, as a simple incident will show. In the early days, he and Bok were opening the mail one Friday full of anxiety because the payroll was due that evening, and there was not enough money in the bank to meet it. From one of the letters dropped a certified check for five figures for a contract equal to five pages in the magazine. It was a welcome sight, for it meant an easy meeting of the payroll for that week and two succeeding weeks. But the check was from a manufacturing patent medicine company. Without a moment's hesitation, Mr. Curtis slipped it back into the envelope, saying: "Of course, *that* we can't take." He returned the check, never gave the matter a second thought, and went out and borrowed more money to meet his payroll!

With all respect to American publishers, there are very few who could have done this—or indeed, would do it today, under similar conditions—particularly in that day when it was the custom for all magazines to accept patent medicine advertising. *The Ladies' Home Journal* was practically the only publication of standing in the country refusing that class of business.

Bok now saw advertising done on a large scale by a man who believed in plenty of white space surrounding the announcement in the advertisement. He paid Mr. Howells $10,000 for his autobiography, and Mr. Curtis spent $50,000 in advertising it. "It is not expense," he would explain to Bok, "it is investment. We are investing in a trademark. It will all come back in time." And when the first $100,000 did not come back as Mr. Curtis figured, he would send another $100,000 after it, and then both came back.

Bok's experience in advertisement writing was now to stand him in excellent stead. He wrote all the advertisements and from that day to his retirement, practically every advertisement of the magazine was written by him.

Mr. Curtis believed that the editor should write the advertisements of a magazine's articles. "You are the one who knows them, what is in them, and your purpose," he said to Bok, who keenly enjoyed this. He put less and less in his advertisements. Mr. Curtis made them larger and larger in the media used. In this way *The Ladies' Home Journal* advertisements became distinctive for their use of white space, and as the advertising world began to say: "You can't miss them." Only one feature was advertised at a time, but the "feature" was always carefully selected for its wide popular appeal, and then Mr. Curtis spared no expense to advertise it abundantly. As much as $400,000 was spent in one year in advertising only a few features— a gigantic sum in those days, approached by no other periodical. But Mr. Curtis believed in showing the advertising world that he was willing to take his own medicine.

Naturally, such a campaign of publicity announcing the most popular attractions offered by any magazine of the day had but one effect: the circulation leaped forward by bounds, and the advertising columns of the magazine rapidly filled up.

The success of *The Ladies' Home Journal* began to look like an assured fact, even to the most skeptical.

As a matter of fact, it was only at its beginning, as both publisher and editor knew. The woman's magazine field was to belong to them!

XVII

Meeting a Reverse or Two

WITH THE hitherto unreached magazine circulation of a million copies a month in sight, Edward Bok decided to give a broader scope to the periodical. He was determined to lay under contribution not only the most famous writers of the day, but also to seek out those well-known persons who usually did not contribute to the magazines, always keeping in mind the popular appeal of his material but likewise aiming constantly to widen its scope and gradually to lift its standard.

Sailing again for England, he sought and secured the acquaintance of Rudyard Kipling, whose alert mind was at once keenly interested in what Bok was trying to do. He was willing to cooperate, with the result that Bok secured the author's new story, *William the Conqueror*. When Bok read the manuscript, he was delighted; he had for some time been reading Kipling's work with enthusiasm, and he saw at once that here was one of the author's best tales.

At that time, Frances E. Willard[1] had brought her

---

[1]Frances Elizabeth Caroline Willard, temperance activist and feminist, was a founder of the Association for the Advancement of Women and the Women's Christian Temperance Union, which, as president, she molded into a potent political force.

agitation for temperance prominently before the public, and Bok had promised to aid her by eliminating
from his magazine, so far as possible, all scenes which
represented alcoholic drinking. It was not an iron-
clad rule, but, both from the principle fixed for his
own life and in the interest of thousands of young people who read his magazine, he believed it would be
better to minimize all incidents portraying alcoholic
drinking or drunkenness. Kipling's story depicted
several such scenes; so when Bok sent the proofs he
suggested that if Kipling could moderate some of
these scenes, it would be more in line with the policy
of the magazine. Bok did not make a special point of
the matter, leaving it to Kipling's judgment to decide
how far he could make such changes and preserve the
atmosphere of the story.

From Kipling's house Bok went to Tunbridge
Wells to visit Mary Anderson,[2] the one-time popular
American actress, who had married Antonio de
Navarro and retired from the stage. A goodly number
of editors had tried to induce the retired actress to
write, just as a number of managers had tried to induce her to return to the stage. All had failed. But Bok
never accepted the failure of others as a final decision

[2]Mary Anderson, a famous American actress, won acclaim for
playing such roles as Galatea in Sullivan's *Pygmalion and Galatea*
and Rosalind in *As You Like It.* Leaving the United States in 1890
to settle permanently in England, she married an American attorney, Antonio de Navarro. Retiring, she became renowned as a
hostess, entertaining eminent playwrights, artists, and musicians.

One of Rudyard Kipling's many literary contributions to the Journal, *October 1901*

Charles Dodgson, better known as Lewis Carroll
Courtesy Library of Congress

for himself; and after two or three visits, he persuaded her to write her reminiscences, which he published with marked success in the magazine.

The editor was very desirous of securing something for his magazine that would delight children, and he hit upon the idea of trying to induce Lewis Carroll[3] to write another *Alice in Wonderland* series. He was told by English friends that this would be difficult, since the author led a secluded life at Oxford and hardly ever admitted anyone into his confidence. But Bok wanted to beard the lion in his den, and an Oxford graduate volunteered to introduce him to an Oxford don through whom, if it were at all possible, he could reach the author. The journey to Oxford was made, and Bok was introduced to the don, who turned out to be no less a person than the original possessor of the highly colored vocabulary of the "White Rabbit" of the *Alice* stories.

"Impossible," immediately declared the don. "You couldn't persuade Dodgson to consider it." Bok, however, persisted, and it so happened that the don liked what he called "American perseverance."

"Well, come along," he said. "We'll beard the lion in his den, as you say, and see what happens. You know, of course, that it is the Reverend Charles L. Dodgson we are going to see, and I must introduce

---

[3]Charles Lutwidge Dodgson was an English mathematician and logician who achieved lasting fame by publishing *Alice's Adventures in Wonderland* in 1865 and *Through the Looking-Glass* in 1872, both under the pseudonym of Lewis Carroll.

you to that person, not to Lewis Carroll. Dodgson is a tutor in mathematics here, as you doubtless know; lives a rigidly secluded life; dislikes strangers; makes no friends; and yet withal is one of the most delightful men in the world if he wants to be."

But as it happened upon this special occasion when Bok was introduced to him in his chambers in Tom Quad, Mr. Dodgson did not "want to be" delightful. There was no doubt that back of the studied reserve was a kindly, charming, gracious gentleman, but Bok's profession had been mentioned and the author was on rigid guard.

When Bok explained that one of the special reasons for his journey from America this summer was to see him, the Oxford mathematician sufficiently softened to ask the editor to sit down. Bok then broached his mission.

"You are quite in error, Mr. Bok," was the Dodgson comment. "You are not speaking to the person you think you are addressing."

For a moment Bok was taken aback. Then he decided to go right to the point.

"Do I understand, Mr. Dodgson, that you are not 'Lewis Carroll'; that you did not write *Alice in Wonderland?*"

For an answer the tutor rose, went into another room, and returned with a book which he handed to Bok. "This is my book," he said simply. It was entitled *An Elementary Treatise on Determinants,* by C. L. Dodgson.

When he looked up, Bok found the author's eyes riveted on him.

"Yes," said Bok. "I know, Mr. Dodgson. If I remember correctly, this is the same book of which you sent a copy to Her Majesty, Queen Victoria, when she wrote to you for a personal copy of your *Alice.*"

Dodgson made no comment. The face was absolutely without expression save a kindly compassion intended to convey to the editor that he was making a terrible mistake.

"As I said to you in the beginning, Mr. Bok, you are in error. You are not speaking to 'Lewis Carroll.'" And then: "Is this the first time you have visited Oxford?"

Bok said it was; and there followed the most delightful two hours with the Oxford mathematician and the Oxford don, walking about and into the wonderful college buildings, and afterward the three had a bite of lunch together. But all efforts to return to "Lewis Carroll" were futile. While saying goodbye to his host, Bok remarked: "I can't help expressing my disappointment, Mr. Dodgson, in my quest in behalf of the thousands of American children who love you and who would so gladly welcome 'Lewis Carroll' back."

The mention of children and their love for him momentarily had its effect. For an instant, a different light came into the eyes, and Bok instinctively realized Dodgson was about to say something. But he checked himself. Bok had almost caught him off his guard.

"I am sorry," he finally said at the parting at the door, "that you should be disappointed, for the sake of the children as well as for your own sake. I only regret that I cannot remove the disappointment."

And as the duo walked to the station, the don said: "That is his attitude toward all, even toward me. He is not 'Lewis Carroll' to anyone; is extremely sensitive on the point, and will not acknowledge his identity. That is why he lives so much to himself. He is in daily dread that some one will mention *Alice* in his presence. Curious, but there it is."

Edward Bok's next quest was to be even more disappointing; he was never even to reach the presence of the person he sought. This was Florence Nightingale, the Crimean nurse.[4] Bok was desirous of securing her own story of her experiences, but on every hand he found an unwillingness even to take him to her house. "No use," said everybody. "She won't see anyone. Hates publicity and all that sort of thing, and

[4]Florence Nightingale was the founder of the modern nursing profession. In the mid-nineteenth century, nursing was regarded as a disreputable occupation. Persevering against fierce parental opposition, and spurning marriage to Richard Monckton Milnes (later Lord Houghton) despite her ardent love for him, she achieved her first success by reorganizing a small hospital in London, after which she was sent on a mission to care for British soldiers wounded in the Crimean War. Taking thirty-eight nurses with her, she exerted nearly superhuman effort in reforming loathsome conditions in military hospitals, winning the adoration of the men and adulation at home as a national heroine. She spent the rest of her long life immersed in nursing education and mystical religious experiences.

shuns the public." Nevertheless, the editor journeyed to the famous nurse's home on South Street in the West End of London, only to be told that "Miss Nightingale never receives strangers."

"But I am not a stranger," insisted the editor. "I am one of her friends from America. Please take my card to her."

This mollified the faithful secretary, but the word instantly came back that Miss Nightingale was not receiving anyone that day. Bok wrote her a letter asking for an appointment, which was never answered. He wrote another, only to receive the message that "Miss Nightingale says there is no answer to the letter."

Bok had with such remarkable uniformity secured whatever he sought, that these experiences were new to him. Frankly, they puzzled him. He was not easily baffled, but baffled he now was, and that twice in succession. Turn as he might, he could find no way in which to reopen an approach to either the Oxford tutor or the Crimean nurse. They were plainly too much for him, and he had to acknowledge defeat. The experience was good for him; he did not realize this at the time, nor did he enjoy the sensation of not getting what he wanted. Nevertheless, a reverse or two was due. Not that his success was having any undesirable effect upon him; his Dutch common sense saved him from any such calamity. But at thirty years of age it is not good for anyone, no matter how well balanced, to have things come his way too fast and too consistently. And here were breaks. He could not have everything he wanted, and it was just as well that, actually, he should find that out.

In his next quest he found himself again opposed by his London friends. Unable to secure a new *Alice in Wonderland* for his child readers, he determined to give them Kate Greenaway.[5] But here he had selected another recluse. Everybody discouraged him. The artist never saw visitors, he was told, and she particularly shunned editors and publishers. Greenaway's own publishers confessed that she was inaccessible to them. "We conduct all our business with her by correspondence. I have never seen her personally myself," said a member of the firm.

Bok inwardly decided that two failures in two days were sufficient, and he made up his mind that there should not be a third. He took a bus for the long ride to Hampstead Heath, where the illustrator lived, and finally stood before a picturesque Queen Anne house that one would have recognized at once, with its lower story of red brick, its upper part covered with red tiles, its windows of every size and shape, as the inspiration of Kate Greenaway's pictures. As it turned out later, Miss Greenaway's sister opened the door and told the visitor that Miss Greenaway was not at home.

"But, pardon me, has not Miss Greenaway re-

[5]Kate Greenaway was a British author of sentimental books about children that she illustrated herself. Her first success was *Under the Window* (1879), which sold more than 100,000 copies. She also wrote *A Apple Pie* (1880), a child's book about the alphabet, and *Mother Goose, or, The Old Nursery Rhymes* (1881). An article by Ethel Mackenzie McKenna, "A Glimpse of Kate Greenaway," appears in *The Ladies' Home Journal*, in the February 1892 issue.

turned? Is not that she?" asked Bok, as he indicated a
figure just coming down the stairs. And as the sister
turned to see, Bok stepped into the hall. At least he
was inside! Bok had never seen a photograph of Miss
Greenaway, he did not know that the figure coming
downstairs was the artist; but his instinct had led him
right, and good fortune was with him.

He now introduced himself to Kate Greenaway,
and explained that one of his objects in coming to
London was to see her on behalf of thousands of
American children. Naturally there was nothing for
the illustrator to do but welcome her visitor. She took
him into the garden, where he saw at once that he was
seated under the apple tree of Miss Greenaway's pictures. It was in full bloom, a veritable picture of spring
loveliness. Bok's love for nature pleased the artist and
when he recognized the cat that sauntered up, he
could see that he was making headway. But when he
explained his profession and stated his errand, the atmosphere instantly changed. Miss Greenaway con-
veyed the unmistakable impression that she had been
trapped, and Bok realized at once that he had a long
and difficult road ahead.

Still, negotiate it he must and he did! And after luncheon in the garden, with the cat in his lap, Miss
Greenaway perceptibly thawed out, and when the editor left late that afternoon he had the promise of the
artist that she would do her first magazine work for
him. That promise was kept monthly; for nearly two
years her articles appeared, with satisfaction to Miss

Greenaway and with great success to the magazine.

The next opposition to Bok's plans arose from the soreness generated by the absence of copyright laws between the United States and Great Britain and Europe. The editor, who had been publishing a series of musical compositions, solicited the aid of Sir Arthur Sullivan.[6] But it so happened that Sir Arthur's most famous composition, "The Lost Chord," had been taken without leave by American music publishers, and sold by the hundreds of thousands with the composer left out on payday. Sir Arthur held forth on this injustice, and said further that no accurate copy of "The Lost Chord" had, so far as he knew, ever been printed in the United States.

"Very well, Sir Arthur," suggested Bok; "with your consent, I will rectify both the inaccuracy and the injustice. Write out a correct version of 'The Lost Chord'; I will give it to nearly a million readers, and so render obsolete the incorrect copies; and I shall be only too happy to pay you the first honorarium for an American publication of the song. You can add to the copy the statement that this is the first American honorarium you have ever received."

[6]Sir Arthur Seymour Sullivan composed many serious works but made his mark chiefly in collaborating with W. S. Gilbert in creating immensely popular operettas, including *H.M.S. Pinafore, The Pirates of Penzance,* and *The Mikado.* His song, "The Lost Chord," which begins with the words, "Seated one day at the organ, I was weary and ill at ease," and culminates with the discovery of a majestic chord that can never be recovered, was enormously appreciated by Victorian audiences and is still sung today.

Kate Greenaway,
whose illustrations appeared in
The Ladies' Home Journal
throughout the late nineteenth century
Courtesy Library of Congress

223

Sir Arthur Sullivan's authorized
version of "The Lost Chord,"
December 1897

Courtesy Library of Congress

224

This argument appealed strongly to the composer, who made a correct transcript of his famous song, and published it with the following note:

This is the first and only copy of "The Lost Chord" which has ever been sent by me to an American publisher. I believe all the reprints in America are more or less incorrect. I have pleasure in sending this copy to my friend, Mr. Edward W. Bok, for publication in *The Ladies' Home Journal* for which he gives me an honorarium, the only one I have ever received from an American publisher for this song.

ARTHUR SULLIVAN.

At least, thought Bok, he had healed one man's soreness toward America. But the next day he encountered another. On his way to Paris, he stopped at Amiens to see Jules Verne.[7] Here he found special difficulty in that the aged author could not speak English, and Bok knew only a few words of casual French. Finally a neighbor's servant who knew a handful of English words was commandeered, and a halting three-cornered conversation was begun.

Bok found two grievances here: the author was incensed at the American public because it had insisted on classing his books as juveniles, and accepting them as stories of adventure, whereas he desired them to

[7]Jules Verne is sometimes called the "father of science fiction." Among his most famous books that secured a mass readership in England and the United States were *Journey to the Center of the Earth, From the Earth to the Moon, Twenty Thousand Leagues Under the Sea,* and *Around the World in Eighty Days.*

be recognized as prophetic stories based on scientific facts—an insistence which, as all the world knows, has since been justified. Bok explained, however, that the popular acceptance of the author's books as stories of adventure was by no means confined to America; that even in his own country the same was true. But Jules Verne came back with the rejoinder that if the French were a pack of fools, that was no reason why the Americans should also be.

The argument weighed somewhat with the author, however, for he then changed the conversation, and pointed out how he had been robbed by American publishers who had stolen his books. So Bok was once more face to face with the old noncopyright conditions; and although he explained the existence then of a new protective law, the old man was not mollified. He did not take kindly to Bok's suggestion for new work, and closed the talk, by declaring that his writing days were over.

But Bok was by no means through with noncopyright echoes, for he was destined next day to take part in an even stormier interview on the same subject with Alexander Dumas *fils*.[8] Bok had been publishing a series of articles in which authors had told how they

[8]Alexandre Dumas became particularly noted for plays defending the institution of marriage, condemning prostitution, and espousing the right of women to seek divorce and to vote. He wrote the novel *La Dame aux camélias* and the play, *Le Demi-monde*. He was the subject of an article by Lucy Hamilton Hooper, "How Dumas Wrote 'Camille'," in the January 1893 issue of *The Ladies' Home Journal*.

had been led to write their most famous books, and Bok wanted Dumas to tell "How I Came to Write 'Camille.' "

To act as translator this time, Bok took a trusted friend along with him, whose services he found were needed, as Dumas was absolutely without knowledge of English. No sooner was the editor's request made known to him than the storm broke. Dumas, hotly excited, denounced the Americans as robbers who had deprived him of his rightful returns on his book and play, and ended by declaring that he would trust no American editor or publisher.

The mutual friend explained the new copyright conditions and declared that Bok intended to treat the author honorably. But Dumas was not to be mollified. He launched forth upon a new arrangement of the Americans; dishonesty was bred in their bones! And they were robbers by instinct. All of this distinctly nettled Bok's Americanism. The interpreting friend finally suggested that the article should be written while Bok was in Paris; that he should be notified when the manuscript was ready, that he should then appear with the actual money in hand in French notes; and that Dumas should give Bok the manuscript when Bok handed Dumas the money.

"After I count it," said Dumas.

This was the last straw!

"Pray ask him," Bok suggested to the interpreter, "what assurance I have that he will deliver the manuscript to me after he has the money." The friend protested against translating this thrust, but Bok insisted, and Dumas, not knowing what was coming, insisted that the message be given him. When it was the man was a study; he became livid with rage.

"But," persisted Bok, "say to Monsieur Dumas that I have the same privilege of distrusting him as he apparently has of distrusting me."

And Bok can still see the violent gesticulations of the storming French author, his face burning with passionate anger, as the two left him.

Edward Bok now sincerely hoped that his encounters with the absence of a law that has been met were at an end!

On his return to London the editor found that Charles Dana Gibson[9] had settled down there for a time. Bok had always wanted Gibson to depict the characters of Dickens; and he felt that this was the opportunity, while the artist was in London and could get the atmosphere for his work. Gibson was as keen for the idea as was Bok, and so the two arranged the series, which was subsequently published.

On his way to his steamer to sail for home, Bok visited "Ian Maclaren,"[10] whose *Bonnie Brier Bush* stories were then in great vogue, and not only contracted

[9]Charles Dana Gibson was an American illustrator who created the "Gibson Girl," who epitomized American beauty in the late nineteenth century. He was the subject of an article by Alice Graham McCollin in *The Ladies' Home Journal,* June 1894, in a series, "A Quartette of Clever Illustrators."

[10]Pseudonym of John Watson, who was a British religious writer and novelist. He wrote a series of stories about Scottish life.

for Dr. Watson's stories of the immediate future, but arranged with him for a series of articles, which for two years thereafter, was published in the magazine.

The editor now sailed for home, content with his assembly of foreign "features."

On the steamer, Bok heard of the recent discovery of some unpublished letters by Louisa May Alcott, written to five girls, and before returning to Philadelphia, he went to Boston, got into touch with the executors of the will of Miss Alcott, brought the letters back with him to read, and upon reaching Philadelphia, wired his acceptance of them for publication.

But the traveler was not at once to enjoy his home. After only a day in Philadelphia he took a train for Indianapolis. Here lived the most thoroughly American writer of the day, in Bok's estimation: James Whitcomb Riley. An arrangement, perfected before his European visit, had secured to Bok practically exclusive rights to all the output of his Chicago friend Eugene Field, and he felt that Riley's work would admirably complement that of Field. This Bok explained to Riley, who readily fell in with the idea, and the editor returned to Philadelphia with a contract to see Riley's next dozen poems. A little later Field passed away. His last poem, "The Dream Ship," and his posthumous story "The Werewolf" later appeared in *The Ladies' Home Journal*.

A second series of articles was also arranged for with Mr. Harrison, in which he was to depict, in a personal way, the life of a president of the United States, the domestic life of the White House, and the financial arrangements made by the government for the care of the chief executive and his family. The first series of articles by the former president had been successful; Bok felt that they had accomplished much in making his women readers familiar with their country and the machinery of its government.

Bok now devoted his attention to strengthening the fiction in his magazine. He sought Mark Twain, and bought his two new stories; he secured from Bret Harte a tale which he had just finished; and then ran the gamut of the best fiction writers of the day, and secured their best output. Marion Crawford, Conan Doyle, Sarah Orne Jewett, John Kendrick Bangs, Kate Douglas Wiggin, Hamlin Garland, Mrs. Burton Harrison, Elizabeth Stuart Phelps, Mary E. Wilkins, Jerome K. Jerome, Anthony Hope, Joel Chandler Harris, and others followed in rapid succession.

He next turned for a moment to his religious department, decided that it needed a freshening of interest, and he then secured Dwight L. Moody, whose evangelical work was then so prominently in the public eye, to conduct "Mr. Moody's Bible Class" in the magazine—practically a study of the stated Bible lesson of the month with explanation in Moody's simple and effective style.

The authors for whom the *Journal* was now publishing attracted the attention of all the writers of the day, and the supply of good material became too great for its capacity. Bok studied the mechanical makeup, and felt that by some method he must find more room in the front portion. He had allotted the first third of the magazine to the general literary contents and the latter two-thirds to departmental features. Toward the close of the number, the departments narrowed down from full pages to single columns with advertisements on each side.

One day Bok was handling a story by Rudyard Kipling which had overrun the space allowed for it in the front. The story had come late, and the rest of the front portion of the magazine had gone to press. The editor was in a quandary what to do with the two remaining columns of the Kipling tale. There were only two pages open, and these were at the back. He remade those pages, and continued the story from pages 6 and 7 to pages 38 and 39.

At once Bok saw that this was an instance where "necessity was the mother of invention." He realized that if he could run some of his front material over to the back he would relieve the pressure at the front, present a more varied contents there, and make his advertisements more valuable by putting them next to the most expensive material in the magazine.

In the next issue he combined some of his smaller departments in the back; and thus, in 1896, he inaugurated the method of "running over into the back," which has now become a recognized principle in the makeup of magazines of larger size. At first, Bok's readers objected, but he explained why he did it. So far as readers can be satisfied with what is, at best, an awkward method of presentation, they were content. Today the practice is undoubtedly followed to excess, some magazines carrying as much as eighty and ninety columns over from the front to the back; from such abuse it will, of course, free itself either by a return to the original method of makeup or by the adoption of some other less irritating plan.

XVIII

A Signal Piece of Constructive Work

THE INFLUENCE of his grandfather and the injunction of his grandmother to her sons that each
"should make the world a better or more beautiful
place to live in" now began to manifest in the grandson. Edward Bok was unconscious that it was this influence. What directly led him to the signal piece of
construction in which he engaged was the wretched
architecture of small houses. As he traveled through
the United States he was appalled by it. Where the
houses were not positively ugly, they were repellently
ornate. Money was wasted on useless turrets, filigree
work, or machine-made ornamentation. Bok found
that these small householders never employed an architect, but that the houses were put up by builders
from their own plans.

Bok felt a keen desire to take hold of the small
American house and make it architecturally better. He
foresaw, however, that the subject would finally include small gardening and interior decoration. He
feared that the subject would become too large for the
magazine, which was already feeling the pressure of
the material which he was securing. He suggested,
therefore, to Mr. Curtis that they purchase a little magazine published in Buffalo, New York, called *Country*

Life,[1] and develop it into a first-class periodical devoted to the general subject of a better American architecture, gardening, and interior decoration, with special application to the small house. The magazine was purchased; while Bok was collecting his material for a number of issues ahead, he edited and issued, for copyright purposes, a four-page magazine.

An opportunity now came to Mr. Curtis to purchase *The Saturday Evening Post,* a Philadelphia weekly of honored prestige, founded by Benjamin Franklin.[2] It was apparent at once that the company could not embark upon the development of two mag-

[1] *Country Life,* which Curtis Publishing owned temporarily before selling it to Doubleday, should not be confused with *Country Gentleman,* a periodical that Curtis published on a long-term basis. Despite the hopes entertained by Curtis for *Country Gentleman,* it never achieved the success of the *Journal* or the *Post.*

[2] *The Saturday Evening Post,* a weekly newspaper and magazine, was founded in Philadelphia in 1821 and was published under various titles until it was purchased, for $1,000, by Cyrus H. K. Curtis in 1897. The *Post* had been in financial distress for some time and its current owner, Albert Smythe, held no copyright on its name. On the basis of no discernible evidence, Curtis decided that the *Post* was descended from Benjamin Franklin's *Pennsylvania Gazette* and used this claim in advertising it. Curtis poured large amounts of money into developing the publication, most of which came from profits earned by *The Ladies' Home Journal,* and gave his editor, George Horace Lorimer, a free hand to make it "a weekly magazine for men, a magazine for businessmen, a national magazine of information and entertainment, and to sell it in direct competition with the newspapers at five cents a copy." To fill its pages, Lorimer went after well-known authors, including Jack London, Booth Tarkington, Ring Lardner, and James Branch Cabell. In its first five years of publication after being acquired by Curtis, the *Post* lost $1,350,000 and Bok, who was jealous of Lorimer

azines at the same time, and as a larger field was seen for *The Saturday Evening Post,* it was decided to leave *Country Life* in abeyance for the present.

Mr. Frank Doubleday, having left the Scribners and started a publishing house of his own, asked Bok to transfer to him the copyright and good will of *Country Life*—seeing that there was little chance for The Curtis Publishing Company to undertake its publication. Mr. Curtis was willing, but he knew that Bok had set his heart on the new magazine and left it for him to decide. The editor realized, as the Doubleday Company could take up the magazine at once, the unfairness of holding indefinitely the field against them by the publication of a mere copyright periodical. And so, with a feeling as if he were giving up his child to another father, Bok arranged that The Curtis Publishing Company should transfer all rights to the title and periodical of which the present beautiful publication *Country Life* is the outgrowth.

Bok now turned to *The Ladies' Home Journal* as his medium for making the small house architecture of America better. He realized the limitation of space, but decided to do the best he could under the circumstances. He believed he might serve thousands of his readers if he could make it possible for them to secure, at moderate cost, plans for well-designed houses

---

and resented the funds he was siphoning from *The Ladies' Home Journal,* argued that the *Post* be dropped. But, soon after the turn of the century, it caught on and skyrocketed to success.

by the leading domestic architects in the country. He consulted a number of architects, only to find them unalterably opposed to the idea. They disliked the publicity of magazine presentation; prices differed too much in various parts of the country; and they did not care to risk the criticism of their contemporaries. It was "cheapening" their profession!

Bok saw that he should have to blaze the way and demonstrate the futility of these arguments. At last he persuaded one architect to cooperate with him, and in 1895 began the publication of a series of houses which could be built, approximately, for from $1,500 to $5,000. The idea attracted attention at once, and the architect-author was swamped with letters and inquiries regarding his plans.

This proved Bok's instinct to be correct as to the public willingness to accept such designs; upon this proof he succeeded in winning over two additional architects to make plans. He offered his readers full building specifications and plans to scale of the houses with estimates from four builders in different parts of the United States for five dollars a set. The plans and specifications were so complete in every detail that any builder could build the house from them.

A storm of criticism now arose from architects and builders all over the country, the architects claiming that Bok was taking "the bread out of their mouths" by the sale of plans, and local builders vigorously questioned the accuracy of the estimates. But Bok knew he was right and persevered.

Slowly but surely he won the approval of the leading architects, who saw that he was appealing to a class of house builders who could not afford to pay an architect's fee, and that, with his wide circulation, he might become an influence for better architecture through these small houses. The sets of plans and specifications sold by the thousands. It was not long before the magazine was able to present small house plans by the foremost architects of the country, whose services the average householder could otherwise never have dreamed of securing.

Bok not only saw an opportunity to better the exterior of the small houses, but he determined that each plan published should provide for two essentials: every servant's room should have two windows to ensure cross ventilation and contain twice the number of cubic feet usually given to such rooms; and in place of the American parlor, which he considered a useless room, should be substituted either a living room or a library. He did not point to these improvements; every plan simply presented the larger servant's room and did not present a parlor. Of the tens of thousands of plans sold, not a purchaser ever noticed the absence of a parlor except one woman in Brookline, Massachusetts, who, in erecting a group of twenty-five "*Journal* houses," discovered after she had built ten that not one contained a parlor!

"*Ladies' Home Journal* houses" were now going up in communities all over the country, and Bok determined to prove that they could be erected for the prices given. Accordingly, he published a prize offer of generous amount for the best set of exterior and interior photographs of a house built after a *Journal* plan within the published price. Five other and smaller prizes were also offered. A legally attested builder's declaration was to accompany each set of photographs. The sets immediately began to come in, until over 5,000 had been received. Bok selected the best of these and awarded the prizes.

Of course this publication gave fresh impetus to the whole scheme; prospective house builders pointed their builders to the proof given, and additional thousands of sets of plans were sold. The little houses became better and better in architecture as the series went on, and occasionally a plan for a house costing as high as $10,000 was given.

For nearly twenty-five years Bok continued to publish pictures of houses and plans. Entire colonies of *"Ladies' Home Journal* houses" have sprung up, and building promoters have built complete suburban developments with them. How many of these homes have been erected it is, of course, impossible to say; the number certainly runs into the thousands.

It was one of the most constructive and far-reaching pieces of work that Bok did during his editorial career—a fact now recognized by all architects. Shortly before Stanford White passed away,[3] he wrote: "I

[3]Stanford White, a famous American architect, designed many residences, churches, and public buildings including Madison Square Garden (1891) and a triumphal arch (based on the Arch of

firmly believe that Edward Bok has more completely influenced American domestic architecture for the better than any man in this generation. When he began, I was short-sighted enough to discourage him and refused to cooperate with him. If Bok came to me now, I would not only make plans for him, but I would waive any fee for them in retribution for my early mistake."

Bok then turned to the subject of the garden for the small house, and the development of the grounds around the homes that he had been instrumental in putting on the earth. He encountered no opposition here. The publication of small gardens for small houses finally ran into hundreds of pages, the magazine supplying planting plans and full directions as to when and how to plant—this time without cost.

Next the editor decided to see what he could do for the better and simpler furnishing of the small American home. Here was a field almost limitless in possible improvement, but he wanted to approach it in a new way. The best method baffled him until one day he met a woman friend who told him that she was on her way to a funeral at a friend's home.

"I didn't know you were so well acquainted with Mrs. S_____," said Bok.

Titus) in New York City's Washington Square (1895). Although Bok refers to White "passing away", he was murdered in June 1906 by millionaire Harry K. Thaw because of an alleged affair with Thaw's wife, Evelyn Nesbit. The scandal resulted in a sensational court trial that was immortalized in films and crime stories.

"I wasn't, as a matter of fact," replied the woman. "I'll be perfectly frank; I am going to the funeral just to see how Mrs. S_____'s house is furnished. She was always thought to have great taste, you know, and, whether you know it or not, a woman is always keen to look into another woman's home."

Bok realized that he had found the method of presentation for his interior furnishing plan if he could secure photographs of the most carefully furnished homes in America. He immediately employed the best available expert, and within six months there came to him an assorted collection of over 1,000 photographs of well-furnished rooms. The best were selected, and a series of photographic pages called "Inside of 100 Homes" was begun. The editor's woman friend had correctly pointed the way to him, for this series won for his magazine the enviable distinction of being the first magazine of standing to reach the then-marvelous record of a circulation of 1 million copies a month. The editions containing the series were sold out as fast as they could be printed.

The editor followed this up with another successful series, again pictorial. He realized that to explain good taste in furnishing by text was almost impossible. So he started a series of all-picture pages called "Good Taste and Bad Taste." He presented a chair that was bad in lines and either useless or uncomfortable to sit in, and explained where and why it was bad; and then put a good chair next to it, and explained where and why it was good.

A Small House with "Lots of Room in It"

By Frank Lloyd Wright

NINTH DESIGN IN THE JOURNAL'S NEW SERIES OF MODEL SUBURBAN HOUSES AT MODERATE COST

SECTIONAL VIEW OF DINING-ROOM

SECTIONAL VIEW OF LIVING-ROOM

SECTIONAL VIEW OF ENTRY

Frank Lloyd Wright's design contribution to The Ladies' Home Journal series on model houses, July 1901

Good Taste and Bad Taste in Dress

By Mrs. Ralston

Drawings by Augusta Reimer and Grace Cochrane Sanger

IT IS the tendency of most women to overdress. By this I do not mean dressing gaudily or choosing too expensive clothes, or even wearing too elaborate and handsome things when only simple ones are required; I mean the very much exaggerated look which so many women give their clothes. When large hats are the style a good many people want them just a little bit larger than anybody's else, thinking they will thus be more in style.

Really good dressing is never complicated by too many distracting details, such as big bows, for instance, long hand chains, or huge, drooping pompadours, all of which seem to hold such a strong place in the affections of many women today. It is hard to define good taste because it is something that is intangible; but certainly it shuns all exaggeration and conspicuousness.

THE first two girls shown on this page are types of the average, every-day girl who needs and wears a separate skirt and shirtwaist; this combination may be said to be the "national constitution" in dress for American girls. Before I say another word on this subject let me first emphasize the fact that there is no difference in expense between clothes in good taste and those in bad taste; really, if you can imagine any difference, bad taste is the more expensive. But as to the type in these first two illustrations: I am sure that most people will recognize the familiar "exaggerated" girl with the huge pompadour and flare hat. I say so well confess in the beginning that personally I like the girl shown here; I believe that the bad taste in her dress not go below the exterior. She wears this kind of clothes only because she has not been trained to wear better, or has not had the chance to know better. Be that as it may, she certainly wears these clothes because, through some mistaken conception, she thinks they are "stylish."

NOTHING that is overdone or exaggerated is ever in good style. It is in the worst possible taste to be conspicuous, and a girl dressed as shown in the second illustration is, I am sorry to say, exceedingly conspicuous. In the first place, look at her hat and her hair: they are out of all proportion to her face and head. Then look at her shirtwaist: it flops over in all directions and looks like a plate of ice cream that has been in the sun too long; it doesn't suggest either neatness or trimness. There is no waist-line to her figure, and see the untidy way that the shoulder-seams droop over the top of her arm, giving her figure a shape that Nature never intended. Such an ornate shock is altogether out of place in a simple shirtwaist. And the beads! A small string of beads is all right, but don't pile them on! And now let us take the other side of the question: observe the girl dressed in a neat, small-checked skirt and a simple shirtwaist. You will see that nothing strikes you with unpleasant force: the girl suits the clothes, and the clothes suit the girl; everything is in proportion, quiet, and low in tone, and yet not without color or snap. The skirt should be of a checked material worn with a white shirtwaist, and the hat of any bright, becoming color, with fancy wings.

THE next two illustrations show an older woman. Here I should like to bring out a few points about some woman's carelessness in dress and also about the appropriateness of certain clothes for certain occasions. I am sure that many of you will recognize the type of woman I have chosen with the very elaborately-trimmed and badly-made skirt of cheap silk, worn with a cotton shirtwaist and a fancy lace collar which she mistakenly thinks is going to make the shirtwaist look "dressed up" as so far to worship with the silk skirt, and that she finishes this costume with a tawdry, ill-fitting collar which doesn't in any way match the shirtwaist or the lace collar. The kind of hat she has on is worn by so many women—unfortunately—that I hear they will not be able to appreciate, even in this picture, what a top-heavy ornament it really is. Nine out of ten women wear hats too big for their heads, and excessively over-trimmed. On this particular hat, you see, there are ribbons, flowers, wings and feathers; the hat is utterly unconnected to the head, and indeed to the entire figure. This, perhaps, is not so much a question of bad taste as of no taste at all—a lack of knowledge as to what is becoming and suitable. For a good gown is worn when one wishes to be dressed up, a costume of the same material is in very much better taste, and it can be made of the most inexpensive goods, from a thirty-seven-cent challie upward. Let me repeat: to dress in good taste is to no sense a question of expense.

NOW we come to the last two illustrations showing a young girl. The question of young girls' clothes is, perhaps, the hardest one to manage, as we should undoubtedly consult the wishes of the girls themselves and must not be too harsh in criticizing their taste. Just notice the general effect of each of these two pictures: you will see that the little girl with the dog could easily have more color and "go" in her appearance and still be dressed in perfectly good taste; while the other girl is not dressed at all in keeping with her years, and presents, on the whole, a rather pathetic little figure—wouldn't she be indignant if she heard me say that! "Well," she would say defiantly, "what is the matter with me, anyhow?"

"Nothing," I should answer, "with you, but a lot in the matter with your clothes. You don't look tidy or trig, you don't look well put together, and your general appearance is exaggerated."

Look her over from head to foot; take the head, for instance: there is too much bow, it makes the whole figure top-heavy, while the braid is too small for the body and so the hair looks "frowsy." Then see the bolero, and the shirtwaist; the unnecessary big bow of tulle at the collar, and the belt which does not, at all answer the purpose of a belt, as it does not fit around the waist-line, and is so dragged down as to give false and badly-proportioned lines to the figure. The skirt is too tight, and it binds the figure instead of giving it the graceful, slim look which was doubtless intended in making such a skirt; the actual result is an uncomfortable look of scantiness and "skimpiness."

An example of Bok's attempt to influence the taste of American women, January 1906

242

The lesson to the eye was simply and directly effective; the pictures told their story as no printed word could have done, and furniture manufacturers and dealers all over the country, feeling the pressure from their customers, began to put on the market the tables, chairs, divans, bedsteads, and dressing tables which the magazine was portraying as examples of good taste.

The next undertaking was a systematic plan for improving the pictures on the walls of the American home. Bok was employing the best artists of the day: Edwin A. Abbey, Howard Pyle, Charles Dana Gibson, W. L. Taylor, Albert Lynch, Will H. Low, W. T. Smedley, Irving R. Wiles, and others. As his magazine was rolled to go through the mails, the pictures naturally suffered; Bok therefore decided to print a special edition of each important picture that he published, an edition on plate paper, without text, and offered to his readers at ten cents a copy. Within a year he had sold nearly 100,000 copies.

Pictures were difficult to advertise successfully; it was before the full color press had become practicable for rapid magazine work; and even the large-page black and white reproductions which Bok would give in his magazine did not, of course, show the beauty of the original paintings, the majority of which were in full color. He accordingly made arrangements with art publishers to print his pictures in their original colors; then he determined to give the public an opportunity to see what the pictures themselves looked like.

He asked his art editor to select the 250 best pictures and frame them. Then he engaged the art gallery of the Philadelphia Art Club and advertised an exhibition of the original paintings. No admission was charged. The gallery was put into gala attire, and the pictures well hung. The exhibition, which was continued for two weeks, was visited by over 50,000 persons.

His success here induced Bok to take the collection to New York. The galleries of the American Art Association were offered him, but he decided to rent the ballroom of the Hotel Waldorf. The hotel was then new; it was the talk not only of the town but of the country, while the ballroom had been pictured far and wide. It would have a publicity value. The exhibition was well advertised; a "private view" was given the evening before the opening day, and when, at nine o'clock the following morning, the doors of the exhibition were thrown open, over a thousand persons were waiting in line.

The hotel authorities had to resort to a special cordon of police to handle the crowds and within four days over 17,000 persons had seen the pictures. On the last evening it was after midnight before the doors could be closed to the waiting line. Boston was next visited, and there, at the Art Club Gallery, the previous successes were repeated. Within two weeks over 28,000 persons visited the exhibition.

Other cities now clamored for a sight of the pictures, and it was finally decided to end the exhibitions by a visit to Chicago. The success here exceeded that in any of the other cities. The banquet hall of the Auditorium Hotel had been engaged; over 2,000 persons were continually in a waiting line outside, and within a week nearly 30,000 persons pushed and jostled themselves into the gallery.

The exhibition was immediately followed by the publication of a portfolio of the ten pictures that had proved the greatest favorites. These were printed on plate-paper and the portfolio was offered by Bok to his readers for one dollar. The first 1,000 were printed, and these were quickly sold out.

Bok's next enterprise was to get his pictures into the homes of the country on a larger scale; he determined to work through the churches. He selected the fifty best pictures, made them into a set, and offered first 100 sets to selected schools, which were at once taken. Then he offered 250 sets to churches to sell at their fairs. The managers were to promise to erect a *Ladies' Home Journal* booth (which Bok knew, of course, would be most effective advertising), and the pictures were to sell at twenty-five and fifty cents each, with some at a dollar each. The set was offered to the churches for five dollars: the actual cost of reproduction and expressage. On the day after the publication of the magazine containing the offer, enough telegraphic orders were received to absorb the entire edition. A second edition was immediately printed; and finally ten editions, 4,000 sets in all, were absorbed before the demand was filled. By this method,

200,000 pictures had been introduced into American homes, and over $150,000 in money had been raised by the churches as their portion.

But all this was simply to lead up to the realization of Bok's cherished dream: the reproduction, in enormous numbers, of the greatest pictures in the world in their original colors. The plan, however, was not for the moment feasible: the cost of the four-color process was at that time prohibitive, and Bok had to abandon it. But he never lost sight of it. He knew the hour would come when he could carry it out, and he bided his time.

It was not until years later that his opportunity came, when he immediately made up his mind to seize it. The magazine had installed a battery of four-color presses; the color work in the periodical was attracting universal attention, and after all stages of experimentation had been passed, Bok decided to make his dream a reality. He sought the cooperation of the owners of the greatest private art galleries in the country: J. Pierpont Morgan, John G. Johnson, Joseph E. Widener, George W. Elkins, Henry C. Frick, Charles P. Taft, Mrs. John L. Gardner, Charles L. Freer, Mrs. Havemeyer, and the owners of the Benjamin Altman Collection, and sought permission to reproduce their greatest paintings.

Although each felt doubtful of the ability of any processes adequately to reproduce their masterpieces, the owners heartily cooperated with Bok. But Bok's coeditors discouraged his plan, since it would involve

endless labor, the exclusive services of a corps of photographers and engravers, and the employment of the
most careful pressman available in the United States.
The editor realized that the obstacles were numerous
and that the expense would be enormous; but he felt
sure that the American public was ready for his idea.

The most wonderful of Rembrandt, Velasquez,
Turner, Hobbema, Van Dyck, Raphael, Frans Hals,
Romney, Gainsborough, Whistler, Corot, Mauve, Ver-
meer, Fragonard, Botticelli, and Titian reproductions
followed in such rapid succession as fairly to daze the
magazine readers. Four pictures were given in each
number, and the faithfulness of the reproductions astonished even their owners. The success of the series
was beyond Bok's own best hopes. He was printing
and selling 1.75 million copies of each issue of his
magazine; and before he was through he had presented to American homes throughout the breadth of
the country over 70 million reproductions of forty
separate masterpieces of art.

The dream of years had come true.

Bok had begun with the exterior of the small American house and made an impression upon it; he had
brought the love of flowers into the hearts of thousands of small householders who had never thought
they could have an artistic garden within a small area;
he had changed the lines of furniture, and he had put
better art on the walls of these homes. He had conceived a full rounded scheme and had carried it out.

It was a peculiar satisfaction to Bok that Theodore

Roosevelt once summed up this piece of work in these words: "Bok is the only man I ever heard of who changed, for the better, the architecture of an entire nation, and he did it so quickly and yet so effectively that we didn't know it was begun before it was finished. That is a mighty big job for one man to have done."

XIX

An Adventure in
Civic and Private Art

EDWARD BOK now turned his attention to those influences of a more public nature where he felt he
could contribute to elevate the standard of public
taste.

He was surprised, on talking with furnishers of
homes, to learn to what extent women whose husbands had recently acquired means would refer to certain styles of decoration and hangings which they had
seen in the Pullman parlor cars. He had never seri-
ously regarded the influence of the furnishings of
these cars upon the travelling public; now he realized
that, in a decorative sense, they were a distinct factor
and a very unfortunate one.

For in those days, twenty years ago, the decoration
of the Pullman parlor car was atrocious. Colors were
in riotous discord; every foot of wood paneling was
carved and ornamented, nothing being left of the grain
of even the most beautiful woods; gilt was recklessly
laid on everywhere regardless of its fitness or relation.
The hangings in the cars were not only in bad taste,
but distinctly unsanitary; the heaviest velvets and
showiest plushes were used; mirrors with bronzed
and red plushed frames were the order of the day;
cord portières, lambrequins, and tasseled fringes were

still in vogue in these cars. It was a riot of the worst ideas.

Bok wrote an editorial calling attention to these facts. The Pullman Company paid no attention to it, but the railroad journals did. With one accord they seized the cudgel which Bok had raised, and a series of hammerings began.

The president of a large western railroad wrote to Bok that he agreed absolutely with his position, and asked whether he had any definite suggestions to offer for the improvement of some new cars which they were about to order. Bok engaged two of the best architects and decorators in the country and submitted the results to the officials of the railroad company, who approved of them heartily. The Pullman Company did not take very kindly, however, to suggestions thus brought to them. But a current had been started; the attention of the travelling public had been drawn for the first time to the wretched decoration of the cars.

The first change came when a new dining car on the Chicago, Burlington, and Quincy Railroad suddenly appeared. It was an artistically treated Flemish oak paneled car with longitudinal beams and cross-beams, giving the impression of a ceiling-beamed room. Between the "beams" was a quiet tone of deep yellow. The sides of the car were wainscoting of plain surface done in a Flemish stain rubbed down to a dull finish. The grain of the wood was allowed to serve as decoration; there was no carving. The whole tone of the car was that of the rich color on the sunflower. The effect upon the public was instantaneous.

The Pullman people now saw the drift, and wisely reorganized their decorative department. Only those who remember the Pullman parlor car of twenty years ago can realize how long a step it is from the atrociously decorated, unsanitary vehicle of that day to the simple car of today.

It was only a step from the Pullman car to the landscape outside, and Bok next decided to see what he could do toward eliminating the hideous billboard advertisements that defaced the landscape along the lines of the principal roads. He found a willing ally in this idea in Mr. J. Horace McFarland,[1] of Harrisburg, Pennsylvania, one of the most skillful photographers in the country, and the president of The American Civic Association. McFarland and Bok worked together; they took an innumerable amount of photographs and began to publish them, calling public attention to the intrusion upon the public eye.

Page after page appeared in the magazine, and after a few months these roused public discussion as to legal control of this class of advertising. Bok meanwhile called the attention of women's clubs and other

[1]John Horace McFarland was a horticulturist and nurseryman who pioneered in developing color-illustrated catalogues of fruits, flowers, and vegetables. He gained national fame by becoming a photographer and writer. Becoming active in the conservation movement, McFarland lectured widely, worked with the Sierra Club and other organizations to preserve natural sites from industrial development, helped establish the National Park Service, and promoted the growing popularity of roses among American gardeners.

civic organizations to the question and urged that they clean their towns of the obnoxious billboards. Legislative measures regulating the size, character, and the location of billboards was introduced in various states, and the agitation began to bear fruit.

Bok now called upon his readers in general to help by offering a series of prizes totaling several thousands of dollars for two photographs, one showing a fence, barn, or outbuilding painted with an advertisement or having a billboard attached to it, or a field with a billboard in it, and a second photograph of the same spot showing the advertisement removed, with an accompanying affidavit of the owner of the property, legally attested, asserting that the advertisement had been permanently removed. Then, hundreds of photographs poured in, scores of prizes were awarded, the results were published, and requests came in for a second series of prizes, which were duly awarded.

While Bok did not solve the problem of billboard advertising, and while in some parts of the country it is a more flagrant nuisance today than ever before, he had started the first serious agitation against billboard advertising of bad design, detrimental, from its location, to landscape beauty. He succeeded in getting rid of a huge billboard which had been placed at the most picturesque spot at Niagara Falls; and hearing of "the largest advertisement sign in the world" to be placed on the rim of the Grand Canyon of the Colorado, he notified the advertisers that a photograph of the sign, if it was erected, would be immediately published in the magazine and the attention of the women of America called to the defacement of one of the most impressive and beautiful scenes in the world. The article to be advertised was a household commodity, purchased by women; and the owners realized that the proposed advertisement would not be to the benefit of their product. The sign was abandoned.

Of course the advertisers whose signs were shown in the magazine immediately threatened the withdrawal of their accounts from *The Ladies' Home Journal,* and even the proposed advertiser of the Grand Canyon, whose business was conspicuous in each number of the magazine, became actively threatening. But Bok contended that the one proposition had absolutely no relation to the other, and that if concerns advertised in the magazine simply on the basis of his editorial policy toward billboard advertising, it was, to say the least, not a sound basis for advertising. No advertising account was ever actually withdrawn.

In their travels about, both Mr. McFarland and Bok began to note the disreputably untidy spots that various municipalities allowed in the closest proximity to the center of their business life, in the most desirable residential sections, and often adjacent to the most important municipal buildings and parks. It was decided to select a dozen cities, pick out the most flagrant instances of spots that were not only an eyesore and a disgrace from a municipal standpoint, but also a menace to health and the potential of depreciation of real estate value.

Lynn, Massachusetts, was the initial city chosen, a number of photographs were taken, and the first of a series of "Dirty Cities" was begun in the magazine. The effect was instantaneous. The people of Lynn rose in protest, and the municipal authorities threatened suit against the magazine; the local newspapers were virulent in their attacks. Without warning, they argued, Bok had held their city to disgrace before the entire country; the attack was unwarranted; in bad taste; every citizen in Lynn should thereafter cease to buy the magazine, and so the criticism ran. In answer Bok merely pointed to the photographs; to the fact that the camera could not lie, and that if he misrepresented conditions he was ready to make amends.

Of course the facts could not be gainsaid; local pride was aroused, and as a result not only were the advertised "dirty spots" cleaned up, but the municipal authorities went out and hunted around for other spots in the city, not knowing what other photographs Bok might have taken.

Trenton, New Jersey, was the next example, and the same storm of public resentment broke loose— with exactly the same beneficial results in the end to the city. Wilkes-Barre, Pennsylvania, was the third one of America's "dirty cities." Here public anger rose particularly high, the magazine practically being barred from the news-stands. But again the result was to the lasting benefit of the community.

Memphis, Tennessee, came next, but here a different spirit was met. Although some resentment was ex-

Some "Beautiful America" Results

Presented by J. Horace McFarland, President of the American Civic Association

The pictures below show some of the results of the offer of prizes made in the issue of THE JOURNAL for July, 1904, for the removal of offensive advertising signs and billboards   A comparison of the two views in each of the five sets will show instantly that the improvement effected is remarkable.

First Prize
awarded to
Mrs. R. F. Fitch,
Troy, New York,
who sent these
pictures.

Mrs. Fitch, whose work in removing a great billboard permanently from the shore of Mount Ida Lake, near Troy, took the first prize, did not have an easy time. When permission failed she raised money among those whom she interested and leased the land carrying the billboards   Then the signs came down, with a written guarantee that they should not again be erected, although the billboard people offered $500 with which to secure adjoining property, and removed the ruins of an unsightly burned building.   A movement is on foot to create a public park along this lake shore.

Second Prize
awarded to
A. A. Zwiebel,
Wilkesbarre,
Pennsylvania.

Even more spectacular was Mr. Zwiebel's effort in Wilkesbarre. The National Government had erected a post-office building costing $125,000, but its lawn was faced with a hideous dead wall, covered with signs. The Federal authorities could only refuse access by way of the lawn to the owner of the wall when he wished to add to or amend his abominations; they could not take away the signs, which simply became more unpleasant as they changed in the weather. Mr. Zwiebel bought the house and quickly cleared away the signs. He will plant vines against the wall this spring.

Winners in Bok's crusade to clean up American cities and countryside, March 1905

pressed, the general feeling was that service had been rendered the city, and that the only wise and practical solution was for the city to meet the situation. The result here was a group of municipal buildings costing millions of dollars, photographs of which *The Ladies' Home Journal* subsequently published with gratification to itself and to the people of Memphis.

Cities throughout the country now began to look around to see whether they had dirty spots within their limits, not knowing when the McFarland photographers might visit them. Bok received letters from various municipalities calling his attention to the fact that they were cognizant of spots in their cities and were cleaning up, and asking that, if he had photographs of these spots, they should not be published.

It happened that in two such instances Bok had prepared sets of photographs for the publication. These he sent to the mayors of the respective cities stating that if they would return them with an additional set showing the spots cleaned up there would be no occasion for their publication. In both cases this was done. Atlanta, Georgia; New Haven, Connecticut; Pittsburgh, Cincinnati, and finally Bok's own city of Philadelphia were duly chronicled in the magazine; local storms broke and calmed down—with the spots in every instance improved.

It was an interesting experiment in photographic civics. The pity of it is that more has not been done along this and similar lines.

XX

Theodore Roosevelt's Influence

W HEN THE virile figure of Theodore Roosevelt
swung down the national highway, Bok was one
of thousands of young men who felt strongly the attraction of his personality. Colonel Roosevelt was only
five years the senior of the editor; he spoke, therefore,
as one of his own years. The energy with which he
said and did things appealed to Bok. He made Americanism something more real, more stirring than Bok
had ever felt it; he explained national questions in a
way that caught Bok's fancy and came within his com-
prehension. Bok's lines had been cast with many of
the great men of the day, but he felt that there was
something distinctive about the personality of this
man; his method of doing things and his way of saying things.

The editor now sought an opportunity to know
personally the man whom he admired. It came at a
dinner at the University Club, and Colonel Roosevelt
suggested that they meet there the following day for a
"talk-fest." For three hours the two talked together.
The fact that Colonel Roosevelt was of Dutch ancestry interested Bok; that Bok was actually of Dutch
birth made a strong appeal to the colonel. With his
tremendous breadth of interests, Roosevelt, Bok

found, had followed him quite closely in his work and was familiar with "its high points," as he called them. "We must work for the same ends," said the colonel, "you in your way, I in mine. But our lines are bound to cross. You and I can each become good Americans by giving our best to make America better. With the Dutch stock there is in both of us, there's no limit to what we can do. Let's go to it." Naturally that talk left the two firm friends.

Bok felt somehow that he had been given a new draft of Americanism: the word took on a new meaning for him; it stood for something different, something deeper and finer than before. Every subsequent talk with Roosevelt deepened the feeling and stirred Bok's deepest ambitions.

One of Theodore Roosevelt's arguments which made a deep impression upon Bok was that no man had a right to devote his entire life to the making of money. "You are in a peculiar position," said the man of Oyster Bay one day to Bok; "you are in that happy position where you can make money and do good at the same time. A man wields a tremendous power for good or for evil who is welcomed into a million homes and read with confidence. That's fine, and is all right so far as it goes, and in your case it goes very far. Still, there remains more for you to do. The public has built up for you a personality: now give that personality to whatever interests you in contact with your immediate fellow men: something in your neighborhood, your city, or your state. With one hand work and write to your national audience: let no fads sway you. Hew close to the line. But, with the other hand, swing into the life immediately around you. Think it over."

Bok did think it over. He was now realizing the dream of his life for which he had worked: his means were sufficient to give his mother every comfort; to install her in the most comfortable surroundings wherever she chose to live; to make it possible for her to spend the winters in the United States and the summers in The Netherlands, and thus to keep in touch with her family and friends in both countries. He had for years toiled unceasingly to reach this point: he felt he had now achieved at least one goal.

He had now turned instinctively to the making of a life for himself. After an engagement of four years he had been married, on 22 October 1896, to Mary Louise Curtis, the only child of Mr. and Mrs. Cyrus H. K. Curtis; two sons had been born to them; he had built and was occupying a house at Merion, Pennsylvania, a suburb six miles from the Philadelphia City Hall. When she was in this country, his mother lived with him, and also his brother, and, with a strong belief in life insurance, he had seen to it that his family was provided for in case of personal incapacity or of his demise. In other words, he felt that he had put his own house in order; he had carried out what he felt is every man's duty: to be, first of all, a careful and adequate provider for his family. He was now at the point where he could begin to work for another goal, the goal that he felt so few American men saw: the point in his life where he could retire from the call of duty and follow the call of inclination.

At the age of forty he tried to look ahead and plan out his life as far as he could. Barring unforeseen obstacles, he determined to retire from active business when he reached his fiftieth year, and give the remainder of his life to those interests and influences which he assumed now as part of his life, and which, at fifty, should seem to him best worthwhile. He realized that in order to do this he must do two things: he must husband his financial resources and he must begin to accumulate a mental reserve.

The wide public acceptance of the periodical he edited naturally brought a share of financial success to him. He had experienced poverty, and as he subsequently wrote, in an article called "Why I Believe in Poverty," he was deeply grateful for his experience. He had known what it was to be poor; he had seen others dear to him suffer for the bare necessities; there was, in fact, not a single step on that hard road that he had not traveled. He could, therefore, sympathize with the fullest understanding with those similarly situated, could help as one who knew from practice and not from theory.

Of course many said to Bok when he wrote the article in which he expressed these beliefs: "That's all very well; easy enough to say, but how can you get out of it?" Bok realized that he could not definitely show anyone the way. No one had shown him. No two persons can find the same way out. Bok determined to lift himself out of poverty because his mother was not born into it, did not belong in it, and could not stand it. That gave him the first essential: a purpose. Then he backed up the purpose with effort and an ever-ready willingness to work, and to work at anything that came his way, no matter what it was, so long as it meant "the way out." He did not pick and choose; he took what came, and did it in the best way he knew how; and when he did not like what he was doing he still did it as well as he could while he was doing it, but always with an eye single to the purpose not to do it any longer than was necessary. He used every rung in the ladder as a rung to the one above. He always gave more than his particular position or salary asked for. He never worked by the clock; always to the job; and saw that it was well done regardless of the time it took to do it. This meant effort, of course, untiring, cease-less, unsparing; and it meant work, hard as nails.

He was particularly careful never to live up to his income; and as his income increased he increased not the percentage of expenditure but the percentage of saving. Thrift was, of course, inborn with him as a Dutchman, but the necessity for it as a prime factor in life was burned into him by his experience with poverty.

At forty, therefore, he felt he had learned the first essential to carrying out his idea of retirement at fifty.

The second essential—varied interests outside of his business upon which he could rely on relinquishing his duties—he had not cultivated. He had quite naturally, in line with his belief that concentration means success, immersed himself in his business to the exclusion of almost everything else. He felt that he could now spare a certain percentage of his time to follow Theodore Roosevelt's ideas and let the breezes of other worlds blow over him. In that way he could do as Roosevelt suggested and as Bok now firmly believed was right; he could develop himself along broader lines, albeit the lines of his daily work were broadening in and of themselves, and he could so develop a new set of inner resources upon which he could draw when the time came to relinquish his editorial position.

He saw, on every side, the pathetic figures of men who could not let go after their greatest usefulness was past; of other men who dropped before they realized their arrival at the end of the road; and, most pathetic of all, of men who having retired, but because of lack of inner resources did not know what to do with themselves, had become a trial to themselves, their families, and their communities.

Bok decided that, given health and mental freshness, he would say goodbye to his public before his public might decide to say goodbye to him. So, at forty, he candidly faced the facts of life and began to prepare himself for his retirement at fifty under circumstances that would be of his own making and not those of others.

And thereby Edward Bok proved that he was still, by instinct, a Dutchman, and had not in his thirty-four years of residence in the United States become so thoroughly Americanized as he believed.

However, it was an American, albeit of Dutch extraction, one whom he believed to be the greatest American in his own day, who had set him thinking and shown him the way.

While Theodore Roosevelt was president of the United States, Bok was sitting one evening talking with him, when suddenly Mr. Roosevelt turned to him and said with his usual emphasis: "Bok, I envy you your power with the public."

The editor was frankly puzzled.

"That is a strange remark from the president of the United States," he replied.

"You may think so," was the rejoinder. "But listen. When do I get the ear of the public? In its busiest moments. My messages are printed in the newspapers and read hurriedly, mostly by men in trolleys or railroad cars. Women hardly ever read them, I should judge. Now you are read in the evening by the fireside or under the lamp, when the day's work is over and the mind is at rest from other things and receptive to what you offer. Don't you see where you have it on me?"

This diagnosis was keenly interesting, and while the president talked during the balance of the evening, Bok was thinking. Finally, he said: "Mr. President, I should like to share my power with you."

"How?" asked Mr. Roosevelt.

"You recognize women do not read your messages;

and yet no president's messages have ever discussed more ethical questions that women should know about and get straight in their minds. As it is, some of your ideas are not at all understood by them; your strenuous-life theory, for instance, your factory-law ideas, and particularly your race-suicide arguments. Men don't fully understand them, for that matter; women certainly do not."

"I am aware of all that," said the president. "What is your plan to remedy it?"

"Have a department in my magazine, and explain your ideas," suggested Bok.

"Haven't time for another thing. You know that," snapped back the president. "Wish I had."

"Not to write it, perhaps, yourself," returned Bok. "But why couldn't you find time to do this: select the writer here in Washington in whose accuracy you have the most implicit faith; let him talk with you for one hour each month on one of those subjects; let him write out your views, and submit the manuscript to you; and we will have a department stating exactly how the material is obtained and how far it represents your own work. In that way, with only an hour's work each month, you can get your views, correctly stated, before this vast audience when it is not in trolleys or railroad cars."

"But I haven't the hour," answered Roosevelt, impressed, however, as Bok saw. "I have only half an hour, when I am awake, when I am really idle, and that is when I am being shaved."

Theodore Roosevelt, who contributed to the magazine during and after his presidency, May 1906

"Well," calmly suggested the editor, "why not two of those half hours a month, or perhaps one?"

"What?" answered the president, sitting upright, his teeth flashing but his smile broadening. "You Dutchman, you'd make me work while I'm getting shaved, too?"

"Well," was the answer, "isn't the result worth the effort?"

"Bok, you are absolutely relentless," said the president. "But you're right. The result would be *worth* the effort. What writer have you in mind: you seem to have thought this thing through."

"How about O'Brien? You think well of him?" (Robert L. O'Brien, now editor of the *Boston Herald,* was then Washington correspondent for the *Boston Transcript*, and he was thoroughly in President Roosevelt's confidence.)

"Fine," said the president. "I trust O'Brien implicitly. All right, if you can get O'Brien to take on the responsibility, I'll try it."

And so the "shaving interviews" were begun; and early in 1906 there appeared in *The Ladies' Home Journal* a department called "The President," with the subtitle: "A Department in which will be presented the attitude of the President on those national questions which affect the vital interests of the home, by a writer intimately acquainted and in close touch with him."

O'Brien talked with Mr. Roosevelt once a month, wrote out the results, the president went over the proofs carefully, and the department was conducted with great success for a year.

But Theodore Roosevelt was again to be the editor of a department in *The Ladies' Home Journal;* this time to be written by himself under the strictest possible anonymity, so closely adhered to that, until this revelation, only five persons have known the authorship.

Feeling that it would be an interesting experiment to see how far Theodore Roosevelt's ideas could stand unsupported by the authority of his vibrant personality, Bok suggested the plan to the colonel. It was just after he had returned from his South American trip.[1] He was immediately interested.

"But how can we keep the authorship really anonymous?" he asked.

"Easily enough," answered Bok, "if you're willing to do the work. Our letters about it must be written in long hand addressed to each other's homes; you must write your manuscript in your own hand; I will copy it in mine, and it will go to the printer in that way. I will personally send you the proofs; you mark your corrections in pencil, and I will copy them in ink; the company will pay me for each article, and I will send you my personal check each month. By this means, the identity of the author will be concealed."

Colonel Roosevelt was never averse to hard work if it was necessary to achieve a worthwhile result.

[1] Roosevelt visited the Amazon region of Brazil in 1914.

"All right," wrote the colonel finally. "I'll try—with you!—the experiment for a year: twelve articles. . . . I don't know that I can give your readers satisfaction but I shall try my very best. I am very glad to be associated with you, anyway. At first I doubted the wisdom of the plan, merely because I doubted whether I could give you just what you wished. I never know what an audience wants: I know what it *ought* to want and sometimes I can give it, or make it accept what I think it needs—and sometimes I cannot. But the more I thought over your proposal, the more I liked it. . . . Whether the wine will be good enough, to attract without any bush I don't know; and besides, in such cases the fault is not in the wine, but in the fact that the consumers decline to have their attention attracted unless there is a bush!"

In the latter part of 1916 an anonymous department called "Men" was begun in the magazine.

The physical work was great. The colonel punctiliously held to his conditions, and wrote the manuscript and letters with his own hand, and Bok carried out his part of the agreement. Nor was this simple, for Colonel Roosevelt's manuscript—particularly when, as in this case, it was written on yellow paper with a soft pencil and generously interlined—was anything but legible. Month after month the two men worked each at his own task. To throw the public off the scent, during the conduct of the department, an article or two by Colonel Roosevelt was published in another part of the magazine under his own name.

It was natural that the appearance of a department devoted to men in a woman's magazine should attract immediate attention. The department took up the various interests of a man's life, such as real efficiency; his duties as an employer and his usefulness to his employees; the employee's attitude toward his employer; the relations of men and women; a father's relations to his sons and daughters; a man's duty to his community; the public school system; a man's relation to his church, and kindred topics.

The anonymity of the articles soon took on interest from the positiveness of the opinions discussed; but so thoroughly had Colonel Roosevelt covered his tracks that, although he wrote in his usual style, in not a single instance was his name connected with the department. Lyman Abbott[2] was the favorite "guess" at first; then after various other public men had been suggested, the newspapers finally decided upon former President Eliot[3] of Harvard University as the writer.

All this intensely interested and amused Colonel

[2] Lyman Abbott was a disciple and biographer of Henry Ward Beecher, who succeeded Beecher as pastor of Brooklyn's Plymouth Congregational Church in 1888. Abbott also became editor of Beecher's journal, the *Christian Union,* and transformed it into *Outlook,* a magazine of current affairs that achieved a circulation of more than 100,000.

[3] Charles William Eliot was elected president of Harvard in 1869 and fashioned it into one of the world's great universities. He also edited the Harvard Classics and, together with Nicholas Murray Butler of Columbia University, pioneered the development of standardized admissions tests.

Roosevelt and he fairly itched with the desire to write a series of criticisms of his own articles to Dr. Eliot. Bok, however, persuaded the colonel not to spend more physical effort than he was already doing on the articles; for, in addition, he was notating answers on the numerous letters received, and those Bok answered "on behalf of the author."

For a year, the department continued. During all that time the secret of the authorship was known to only one man, besides the colonel and Bok, and their respective wives!

When the colonel sent his last article in the series to Bok, he wrote:

Now that the work is over, I wish most cordially to thank you, my dear fellow, for your unvarying courtesy and kindness. I have not been satisfied with my work. This is the first time I ever tried to write precisely to order, and I am not one of those gifted men who can do so to advantage. Generally I find that the 3,000 words is not the right length and that I wish to use 2,000 or 4,000! And in consequence feel as if I had either padded or mutilated the article. And I am not always able to feel that every month I have something worth saying on a given subject.

But I hope that you have not been too disappointed.

Bok had not been, and neither had the public!

XXI

The President and the Boy

O NE OF the incidents connected with Edward Bok that Theodore Roosevelt never forgot was when Bok's eldest boy[1] chose the colonel as a Christmas present. And no incident better portrays the wonderful character than did his remarkable response to the compliment.

A vicious attack of double pneumonia had left the heart of the boy very weak—and Christmas was close by! So the father said: "It's a quiet Christmas for you this year, boy. Suppose you do this: think of the one thing in the world that you would rather have than anything else and I'll give you that."

"I know now," came the instant reply.

"But the world is a big place, and there are lots of things in it, you know."

"I know that," said the boy, "but this is something I have wanted for a long time, and would rather have than anything else in the world."

[1]William Curtis Bok was the first of two sons (the other being Cary W. Bok) born to Edward W. and Mary Louise Curtis Bok. After graduating from Williams College he took a law degree at the University of Virginia and established a law practice that led to his becoming judge of the Court of Common Pleas in Philadelphia and justice of the Pennsylvania Supreme Court. He wrote several books but never became active in Curtis Publishing.

"Well, out with it, then, if you're so sure."

And to the father's astonished ears came his son's request:

"Take me to Washington as soon as my heart is all right, introduce me to President Roosevelt, and let me shake hands with him."

"All right," said the father, after recovering from his surprise. "I'll see whether I can fix it." And that morning a letter went to the president saying that he had been chosen as a Christmas present. Naturally, any man would have felt pleased, no matter how high his station, and for Theodore Roosevelt, father of boys, the message had a special appeal.

The letter had no sooner reached Washington than back came an answer, addressed not to the father but to the boy! It read:

> The White House, Washington
> November 13th, 1907.

DEAR CURTIS:

Your father has just written me, and I want him to bring you on and shake hands with me as soon as you are well enough to travel. Then I am going to give you, myself, a copy of the book containing my hunting trips since I have been president; unless you will wait until the new edition, which contains two more chapters, is out. If so, I will send it to you, as this new edition probably won't be ready when you come on here. Give my warm regards to your father and mother.

> Sincerely yours,
> THEODORE ROOSEVELT.

Here was joy serene! But the boy's heart had acted queerly for a few days, and so the father wrote, thanked the president, and said that as soon as the heart moderated a bit the letter would be given the boy. It was a rare bit of consideration that now followed. No sooner had the father's letter reached the White House than an answer came back by first post—this time with a special delivery stamp on it.

Dear Mr. Bok:—
I have your letter of the 16th instant. I hope the little fellow will soon be all right. Instead of giving him my letter, give him a message from me based on the letter, if that will be better for him. Tell Mrs. Bok how deeply Mrs. Roosevelt and I sympathize with her. We know just how she feels.

Sincerely yours,
Theodore Roosevelt.

"That's pretty fine consideration," said the father. He got the letter during a business conference and he read it aloud to the group of business men. Some there were in that group who keenly differed with the president on national issues, but they were all fathers, and two of the sturdiest turned and walked to the window as they said: "Yes, that *is* fine!"

Then came the boy's pleasure when he was handed the letter; the next few days were spent inditing an answer to "my friend, the president." At last the momentous epistle seemed satisfactory, and off to the busy presidential desk went the boyish note, full of thanks and assurances that he would come just as soon as he could, and that Mr. Roosevelt must not get impatient!

The "soon as he could" time, however, did not come as quickly as all had hoped!—a little heart pumped for days full of oxygen and accelerated by hypodermic injections is slow to mend. But the president's framed letter, hanging on the spot of the wall first seen in the morning, was a daily consolation.

Then, in March, although four months after the promise—and it would not have been strange, in his busy life, for the president to have forgotten or at least overlooked it—on the very day that the book was published came a special "large paper" copy of *The Outdoor Pastimes of an American Hunter.* On the flyleaf there greeted the boy, in the president's own hand:

To MASTER CURTIS BOK,
With the best wishes of his friend,
THEODORE ROOSEVELT.
March 11, 1908.

The boy's cup was now full, and so said his letter to the president. And the president wrote back to the father: "I am really immensely amused and interested, and shall be mighty glad to see the little fellow."

In the spring, on a beautiful May day, came the great moment. The mother had to go along, the boy insisted, to see the great event, and so the trio found themselves shaking the hand of the president's secretary at the White House.

"Oh, the president is looking for you, all right," he

said to the boy, and then the next moment the three were in a large room. Mr. Roosevelt, with beaming face, was already striding across the room, and with a "Well, well, and so this is my friend Curtis!" the two stood looking into each other's faces, each fairly wreathed in smiles, and each industriously shaking the hand of the other.

"Yes, Mr. President, I'm mighty glad to see you!" said the boy.

"I am glad to see you, Curtis," returned the president of the United States.

Then there came a white rose from the presidential desk for the mother, but after that father and mother might as well have faded away. Nobody existed save the president and the boy. The anteroom was full; in the Cabinet room a delegation waited to be addressed. But affairs of state were at a complete standstill as, with boyish zeal, the president became oblivious to all but the boy before him.

"Now, Curtis, I've got some pictures here of bears that a friend of mine has just shot. Look at that whopper, 1,500 pounds—that's as much as a horse weighs, you know. Now, my friend shot him"—and it was a toss up who was the more keenly interested, the real boy or the man-boy, as picture after picture came out and bear adventure crowded upon the heels of bear adventure.

"Gee, he's a corker, all right!" came from the boy at one point, and then, from the president: "That's right, he *is* a corker. Now you see his head here."

The private secretary came in at this point and whispered in the president's ear.

"I know, I know. I'll see him later. Say that I am very busy now." And the face beamed with smiles.

"Now, Mr. President—" began the father.

"No, sir; no, sir; not at all. Affairs can wait. This is a long standing engagement between Curtis and me, and that must come first. Isn't that so, Curtis?"

Of course the boy agreed.

Suddenly the boy looked around the room and said:

"Where's your gun, Mr. President? Got it here?"

"No," laughingly came from the president, "but I'll tell you"—and then the two heads were together again.

A moment for breathtaking came, and the boy said:

"Aren't you ever afraid of being shot?"

"You mean while I am hunting?"

"Oh, no. I mean as president."

"No," replied the smiling president. "I'll tell you, Curtis; I'm too busy to think about that. I have too many things to do to bother about anything of that sort. When I was in battle I was always too anxious to get to the front to think about the shots. And here— well, here I'm too busy too. Never think about it. But I'll tell you, Curtis, there are some men down there," pointing out of the window in the direction of the capitol, "called the Congress, and if they would only give me the four battleships I want, I'd be perfectly willing to have any one take a crack at me." Then, for the first time recognizing the existence of the parents, the president said: "And I don't know but if they did pick me off I'd be pretty well ahead of the game."

Just in that moment only did the boy-knowing president get a single inch above the boy-interest. It was astonishing to see the natural accuracy with which the man gauged the boy-level.

"Now, how would you like to see a bear, Curtis?" came next. "I know where there's a beauty, 1,200 pounds."

"Must be some bear!" interjected the boy.

"That's what it is," put in the president. "Regular cinnamon brown type"—and then off went the talk of the big bear of the Washington "Zoo" where the president was to send the boy.

Then, after a little: "Now, Curtis, see those men over there in that room. They've traveled from all parts of the country to come here at my invitation, and I've got to make a little speech to them, and I'll do that while you go off to see the bear."

And then the hand came forth to say goodbye. The boy put his in it, each looked into the other's face, and on neither was there a place big enough to put a ten-cent piece that was not wreathed in smiles. "He certainly is all right," said the boy to the father, looking wistfully after the president.

Almost to the other room had the president gone when he, too, instinctively looked back to find the boy following him with his eyes. He stopped, wheeled around, and then the two instinctively sought each other again. The president came back, the boy went forward. This time each held out both hands, and as each looked once more into the other's eyes a world of complete understanding was in both faces, and every looker-on smiled with them.

"Goodbye, Curtis," came at last from the president.

"Goodbye, Mr. President," came from the boy.

Then, with another pump-handly shake and with a "Gee, but he's great, all right!" the boy went out to see the cinnamon bear at the "Zoo," and to live it all over in the days to come.

Two boy-hearts had met, although one of them belonged to the president of the United States.

XXII

The Literary Backstairs

H IS COMPLETE absorption in the magazine work now compelled Bok to close his newspaper syndicate in New York and end the writing of his weekly newspaper literary letter. He decided, however, to transfer to the pages of his magazine his idea of making the American public more conversant with books and authors. Accordingly, he engaged Robert Bridges (the present editor of *Scribner's Magazine*) to write a series of conversational book-talks under his *nom de plume* of "Droch." Later, this was supplemented by the engagement of Hamilton W. Mabie, who for years reviewed the newest books.

In almost every issue of the magazine there appeared also an article addressed to the literary novice. Bok was eager, of course, to attract the new authors to the magazine; but, particularly, he had in mind the correction of the popular notion, then so prevalent (less so today, fortunately, but still existent), that only the manuscripts of famous authors were given favorable reading in editorial offices; that in these offices there really existed a clique, and that unless the writer knew the literary backstairs he had a slim chance to enter and be heard.

In the minds of these misinformed writers, these

backstairs are gained by "knowing the editor" or through "having some influence with him." These writers have conclusively settled two points in their own minds: first, that an editor is antagonistic to the struggling writer; and, second, that a manuscript sent in the ordinary manner to an editor never reaches him. Hence, some "influence" is necessary, and they set about to secure it.

Now, the truth is, of course, that there are no "literary backstairs" to the editorial office of the modern magazine. There cannot be. The making of a modern magazine is a business proposition; the editor is there to make it pay. He can do this only if he is of service to his readers, and that depends on his ability to obtain a class of material essentially the best of its kind and varied in its character.

The "best," while it means good writing, means also that it shall say something. The most desired writer in the magazine office is the man who has something to say, and knows how to say it. Variety requires that there shall be many of these writers, and it is the editor's business to ferret them out. It stands to reason, therefore, that there can be no such thing as a "clique"; limitation by the editor of his list of authors would mean being limited to the style of the few and the thoughts of a handful. And with a public that easily tires even of the best where it continually comes from one source, such policy would be suicidal.

Hence, if the editor is more keenly alert for one thing than for another, it is for the new writer. The frequency of the new note in his magazine is his salvation; for just in proportion as he can introduce that new note is his success with his readers. A successful magazine is exactly like a successful store: it must keep its wares constantly fresh and varied.

With an editor ever alive to the new message, the new note, the fresh way of saying a thing, the new angle on a current subject, whether in article or story— since fiction is really today only a reflection of modern thought—the foolish notion that an editor must be approached through "influence", by a letter of introduction from some friend or other author, falls of itself. There is no more powerful lever to open the modern magazine door than a postage stamp on an envelope containing a manuscript that says something. No influence is needed to bring that manuscript to the editor's desk or to his attention. That he will receive it the sender need not for a moment doubt; his mail is too closely scanned for that very envelope.

The most successful authors have "broken into" the magazines very often without even a letter accompanying their first manuscript. The name and address in the right hand corner of the first page; some "return" stamps in the left corner, and all that the editor requires is there. The author need tell nothing about the manuscript; if what the editor wants is in it he will find it. An editor can stand a tremendous amount of letting alone. If young authors could be made to realize how simple is the process of "breaking into" the modern magazine, which apparently gives them such needless heartburn, they would save themselves infinite pains, time and worry.

Despite all the rubbish written to the contrary, manuscripts sent to the magazine of today are, in every case, read, and frequently more carefully read than the author imagines. Editors know that, from the standpoint of good business alone, it is unwise to return a manuscript unread. Literary talent has been found in many instances where it was least expected.

This does not mean that every manuscript received by a magazine is read from first page to last. There is no reason why it should be, any more than that all of a bad egg should be eaten to prove that it is bad. The title alone sometimes decides the fate of the manuscript. If the subject discussed is entirely foreign to the aims of the magazine, it is simply a case of misapplication on the author's part; and it would be a waste of time for the editor to read something which he knows from its subject he cannot use.

This, of course, applies more to articles than to other forms of literary work, although unsuitability in a poem is naturally as quickly detected. Stories, no matter how unpromising they may appear at the beginning, are generally read through, since gold in a piece of fiction has often been found almost at the close. This careful attention to manuscripts in editorial offices is fixed by rules, and an author's endorsement or a friend's judgment never affects the custom.

At no time does the fallacy hold in a magazine office that "a big name counts for everything and an unknown name for nothing." There can be no denial of the fact that where a name of repute is attached to a meritorious story or article the combination is ideal. But as between an indifferent story and a well-known name and a good story with an unknown name the editor may be depended upon to accept the latter. Editors are very careful nowadays to avoid the public impatience that invariably follows upon publishing of material simply on account of the name attached to it. Nothing so quickly injures the reputation of a magazine in the estimation of its readers. If a person, taking up a magazine, reads a story attracted by a famous name, and the story disappoints, the editor has a doubly disappointed reader on his hands: a reader whose high expectations from the name have not been realized and who is disappointed with the story.

It is a well known fact among successful magazine editors that their most striking successes have been made by material to which unknown names were attached, where the material was fresh, the approach new, the note different. That is what builds up a magazine; the reader learns to have confidence in what he finds in the periodical, a famous name or not.

Nor must the young author believe that the best work in modern magazine literature "is dashed off at white heat." What is dashed off *reads dashed off,* and one does not come across it in the well-edited magazine, because it is never accepted. Good writing is laborious writing, the result of revision upon revision. The work of masters such as Robert Louis Stevenson and Rudyard Kipling represents never less than eight or ten revisions, and often a far greater number. It was Stevenson who once said to Edward Bok, after a laborious correction of certain proofs: "My boy, I could be a healthy man, I think, if I did something else than writing. But to write, as I try to write, takes every ounce of my vitality."

But the author must also know when to let his material alone. In his excessive regard for style even so great a master as Robert Louis Stevenson robbed his work of much of the spontaneity and natural charm found, for example, in his *Vailima Letters.* The main thing is for a writer to say what he has to say in the best way, natural to himself, in which he can say it, and then let it alone—always remembering that, provided he has made himself clear, the message itself is of greater import than the manner in which it is said. Up to a certain point only is a piece of literary work an artistic endeavor. A readable, lucid style is far preferable to what is called a "literary style"—a foolish phrase, since it often means nothing except a complicated method of expression which confuses rather than clarifies thought. What the public wants in its literature is human nature, and that human nature simply and forcibly expressed. This is fundamental, and this is why true literature has no fashion and knows no change, despite the cries of the modern weaklings who affect weird forms. The clarity of Shakespeare is the clarity of today and will be that of tomorrow.

XXIII

Women's Clubs and Woman Suffrage

E DWARD BOK was now jumping from one sizzling
frying pan into another. He had become vitally interested in the growth of women's clubs as a power for
good, and began to follow their work and study their
methods. He attended meetings; he had his editors
attend others and give him reports; he collected and
read the yearbooks of scores of clubs, and he secured
and read a number of papers that had been presented
by members at these meetings. He saw at once that
what might prove a wonderful power in the civic life
of the nation was being misdirected into gatherings
of pseudo-culture, where papers ill-digested and
mostly copied from books were read and superficially
discussed.

Apparently the average club thought nothing of disposing of the works of the Victorian poets in one afternoon; the Italian Renaissance was "fully treated and
most ably discussed," according to one program, at a
single meeting; Rembrandt and his school were likewise disposed of in one afternoon, and German literature was "adequately treated" at one session "in able
papers."

Bok gathered a mass of this material, then paid his
respects to it in the magazine. He recited his evidence

and then expressed his opinion of it. He realized that his arraignment of the clubs would cost the magazine hundreds of friends; but, convinced of the great power of the woman's club with its activities rightly directed, he concluded that he could afford to risk incurring displeasure if he might point the way to more effective work. The one was worth the other.

The displeasure was not slow in making itself manifest. It came to maturity overnight, as it were, and expressed itself in no uncertain terms. Every club flew to arms, and Bok was intensely interested to note that the clubs whose work he had taken as "horrible examples," although he had not mentioned their names, were the most strenuous in denials of the methods outlined in the magazine, and that the members of those clubs were particularly heated in their attacks upon him.

He soon found that he had stirred up quite as active a hornet's nest as he had anticipated. Letters by the hundred poured in attacking and reviling him. In nearly every case the writers fell back upon personal abuse, ignoring his arguments altogether. He became the subject of heated debates at club meetings, at conventions, in the public press; and soon long petitions demanding his removal as editor began to come to Mr. Curtis. These petitions were signed by hundreds of names. Bok read them with absorbed interest, and bided his time for action. Meanwhile he continued his articles of criticism in the magazine, and these, of course, added fuel to the conflagration.

Former President Cleveland[1] now came to Bok's side, and in an article in the magazine went even further than Bok had ever thought of going in his criticism of women's clubs. This article had deflected the criticism from Bok momentarily, and Mr. Cleveland received a grilling to which his experiences in the White House were "as child's play," as he expressed it. The two men, the editor and the former president, were now bracketed as copartners in crime in the eyes of the club women, and nothing too harsh could be found to say or write of either.

Meanwhile Bok had been watching the petitions for his removal which kept coming in. He was looking for an opening, and soon found it. One of the most prominent women's clubs sent a protest condemning his attitude and advising him by resolutions, which were enclosed, that unless he ceased his attacks, the members of the _____ Woman's Club had resolved "to unitedly and unanimously boycott *The Ladies' Home Journal* and had already put the plan into effect with the current issue."

Bok immediately engaged counsel in the city where the club was situated, and instructed his lawyer to begin proceedings, for violation of the Sherman Act,

[1]Grover Cleveland, president of the United States, 1885-1889 and 1893-1897, was nominated in 1885 and won in a close race against James G. Blaine. Defeated for reelection by Benjamin Harrison in 1889, he prevailed over Harrison in 1893, thereby becoming the only president to serve two discontinuous terms. After leaving the White House, Cleveland became a trustee of Princeton University.

against the president and the secretary of the club, and three other members; counsel to take particular pains to choose, if possible, the wives of three lawyers.[2]

Within forty-eight hours Bok heard from the husbands of the five wives, who pointed out to him that the women had acted in entire ignorance of the law, and suggested a reconsideration of his action. Bok replied by quoting from the petition which set forth that it was signed "by the most intelligent women of _____ who were thoroughly versed in civic and national affairs"; and if this were true, Bok argued, it naturally followed that they must have been cognizant of a legislative measure so well known and so widely discussed as the Sherman Act. He was basing his action, he said, merely on their declaration.

Bok could easily picture to himself the chagrin and wrath of the women, with the husbands laughing up their sleeves at the turn of affairs. "My wife never could see the humor in the situation," said one of these husbands to Bok, when he met him years later. Bok capitulated, and then with great reluctance, only when the club sent an official withdrawal of the protest and an apology for "its ill-considered action." It was years after that one of the members of the club, upon meeting Bok, said to him: "Your action did not increase the club's love for you, but you taught it a

[2]The Sherman Antitrust Act of 1890 was at best a half-hearted attempt to outlaw monopolies. Bok presumably used the portion of the law that refers to "restraint of trade" when threatening to bring suit against the club.

much-needed lesson which has never been forgotten."

Up to this time, Bok had purposely been destructive in his criticism. Now, he pointed out a constructive plan whereby the woman's club could make itself a power in every community. He advocated less of the cultural and more of the civic interest, and urged that the clubs study the numerous questions dealing with the life of their communities. This seems strange, in view of the enormous amount of civic work done by women's clubs today. But at that time, when the woman's club movement was unformed, these civic matters found but a small part in the majority of programs; in a number of cases none at all.

Of course, the clubs refused to accept or even to consider his suggestions; they were quite competent to decide for themselves the particular subjects for their meetings, they argued; they did not care to be tutored or guided, particularly by Bok. They were much too angry with him even to admit that his suggestions were practical and in order. But he knew, of course, that they would adopt them of their own volition—under cover, perhaps, but that made no difference, so long as the end was accomplished. One club after another, during the following years, changed its program, and soon the supposed cultural interest had yielded first place to the needful civic questions.

For years, however, the club women of America did not forgive Bok. They refused to buy or countenance his magazine, and periodically they attacked it or made light of it. But he knew he had made his point, and was content to leave it to time to heal the wounds. This came years afterward, when Mrs. Pennypacker became the president of the General Federation of Women's Clubs and Mrs. Rudolph Blankenburg, vice-president.

Those two far-seeing women and Bok arranged that an official department of the Federation should find a place in *The Ladies' Home Journal,* with Mrs. Pennypacker as editor and Mrs. Blankenburg, who lived in Philadelphia, as the resident consulting editor. The idea was arranged agreeably to all three; the Federation officially endorsed its president's suggestion, and for several years the department was one of the most successful in the magazine.

The breach had been healed; two powerful forces were working together, as they should, for the mutual good of the American woman. No relations could have been pleasanter than those between the editor-in-chief of the magazine and the two departmental editors. The report was purposely set afloat that Bok had withdrawn from his position of antagonism toward women's clubs, and this gave great satisfaction to thousands of women club members and made everybody happy!

At this time the question of suffrage for women was fast becoming a prominent issue, and naturally Bok was asked to take a stand on the question in his magazine. No man sat at a larger gateway to learn the sentiments of numbers of women on any subject. He read his vast correspondence carefully. He consulted women of every grade of intelligence and in every station in life. Then he caused a straw-vote to be taken among a selected list of thousands of his subscribers in large cities and in small towns. The result of all these inquiries was most emphatic and clear: by far the overwhelming majority of the women approached either were opposed to the ballot or were indifferent to it. Those who desired to try the experiment were negligible in number. So far as the sentiment of any wide public can be secured on any given topic, this seemed to be the dominant opinion.

Bok then instituted a systematic investigation of conditions in those states where women had voted for years; but he could not see, from a thoughtful study of his investigations, that much had been accomplished. The results certainly did not measure up to the prophecies constantly advanced by the advocates of a nationwide equal suffrage.

The editor now carefully looked into the speeches of the suffragists, examined the platform of the national body in favor of woman suffrage, and talked at length with such leaders in the movement as Susan B. Anthony, Julia Ward Howe, Anna Howard Shaw, and Jane Addams.[3]

All this time Bok had kept his own mind open. He

[3]Susan Brownell Anthony became one of the two central figures (the other being Elizabeth Cady Stanton) in female suffrage. She traveled ceaselessly throughout the United States, helped organize the National Woman Suffrage Association, and did more than any other person to bring about adoption of the Nineteenth

was ready to have the magazine, for whose editorial policy he was responsible, advocate that side of the issue which seemed for the best interests of the American woman.

The arguments that a woman should not have a vote because she was a woman; that it would interfere with her work in the home; that it would make her more masculine; that it would take her out of her own home; that it was a blow at domesticity and an actual menace to the home life of America—these did not weigh with him. There was only one question for him to settle: Was the ballot something which, in its demonstrated value or in its potentiality, would serve the best interests of American womanhood?

After all his investigations of both sides of the question, Bok decided upon a negative answer. He felt that American women were not ready to exercise the privilege intelligently and their attitude was against it.

———

Amendment. Julia Ward Howe, author of "The Battle Hymn of the Republic," joined the feminist movement and became associated with the conservative wing of the crusade for woman suffrage. Anna Howard Shaw, born in England, became one of the earliest female ministers and physicians in the United States, a leader in the Women's Christian Temperance Union, and a crusader for women's suffrage. She eventually became the president of the National American Woman Suffrage Association. Jane Addams, a settlement house pioneer, social reformer, and peace advocate, became best known for joining a companion, Ellen Starr, in transforming a Chicago mansion into Hull House, a center that offered social and cultural services to poor immigrants. She was co-winner (with Nicholas Murray Butler) of the Nobel Peace Prize in 1931.

Forthwith he said so in his magazine. And the storm broke. The denunciations brought down upon him by his attitude toward women's clubs was as nothing compared to what was now let loose. The attacks were bitter. His arguments were ignored; and the suffragists evidently decided to concentrate their criticisms upon the youthful years of the editor. They regarded this as a most vulnerable point of attack, and reams of paper were used to prove that the opinion of a man so young in years and so necessarily unformed in his judgment was of no value.

Unfortunately, the suffragists did not know, when they advanced this argument, that it would be overthrown by the endorsement of Bok's point of view by such men and women of years and ripe judgment as Dr. Eliot, then president of Harvard University, former President Cleveland, Lyman Abbott, Margaret Deland,[4] and others.

When articles by these opponents to suffrage appeared, the argument of youth hardly held good; and the attacks of the suffragists were quickly shifted to the ground of "narrow-mindedness and old fashioned fogyism."

[4]Margaret Deland became one of America's leading female writers. Like Bok, she had reformist tendencies but took a conservative stance on such matters as female suffrage. Her work fell rapidly out of favor in the postwar period, but she continued to publish in magazines like *The Ladies' Home Journal.* An article, "Margaret Deland," by Marguerite Merington is in the magazine, October 1892, as Part III of a series, "Literary Women In Their Homes."

The article by former President Cleveland particularly stirred the ire of the attacking suffragists, and Miss Anthony hurled a broadside at the former president in a newspaper interview. Unfortunately for her best judgment, and the strength of her argument, the attack became intensely personal; and of course nullified its force. But it irritated Mr. Cleveland, who called Bok to his Princeton home and read him a draft of a proposed answer written for publication in Bok's magazine.

Those who knew Mr. Cleveland were well aware of the force that he could put into his pen when he chose, and in this proposed article he certainly chose! It would have made very unpleasant reading for Miss Anthony in particular, as well as for her friends. Bok argued strongly against the article. He reminded Mr. Cleveland that it would be undignified to make such an answer; that it was always an unpopular thing to attack a woman in public, especially a woman who was old and ill; that she would again strive for the last word; that there would be no point to the controversy and nothing gained by it. He pleaded with Mr. Cleveland to meet Miss Anthony's attack by only a dignified silence.

These arguments happily prevailed. In reality, Mr. Cleveland was not keen to attack Miss Anthony or any other woman; such a thought was foreign to his nature. He summed up his feeling to Bok when he tore up the draft of his article and smilingly said: "Well, I've got it off my chest, that is the main thing. I wanted to get it out of my system, and talking it over has driven it out. It is better in the fire," and he threw the torn paper into an open grate.

As events turned out, it was indeed fortunate that the matter had been so decided; for the article would have appeared in the number of Bok's magazine published on the day that Miss Anthony passed away.[5] It would have been a most unfortunate moment, to say the least, for the appearance of an attack such as Mr. Cleveland had in mind.

This incident, like so many instances that might be adduced, points with singular force to the value of that editorial discrimination which the editor often makes between what is wise or unwise for him to publish. Bok realized that had he encouraged Mr. Cleveland to publish the article, he could have exhausted any edition he might have chosen to print. Times without number, editors make such decisions directly against what would be of temporary advantage.

More often than not the editor hears "stories" that, if printed, would be a "scoop" which would cause his publication to be talked about from one end of the country to the other. The public does not give credit to the editor, particularly of the modern newspaper, for the high code of honor which constantly actuates him in his work. The prevailing notion is that an editor prints all that he knows, and much that he does not know. Outside of those in inner government circles,

[5]Susan B. Anthony died on 13 March 1906.

no group of men, during the Great War, had more information of a confidential nature constantly given or brought to them, and more zealously guarded it, than the editors of the newspapers of America. Among no other set of professional men is the code of honor so high; and woe betide the journalist who, in the eyes of his fellow workers, violates, even in the slightest degree, that code of editorial ethics. Public men know how true is this statement; the public at large, however, has not the first conception of it. If it had, it would have a much higher opinion of its periodicals and newspapers.

At this juncture, Rudyard Kipling unconsciously came into the very center of the suffragists' maelstrom of attack when he sent Bok his famous poem: "The Female of the Species."[6] The suffragists at once took the argument in the poem as personal to themselves, and now Kipling got the full benefit of their vitriolic abuse. Bok had sent a handful of these criticisms to Kipling, who was very gleeful about them. "I owe you a good laugh over the clippings," he wrote. "They were delightful. But what a quantity of spare time some people in this world have to burn!"

It was a merry time; and the longer it continued the more heated were the attacks. The suffragists now had a number of targets, and they took each in turn and proceeded to riddle it. That Bok was publishing arti-

[6]Kipling's poem, "The Female of the Species," published in 1911, repeatedly uses "For the female of the species is more deadly than the male" as a refrain.

cles explaining both sides of the question, presenting arguments by the leading suffragists as well as known antisuffragists, did not matter in the least. These were either conveniently overlooked, or, when referred to at all, were considered in the light of the "sops" to the offended women.

At last Bok reached the stage where he had exhausted all the arguments worth printing, on both sides of the question, and soon the storm calmed down.

It was always a matter of gratification to him that the woman who had most bitterly assailed him during the suffrage controversy, Anna Howard Shaw, became in later years one of his stanchest friends, and was an editor on his payroll. When the United States entered the Great War, Bok saw that Dr. Shaw had undertaken a gigantic task in promising, as chairman, to direct the activities of the National Council for Women. He went to see her in Washington, and offered his help and that of the magazine. Dr. Shaw, kindliest of women in her nature, at once accepted the offer; Bok placed the entire resources of the magazine and of its Washington editorial force at her disposal; and all through America's participation in the war, she successfully conducted a monthly department in *The Ladies' Home Journal.*

"Such help," she wrote at the close, "as you and your associates have extended me and my coworkers; such unstinted cooperation and such practical guidance I never should have dreamed possible. You made your magazine a living force in our work; we do not see now how we could have done without it. You came into our activities at the psychological moment, when we most needed what you could give us, and none could have given with more open hands and fuller hearts."

So the contending forces in a bitter word-war came together and worked together, and a mutual regard sprang up between the woman and the man who had once so radically differed.

XXIV

Going Home with Kipling and as a Lecturer

I T WAS in June 1899, when Rudyard Kipling, after
the loss of his daughter and his own almost fatal ill
ness from pneumonia in America,[1] sailed for his English home on the White Star liner, *Teutonic.* The party
consisted of Kipling, his wife, his father J. Lockwood
Kipling,[2] Mr. and Mrs. Frank N. Doubleday, and Bok.

---

[1] In 1892, Rudyard Kipling married Caroline Balestier, an
American, and settled on her family's estate near Brattleboro, Ver-
mont. There he wrote some of his best and most famous works,
including *The Jungle Book* (1894) and *Second Jungle Book* (1895),
and most of *Captains Courageous* (1897). In 1896, after a falling-
out with a brother-in-law, Kipling and his wife, Caroline, went to
England. Early in 1899 they returned to the United States to visit
Caroline's family, landing in New York after a stormy winter crossing of the Atlantic Ocean. Late in February, soon after their arrival,
their daughter Josephine became ill with a high fever and Kipling
himself developed lung congestion so severe that his attending
physicians gave no hope for his recovery. After Caroline took
Josephine to a friend's estate on Long Island, Kipling rallied and
survived without knowing for a time that Josephine had died.
Kipling, whose writings had become controversial with the publication of "Recessional" in 1907 and "The White Man's Burden"
in 1898, never got over Josephine's death and became obsessed
with his privacy.

[2] A sculptor, John Lockwood Kipling met Methodist minister
Frederick Macdonald's sister, Alice, who became his wife. Soon
thereafter, Lockwood Kipling accepted a position as principal of
the Jeejeebhoy School of Art in Bombay, India, where their first

It was only at the last moment that Bok decided to join the party, and the steamer having its full complement of passengers, he could only secure one of the officers' large rooms on the upper deck. Owing to the sensitive condition of Kipling's lungs, it was not wise for him to be out on deck except in the most favorable weather. The atmosphere of the smoking room was forbidding, and as the rooms of the rest of the party were below deck, it was decided to make Bok's convenient room the headquarters of the party. Here they assembled for the best part of each day; the talk ranged over literary and publishing matters of mutual interest, and Kipling promptly labeled the room "The Hatchery"—from the plans and schemes that were hatched during these discussions.

It was decided on the first day out that the party, too active minded to remain inert for any length of time, should publish a daily newspaper to be written on large sheets of paper and to be read each evening to the group. It was called *The Teuton Tonic;* Mr. Doubleday was appointed publisher and advertising manager; Mr. Lockwood Kipling was made art director to embellish the news; Rudyard Kipling was the star reporter, and Bok was editor.

---

child, Joseph Rudyard Kipling, was born 30 December 1865. Philip Mason, one of Rudyard Kipling's biographers, states that "His father was wise, gentle, and kindly, a maker of things. He drew, modeled, carved, designed; everyone knows his illustrations for *Kim*. . . . His son loved and admired him and submitted work for his judgment."

Kipling, just released from his long confinement, like a boy out of school, was the life of the party—and when, one day, he found a woman aboard reading a copy of *The Ladies' Home Journal* his joy knew no bounds; he turned in the most inimitable "copy" to the *Tonic*, describing the woman's feelings as she read the different departments in the magazine. Of course, Bok, as editor of the *Tonic*, promptly pigeon holed the reporter's "copy"; then relented, and in a fine spirit of large mindedness, "printed" Kipling's pœans of rapture over Bok's subscriber. The preparation of the paper was a daily joy: it kept the different members busy, and each evening the copy was handed to "the large circle of readers"—the two women of the party—to read aloud. At the end of the sixth day, it was voted to "suspend publication," and the daily of six issues was unanimously bequeathed to the little daughter of Mr. Lockwood de Forest, a close friend of the Kipling family—a choice bit of Kiplingania.

Bok derived special pleasure on this trip from his acquaintance with Father Kipling, as the party called him. Rudyard Kipling's respect for his father was the tribute of a loyal son to a wonderful father.

"What annoys me," said Kipling, speaking of his father one day, "is when the pater comes to America to have him referred to in the newspapers as 'the father of Rudyard Kipling.' It is in India where they get the relation correct: there I am always 'the son of Lockwood Kipling.'"

Father Kipling was, in every sense, a choice spirit:

gentle, kindly, and of a most remarkably even temperament. His knowledge of art, his wide reading, his extensive travel, and an interest in every phase of the world's doings, made him a rare conversationalist, when inclined to talk, and an encyclopedia of knowledge as extensive as it was accurate. It was very easy to grow fond of Father Kipling, and he won Bok's affection as few men ever did.

Father Kipling's conversation was quite remarkable in that he was exceedingly careful of language and wasted few words.

One day Kipling and Bok were engaged in a discussion of the Boer problem,[3] which was then most pressing. Father Kipling sat by listening, but made no comment of the different views since, Kipling holding the English side of the question and Bok the Dutch side, it followed that they could not agree. Finally Father Kipling arose and said: "Well, I will take a stroll and see if I can't listen to the water and get all this din out of my ears."

Both men felt gently but firmly rebuked and the discussion was never taken up again.

During the years which intervened until his passing away, Bok sought to keep in touch with Father Kipling,

---

[3]"Boer" is the Dutch form for the German word "Bauer," for "farmer" or "husbandman." "Boer" came to be applied to South Africans of Dutch (or French Huguenot) descent, particularly to inhabitants of Transvaal and the Orange Free State, with whom Great Britain fought the Boer War between October 1899 and May 1902 to which Bok refers.

and received the most wonderful letters from him. One day he enclosed in a letter a drawing which he had made showing Sakia Muni[4] sitting under the bo-tree with two of his disciples, a young man and a young woman, gathered at his feet. It was a piece of ex-quisite drawing. "I like to think of you and your work in this way," wrote Mr. Kipling, "and so I sketched it for you." Bok had the sketch enlarged, engaged John La Farge to translate it into glass, and inserted it in a window of the living room of his home in Merion.

After Father Kipling had passed away, the express brought to Bok one day a beautiful plaque of red clay, showing the elephant's head, the lotus, as well as the swastika, which the father had made for the son. It was the original model of the insignia which, as a wa-termark, is used in the pages of Kipling's books.

"I am sending with this for your acceptance," wrote Kipling to Bok, "as some little memory of my father to whom you were so kind, the original of one of the plaques that he used to make for me. I thought it being the swastika would be appropriate for *your* swastika.[5] May it bring you even more good fortune."

To those who knew Lockwood Kipling, it is easier

[4] A name his disciples gave Guatama Buddha because he came from the warrior caste, the Sakyas.

[5] Bok's home in Merion was named Swastika. The swastika is one of the most ancient of all human symbols, standing for good luck. For centuries it had no negative connotations until it was adopted by the Nazi party in the 1920s and became odious by virtue of its association with Adolf Hitler's infamous Third Reich, anti-Semitism, and the Holocaust.

to understand the genius and the kindliness of the son. For the sake of the public's knowledge, it is a distinct loss that there is not a better understanding of the real sweetness of character of the son. The public's only idea of the great writer is naturally one derived from writers who do not understand him, or from reporters whom he refused to see, while Kipling's own slogan is expressed in his own words: "I have always managed to keep clear of 'personal' things as much as possible."

The lecture bureaus now desired that Edward Bok should go on the platform. Bok had never appeared in the role of a lecturer, but he reasoned that through the medium of the rostrum he might come in closer contact with the American public, meet his readers, and secure some first hand constructive criticism of his work. This last he always encouraged. It was a naïve conception of a lecture tour, but Bok believed it and he contracted for a tour beginning at Richmond, Virginia, and continuing through the South and Southwest as far as Saint Joseph, Missouri, and then back home by way of the Middle West.

Large audiences greeted him wherever he went, but he had not gone far on his tour when he realized that he was not getting what he thought he would. There was much entertaining and lionizing, but nothing to help him in his work by pointing out to him where he could better it. He shrank from the pitiless publicity that was inevitable; he became more and more self-conscious when during the first five minutes on the stage he felt the hundreds of opera glasses leveled at him, and he and Mrs. Bok, who accompanied him, had not a moment to themselves from early morning to midnight. Yet his large correspondence followed him from the office, and the inevitable invitations in each city had at least to be acknowledged. Bok realized he had miscalculated the benefits of a lecture tour to his work and began hopefully to wish for the ending of the circuit.

One afternoon as he was returning with his manager from a large reception, the "impresario" said to him: "I don't like these receptions. They hurt the house."

"The house?" echoed Bok.

"Yes, the attendance."

"But you told me the house for this evening was sold out?" said the lecturer.

"That is true enough. House, and even the stage. Not a seat unsold. But hundreds just come to see you and not to hear you lecture, and this exposure of a lecturer at so crowded a reception as this, before the talk, satisfies the people without their buying a ticket. My rule is that a lecturer should not be seen in public before his lecture, and I wish you would let me enforce the rule with you. It wears you out, anyway, and no receptions until afterward will give you more time for yourself and save your vitality for the talk."

Bok was entirely acquiescent. He had no personal taste for the continued round of functions, but he had accepted it as part of the game.

The idea from this talk that impressed Bok, however, with particular force, was that the people who crowded his houses came to see him and not to hear his lecture. Personal curiosity, in other words. This was a new thought. He had been too busy to think of his personality; now he realized a different angle to the situation. And, much to his manager's astonishment, two days afterwards Bok refused to sign an agreement for another tour later in the year. He had had enough of exhibiting himself as a curiosity. He continued his tour; but before conclusion fell ill—a misfortune with a pleasant side to it, for three of his engagements had to be cancelled.

The Saint Joseph engagement could not be cancelled. The house had been oversold; it was for the benefit of a local charity which besought Bok by wire after wire to keep a postponed date. He agreed, and he went. He realized that he was not well, but did not realize the extent of his mental and physical exhaustion until he came out on the platform and faced the crowded auditorium. Barely sufficient space had been left for him and for the speaker's desk; the people on the stage were close to him, and he felt distinctly uncomfortable.

Then, to his consternation, it suddenly dawned upon him that his tired mind had played a serious trick on him. He did not remember a line of his lecture; he could not even recall how it began! He arose after his introduction in a bath of cold perspiration. The applause gave him a moment to recover himself,

THE MOST POPULAR YOUNG MAN IN AMERICA

EDWARD BOK EDITOR OF THE LADIES HOME JOURNAL

Promotional illustration for Bok's lecture tour in the early 1900s

but not a word came to his mind. He sparred for time by some informal prefatory remarks expressing regret at his illness and that he had been compelled to disappoint his audience a few days before, and then he stood helpless! In sheer desperation he looked at Mrs. Bok sitting in the stage box, who, divining her husband's plight, motioned to the inside pocket of his coat. He put his hand there and pulled out a copy of his lecture which she had placed there! The whole tragic comedy had happened so quickly that the audience was absolutely unaware of what had occurred, and Bok went on and practically read his lecture. But it was not a successful evening for his audience or for himself, and the one was doubtless as glad when it was over as the other.

When he reached home, he was convinced that he had had enough lecturing! He had to make a second short tour, however, for which he had contracted with another manager before embarking on the first. This tour took him to Indianapolis, and after the lecture, James Whitcomb Riley gave him a supper. There were some thirty men in the party; the affair was an exceedingly happy one; the happiest that Bok had ever attended.

One day Bok got a distinctly amusing line on himself from a chance stranger. He was riding from Washington to Philadelphia in the smoking compartment when the newsboy stuck his head in the door and yelled: "*Ladies' Home Journal,* out today." He had heard this many times before; but on this particular day, upon hearing the title of his own magazine yelled almost in his ears, he gave an involuntary start.

Opposite to him sat a most companionable young fellow, who, noticing Bok's start, leaned over and with a smile said: "I know, I know just how you feel. That's the way I feel whenever I hear the name of that damned magazine. Here, boy," he called to the retreating magazine carrier, "give me a copy of that *Ladies' Home Disturber:* I might as well buy it here as in the station."

Then to Bok: "Honest, if I don't bring home that sheet on the day it is out, the wife is in a funk. She runs her home by it literally. Same with you?"

"The same," answered Bok. "As a matter of fact, in our family, we live by it, on it, and from it."

Bok's neighbor, of course, couldn't get the real point of this, but he thought he had it.

"Exactly," he replied. "So do we. That fellow Bok certainly has the women buffaloed for good. Ever see him?"

"Oh, yes," answered Bok.

"Live in Philadelphia?"

"Yes."

"There's where the thing is published, all right. What does Bok look like?"

"Oh," answered Bok carelessly, "just like, well, like all of us. In fact, he looks something like me."

"Does he, now?" echoed the man. "Shouldn't think it would make you very proud."

And, the train pulling in at Baltimore, Bok's genial

neighbor sent him a hearty goodbye and ran out with the much maligned magazine under his arm.

He had an occasion or two now to find out what women thought of him!

He was leaving the publication building one evening after office hours when just as he opened the front door, a woman approached. Bok explained that the building was closed.

"Well, I am sorry," said the woman in a dejected tone, "for I don't think I can manage to come again."

"Is there anything I can do?" asked Bok. "I am employed here."

"No-o," said the woman. "I came to see Mr. Curtis on a personal matter."

"I shall see him this evening," suggested Bok, "and can give him a message for you if you like."

"Well, I don't know if you can. I came to complain to him about Mr. Bok," announced the woman.

"Oh, well," answered Bok, with a slight start at the matter-of-fact announcement, "that is serious; quite serious. If you will explain your complaint, I will surely see that it gets to Mr. Curtis."

Bok's interest grew.

"Well, you see," said the woman, "it is this way. I live in a three-family flat. Here is my name and card," and a card came out of a bag. "I subscribe to *The Ladies' Home Journal.* It is delivered to my house each month by Mr. Bok. Now I have told that man three times over that when he delivers the magazine, he must ring the bell twice. But he just persists in ringing once and then that cat who lives on the first floor gets my magazine, reads it, and keeps it sometimes for three days before I get it! Now, I want Mr. Curtis to tell Mr. Bok that he must do as I ask and ring the bell twice. Can you give him that message for me? There's no use talking to Mr. Bok; I've done that, as I say."

And Bok solemnly assured his subscriber that he would!

The *Journal* had been calling the attention of its readers to the defacement of the landscape by billboard advertisers. One day on his way to New York he found himself sitting in a sleeping car section opposite a woman and her daughter.

The mother was looking at the landscape when she suddenly commented: "There are some of those ugly advertising signs that Mr. Bok says are such a defacement to the landscape. I never noticed them before, but he is right, and I am going to write and tell him so."

"Oh, mamma, don't," said the girl. "That man is pampered enough by women. Don't make him worse. Ethel says he is now the vainest man in America."

Bok's eyes must have twinkled, and just then the mother looked at him, caught his eye; she gave a little gasp, and Bok saw that she had telepathically discovered him!

He smiled, raised his hat, presented his card to the mother, and said: "Excuse me, but I do want to defend myself from that last statement, if I may. I couldn't help overhearing it."

The mother, a woman of the world, read the name on the card quickly and smiled, but the daughter's face was a study as she leaned over and glanced at the card. She turned scarlet and then white.

"Now, do tell me," asked Bok of the daughter, "who 'Ethel' is, so that I may try at least to prove that I am not what she thinks."

The daughter was completely flustered. For the rest of the journey, however, the talk was informal; the girl became more at ease, and Bok ended by dining with the mother and daughter at their hotel that evening.

But he never found out "Ethel's" other name!

There were curiously amusing sides to a man's editorship of a woman's magazine!

XXV

An Excursion into the Feminine Nature

THE STRANGLING hold which the Paris couturiers had secured on the American woman in their absolute dictation as to her fashions in dress, had interested Edward Bok for some time. As he studied the question, he was constantly amazed at the audacity with which these French dressmakers and milliners, often themselves of little taste and scant morals, cracked the whip, and the docility with which the American woman blindly and unintelligently danced to their measure. The deeper he went into the matter, too, the more deceit and misrepresentation did he find in the situation. It was inconceivable that the American woman should submit to what was being imposed upon her if she knew the facts. He determined that she should. The process of Americanization going on within him decided him to expose the Paris conditions and advocate and present American designed fashions for women.

The *Journal* engaged the best-informed woman in Paris frankly to lay open the situation to the American women; she proved that the designs sent over by the so-called Paris arbiters of fashion were never worn by the French woman of birth and good taste; that they were especially designed and specifically intended for

313

"the bizarre American trade," as one polite Frenchman called it; and that the only women in Paris who wore these grotesque and often immoderate styles were of the demimonde.[1]

This article was the opening gun of the campaign, and this was quickly followed by a second equally convincing—both articles being written from the inside of the gilded circles of the couturiers' shops. Madame Sarah Bernhardt was visiting the United States at the time, and Bok induced the great actress to verify the statements printed. She went farther and expressed amazement at the readiness with which the American woman had been duped; and indicated her horror on seeing American women of refined sensibilities and position dressed in the gowns of the *déclassé* street women of Paris. The somewhat sensational nature of the articles attracted the attention of the American newspapers, which copied and commented on them; the gist of them was cabled over to Paris, and, of course, the Paris couturiers denied the charges. But their denials were in general terms; and no convincing proof of the falsity of the charges was furnished. The French couturier simply resorted to a shrug of the shoulder and a laugh, implying that the accusations were beneath his notice.

Bok now followed the French models of dresses and millinery to the United States, and soon found

[1]demimonde: from French for "half world," where women of dubious virtue were mistresses of wealthy lovers. A woman of this type is called a demimondaine.

that for every genuine Parisian model sold in the large cities at least ten were copies, made in New York shops, but with the labels of the French dressmakers and milliners sewed on them. He followed the labels to their source, and discovered a firm, one of whose specialties was the making of these labels bearing the names of the leading French designers. They were manufactured by the gross, and sold in bundles to the retailers. Bok secured a list of the buyers of these labels and found that they represented some of the leading merchants throughout the country. All these facts he published. The retailers now sprang up in arms and denied the charges, but again the denials were in general terms. Bok had the facts and they knew it. These facts were too specific and too convincing to be controverted.

The editor had now presented a complete case before the women of America as to the character of the Paris-designed fashions and the manner in which women were being hoodwinked in buying imitations.

Meanwhile, he had engaged the most expert designers in the world of women's dress and commissioned them to create American designs. He sent one of his editors to the West to get first hand *motifs* from Indian costumes and adapt them as decorative themes for dress embroideries. Three designers searched the Metropolitan Museum for new and artistic ideas, and he induced his company to install a battery of four-color presses in order that the designs might be given in all the beauty of their original colors. For months designers and artists worked; he had the designs passed upon by a board of judges composed of New York women who knew good clothes, and then he began their publication.

The editor of The *New York Times* asked Bok to conduct for that newspaper a prize contest for the best American-designed dresses and hats, and edit a special supplement presenting them in full colors, the prizes to be awarded by a jury of six of the leading New York women best versed in matters of dress. Hundreds of designs were submitted, the best were selected, and the supplement issued under the most successful auspices.

In his own magazine, Bok published many pages of American-designed fashions: their presence in the magazine was advertised far and wide; conventions of dressmakers were called to consider the salability of domestic-designed fashions, and a campaign with the slogan "American Fashions for American Women" was soon in full swing.

But there it ended. The women looked the designs over with interest, as they did all designs of new clothes, and paid no further attention to them. The very fact that they were of American design prejudiced the women against them. America never had designed good clothes, they argued: she never would. Argument availed naught. The Paris germ was deep rooted in the feminine mind of America: the women acknowledged that they were, perhaps, being hoodwinked by spurious French dresses and hats; that the case presented by Bok seemed convincing enough, but the temptation to throw a coat over a sofa or a chair to expose a Parisian label to the eyes of some other woman was too great; there was always a gambling chance that her particular gown, coat, or hat was an actual Paris creation.

Bok called upon the American woman to come out from under the yoke of the French couturiers, show her patriotism, and encourage American design. But it was of no use. He talked with women on every hand; his mail was full of letters commending him for his stand; but as for actual results, there were none. One of his most intelligent woman friends finally summed up the situation for him:

"You can rail against the Paris domination all you like; you can expose it for the fraud that it is, and we know that it is; but it is all to no purpose, take my word. When it comes to the question of her personal adornment, a woman employs no reason; she knows no logic. She knows that adornment of her body is all that she has to match the other woman and outdo her, and to attract the male, and nothing that you can say will influence her a particle. I know this all seems incomprehensible to you as a man, but that is the feminine nature. You are trying to fight something that is unfightable."

"Has the American woman no instinct of patriotism, then?" asked Bok.

"Not the least," was the answer, "when it comes to her adornment. What Paris says, she will do, blindly and unintelligently if you will, but she will do it. She will sacrifice her patriotism; she will even justify a possible disregard of the decencies. Look at the present Parisian styles. They are absolutely indecent. Women know it, but they follow them just the same, and they will. It is all very unpleasant to say this, but it is the truth and you will find it out. Your effort, fine as it is, will bear no fruit."

Wherever Bok went, women upon whose judgment he felt he could rely, told him, in effect, the same thing. They were all regretful, in some cases ashamed of their sex, universally apologetic; but one and all declared that such is "the feminine nature," and Bok would only have his trouble for nothing.

And so it proved. For a period, the retail shops were more careful in the number of genuine French models of gowns and hats which they exhibited, and the label firm confessed that its trade had fallen off. But this was only temporary. Within a year after the *Journal* stopped the campaign, baffled and beaten, the trade in French labels was greater than ever, hundreds of French models were sold that had never crossed the ocean, the American woman was being hoodwinked on every hand, and the reign of the French couturier was once more supreme.

There was no disguising the fact that the case was hopeless, and Bok recognized and accepted the inevitable. He had, at least, the satisfaction of having made an intelligent effort to awaken the American woman to her unintelligent submission. But she refused to be awakened. She preferred to be a tool: to be made a fool of.

Bok's probe into the feminine nature had been keenly disappointing. He had earnestly tried to serve the American woman, and he had failed. But he was destined to receive a still greater and deeper disappointment on his next excursion into the feminine nature, although, this time, he was to win.

During his investigations into women's fashions, he had unearthed the origin of the fashionable aigrette, the most desired of the feathered possessions of womankind.[2] He had been told of the cruel torture of the mother heron, who produced the beautiful aigrette only in her period of maternity and who was cruelly slaughtered, usually left to die slowly rather than killed, leaving her whole nest of baby birds to starve while they awaited the return of the mother bird.

Bok was shown the most heart-rending photographs portraying the butchery of the mother and the starvation of her little ones. He collected all the photographs that he could secure, had the most

[2] aigrette: the tail feathers of the egret, once highly prized as decorations for women's hats. The feathers caused the birds to be hunted virtually to extinction. Several laws were enacted to make illegal this type of predatory hunting. In 1900, Congress passed the Lacey Act, which "prohibited game taken illegally in one state to be shipped across state boundaries contrary to the laws of the state where taken." Problems in enforcement led to the Weeks-McLean Law of 1913, which was designed to stop commercial market hunting of migratory birds. The Migratory Bird Treaty Act of 1918 decreed that all migratory birds and their parts (including eggs, nests, and feathers) were fully protected.

graphic text written to them, and began their publication. He felt certain that the mere publication of the frightfully convincing photographs would be enough to arouse the mother instinct in every woman and stop the wearing of the so highly prized feather. But for the second time in his attempt to reform the feminine nature he reckoned beside the mark.

He published a succession of pages showing the frightful cost at which the aigrette was secured. There was no challenging the actual facts as shown by the photographic lens: the slaughter of the mother bird, and the starving baby birds; and the importers of the feather wisely remained quiet, not attempting to answer Bok's accusations. Letters poured in upon the editor from Audubon Society workers; from lovers of birds, and from women filled with the humanitarian instinct. But Bok knew that the answer was not with those few: the solution lay with the larger circle of American womanhood from which he did not hear.

He waited for results. They came. But they were not those for which he had striven. After four months of his campaign, he learned from the inside of the importing houses which dealt in the largest stocks of aigrettes in the United States that the demand for the feather had more than quadrupled! Bok was dumbfounded! He made inquiries in certain channels from which he knew he could secure the most reliable information, and after all the importers had been interviewed, the conviction was inescapable that just in proportion as Bok had dwelt upon the desirability of the aigrette as the hallmark of wealth and fashion, upon its expense, and the fact that women regarded it as the last word in feminine adornment, he had by so much made these facts familiar to thousands of women who had never before known of them, and had created the desire to own one of the precious feathers.

Bok could not and would not accept these conclusions. It seemed to him incredible that women would go so far as this in the question of personal adornment. He caused the increased sales to be traced from wholesaler to retailer, and from retailer to customer, and was amazed at the character and standing of the latter. He had a number of buyers who lived in adjacent cities, privately approached and interviewed, and ascertained that, save in two instances, they were all his readers, had seen the gruesome pictures he had presented, and then had deliberately purchased the coveted aigrette.

Personally again he sought the most intelligent of his woman friends, talked with scores of others, and found himself facing the same trait in feminine nature which he had encountered in his advocacy of American fashions. But this time it seemed to Bok that the facts he had presented went so much deeper.

"It will be hard for you to believe," said one of his most trusted woman friends. "I grant your arguments: there is no gainsaying them. But you are fighting that which you do not understand. The feminine nature that craves outer adornment will secure it at any cost."

"Yes," argued Bok. "But if there is one thing above everything else that we believe a woman feels and understands, it is the mother instinct. Do you mean to tell me that it means nothing to her that these birds are killed in their period of motherhood, and that a whole nest of starving baby birds is the price of every aigrette?"

"I won't say that this does not weigh with a woman. It does, naturally. But when it comes to her possession of an ornament of beauty, as beautiful as the aigrette, it weighs with her, but it doesn't tip the scale against her possession of it. I am sorry to have to say this to you, but it is a fact. A woman will regret that the mother bird must be tortured and her babies will starve, but she will *have* the aigrette. She simply trains herself to forget the origin."

But Bok was determined that this time he would not fail. His sense of justice and protection to the mother bird and her young was now fully aroused. He resolved that he would, by compulsion, bring about what he had failed to do by persuasion. He would make it impossible for women to be untrue to their most sacred instinct. He sought legal talent, had a bill drawn up making it a misdemeanor to import, sell, purchase, or wear an aigrette. Armed with this measure, and the photographs and articles which he had published, he sought and obtained the interest and promise of support of the most influential legislators in several states. He felt a sense of pride in his own sex that he had no trouble in winning the immediate interest of every legislator with whom he talked.

Where he had failed with women, he was succeeding with men! The outrageous butchery of the birds and the circumstances under which they were tortured appealed with direct force to the sporting instinct in every man, and aroused him. Bok explained to each that he need expect no support for such a measure from women save from the members of the Audubon Societies, and a few humanitarian women and bird lovers. Women, as a whole, he argued from his experiences, while they would not go so far as openly to oppose such a measure, for fear of public comment, would do nothing to further its passage, for in their hearts they preferred failure to success for the legislation. They had frankly told him so: he was not speaking from theory.

In one state after another Bok got into touch with legislators. He counseled, in each case, a quiet passage for the measure instead of one that would draw public attention to it.

Meanwhile, a strong initiative had come from the Audubon Societies throughout the country, and from the National Association of Audubon Societies, at New York. This latter society also caused to be introduced bills of its own to the same and in various legislatures, and here Bok had a valuable ally. It was a fact that Audubon officials encountered their strongest resistance in Bok's own state: Pennsylvania. But Bok's personal acquaintance with legislators in his Keystone State helped here materially.

The demand for the aigrette constantly increased and rose to hitherto unknown figures. In one state where Bok's measure was pending before the legislature, he heard of the coming of an unusually large shipment of aigrettes to meet this increased demand. He wired the legislator in charge of the measure to apprise him of this fact, of what he intended to do, and urging speed in securing the passage of the bill. Then he caused the shipment to be seized at the dock on the ground of illegal importation.

The importing firm at once secured an injunction restraining the seizure. Bok replied by serving a writ setting the injunction aside. The lawyers of the importers got busy, of course, but meanwhile the legislator, taking advantage of a special evening session, had the bill passed, and induced the governor to sign it, the act taking effect at once.

This was exactly what Bok had been playing for. The aigrettes were now useless; they could not be reshipped to another state, they could not be offered for sale. The suit was dropped, and Bok had the satisfaction of seeing the entire shipment, valued at $160,000, destroyed. He had not saved the lives of the mother birds, but, at least, he had prevented hundreds of American women from wearing the odious hallmark of torture.

State after state now passed an aigrette-prohibition law until fourteen of the principal states, including practically all the large cities, fell into line.

Later, the National Association of Audubon Societies had introduced into the United States Congress and passed a bill prohibiting the importation of bird feathers into the country, thus bringing a federal law into existence.[3]

Bok had won his fight, it is true, but he derived little satisfaction from the character of his victory. His ideal of womanhood had received a severe jolt. Women had revealed their worst side to him, and he did not like the picture. He had appealed to what he had been led to believe was the most sacred instinct in a woman's nature. He received no response. Moreover, he saw the deeper love for personal vanity and finery absolutely dominate the mother instinct. He was conscious that something had toppled off its pedestal which could never be replaced.

He was aware that his mother's words, when he accepted his editorial position, were coming terribly true: "I am sorry you are going to take this position. It will cost you the high ideal you have always held of your mother's sex. But a nature, as is the feminine nature, wholly swayed inwardly by emotion, and outwardly influenced by an insatiate love for personal adornment, will never stand the analysis you will give it."

He realized that he was paying a high price for his success. Such experiences as these—and, unfortunately, they were only two of several—were doubtless

[3]See footnote 2 in this chapter for information on legislation enacted.

in his mind when, upon his retirement, the newspapers clamored for his opinions of women. "No, thank you," he said to one and all, "not a word."

He did not give his reasons.

He never will.

XXVI

Cleaning Up
Patent Medicine and Other Evils

I N 1892, *The Ladies' Home Journal* announced that
it would thereafter accept no advertisements of
patent medicines for its pages. It was a pioneer stroke.
During the following two years, seven other newspapers and periodicals followed suit. The American
people were slaves to self-medication, and the patent
medicine makers had it all their own way. There was
little or no legal regulation as to the ingredients in
their nostrums; the mails were wide open to their circulars, and the pages of even the most reputable periodicals welcomed their advertisements. The patent
medicine business in the United States ran into the
hundreds of millions of dollars annually. The business is still large; then it was enormous.

Into this army of deceit and spurious medicines,
The Ladies' Home Journal fired the first gun. Neither
the public nor the patent medicine people paid much
attention to the first attacks. But as they grew, and the
evidence multiplied, the public began to comment
and the nostrum makers began to get uneasy.

The magazine attacked the evil from every angle. It
aroused the public by showing the actual contents of
some of their pet medicines, the absolute worthless-
ness of them. The editor got the Women's Christian

328 The Americanization of Edward Bok

Temperance Union into action against various periodicals for publishing advertisements of medicines containing as high as forty percent alcohol. He showed that the most confidential letters written by women with private ailments were opened by young clerks of both sexes, laughed at and gossiped over, and that afterward their names and addresses, which they had been told were held in strictest confidence, were sold to other lines of business for five cents each. He held the religious press up to the scorn of church members for accepting advertisements which the publishers knew and which he proved to be not only fraudulent, but actually harmful. He called the United States Post Office authorities to account for accepting and distributing obscene circular matter.

He cut an advertisement out of a newspaper which ended with the statement:

"Mrs. Pinkham, in her laboratory at Lynn, Massachusetts, is able to do more for the ailing women of America than the family physician. Any woman, therefore, is responsible for her own suffering who will not take the trouble to write to Mrs. Pinkham for advice."

Next to this advertisement representing Mrs. Lydia Pinkham as "in her laboratory," Bok simply placed the photograph of Mrs. Pinkham's tombstone in Pine Grove Cemetery, at Lynn, showing that Mrs. Pinkham had passed away twenty-two years before!

It was one of the most effective pieces of copy that the magazine used in the campaign. It told its story with absolute simplicity, but with deadly force.

MRS. LYDIA E. PINKHAM'S MONUMENT
in Pine Grove Cemetery, Lynn, Massachusetts.
Mrs. Pinkham Died May 17, 1883 (22 Years Ago).

False patent medicine advertising, as exposed by
Bok in the magazine, September 1905

329

The dangers of narcotics in patent medicines,
as cautioned by Bok in The Ladies' Home Journal, *September 1905*

The proprietors of "Mrs. Winslow's Soothing Syrup" had strenuously denied the presence of morphine in their preparation. Bok simply bought a bottle of the syrup in London, where, under the English Pharmacy Act, the authorities compelled the proprietors of the syrup to affix the following declaration on each bottle: "This preparation, containing, among other valuable ingredients, a small amount of morphine is, in accordance with the Pharmacy Act, hereby labeled 'Poison'." The magazine published a photograph of the label, and it told its own convincing story. It is only fair to say that the makers of this remedy now publish their formula.

Bok now slipped a cog in his machinery. He published a list of twenty-seven medicines, by name, and told what they contained. One preparation, he said, contained alcohol, opium, and digitalis. He believed he had been extremely careful in this list. He had consulted the highest medical authorities, physicians, and chemists. But in the instance of one preparation referred to above he was wrong.

The analysis had been furnished by the secretary of The State Board of Health of Massachusetts; a recognized expert, who had taken it from the analysis of a famous German chemist. It was in nearly every standard medical authority, and was accepted by the best medical authorities. Bok accepted these authorities as final. Nevertheless, the analysis and the experts were wrong. A suit for $200,000 was brought by the patent medicine company against The Curtis Publishing

Company and, of course, it was decided in favor of
the former. But so strong a public sentiment had been
created against the whole business of patent medicines by this time that the jury gave a verdict of only
$16,000, with costs, against the magazine.

Undaunted, Bok kept on. He now engaged Mark
Sullivan,[1] then a young lawyer in downtown New York,
induced him to give up his practice, and bring his legal
mind to bear upon the problem. It was the beginning of
Sullivan's subsequent journalistic career. He justified
Bok's confidence in him. He exposed the testimonials
to patent medicines from senators and congressmen
then so widely published, showed how they were obtained by a journalist in Washington who made a business of it. He charged seventy-five dollars for a senator's
testimonial, forty dollars for that of a congressman, and
accepted no contract for less than $5,000.

Sullivan next exposed the disgraceful violation of
the confidence of women by these nostrum vendors in
selling their most confidential letters to anyone who
would buy them. Sullivan himself bought thousands
of these letters and names, and then wrote about them
in the magazine. One prominent firm indignantly denied the charge, asserting that whatever others might
have done, their names were always held sacred. In

[1]Mark Sullivan, a distinguished American journalist and popular historian, became a newspaperman who was well known for
writing muckraking articles, including his exposé of the patent
medicine industry published by Edward Bok in *The Ladies' Home
Journal*.

answer to this declaration Sullivan published an advertisement of this righteous concern offering 50,000 of their names for sale.

Bok had now kept up the fight for over two years, and the results were apparent on every hand. Reputable newspapers and magazines were closing their pages to the advertisements of patent medicines; legislation was appearing in several states; the public had been awakened to the fraud practiced upon it, and a Federal Pure Food and Drug Act was beginning to be talked about.

Single handed, *The Ladies' Home Journal* kept up the fight until Mark Sullivan produced an unusually strong article, but too legalistic for the magazine. He called the attention of Norman Hapgood, then editor of *Collier's Weekly,* to it, who accepted it at once, and, with Bok's permission, engaged Sullivan, who later succeeded Hapgood as editor of *Collier's.* Robert J. Collier now brought Samuel Hopkins Adams[2] to Bok's attention and asked the latter if he should object if *Collier's Weekly* joined him in his fight. The Philadelphia editor naturally welcomed the help of the weekly and Adams began his wonderfully effective campaign.

The weekly and the monthly now pounded away

[2]Samuel Hopkins Adams was a reporter and writer for the *New York Sun, McClure's Magazine,* and *Collier's Weekly* who worked with other journalists of the "muckraking" school to expose fraud and corruption. His articles on the patent medicine industry helped lead to passage of the Pure Food and Drug Act in 1906. The prize-winning film *It Happened One Night* was based on one of his short stories.

together; other periodicals and newspapers, seeing success ahead, and desiring to be part of it and share the glory, came into the conflict, and it was not long before so strong a public sentiment had been created as to bring about the passage of the United States Food and Drug Act, and the patent medicine business of the United States had received a blow from which it has never recovered. Today the pages of every newspaper and periodical of recognized standing are closed to the advertisements of patent medicines; the Drug Act regulates the ingredients, and the post office officials scan the literature sent through the United States mails.

There are distinct indications that the time has come once more to scan the patent medicine horizon carefully, but the conditions existing in 1920 are radically different from those prevailing in 1904.

One day when Bok was at luncheon with Dr. Lyman Abbott, the latter expressed the wish that Bok would take up the subject of venereal disease as he had the patent medicine question.

"Not our question," answered Bok.

"It is most decidedly your question," was the reply.

Bok cherished the highest regard for Dr. Abbott's opinion and judgment, and this positive declaration amazed him.

"Read up on the subject," counseled Dr. Abbott, "and you will find that the evil has its direct roots in the home with the parents. You will agree with me before you go very far that it *is* your question."

Bok began to read on the unsavory subject. It was exceedingly unpleasant reading, but for two years Bok persisted, only to find that Dr. Abbott was right. The root of the evil lay in the reticence of parents with children as to the mystery of life; boys and girls were going out into the world blindfolded as to any knowledge of their physical selves; "the bloom must not be rubbed off the peach," was the belief of thousands of parents, and the results were appalling. Bok pursued his investigations from books direct into the "Homes of Refuge," "Doors of Hope," and similar institutions, and unearthed a condition, the direct results of the false modesty of parents, that was almost unbelievable.

Bok had now all his facts, but realized that for his magazine, of all magazines, to take up this subject would be like a bolt from the blue in tens of thousands of homes. But this very fact, the unquestioned position of the magazine, the remarkable respect which its readers had for it, and the confidence with which parents placed the periodical on their home tables—all this was, after all, Bok thought, the more reason why he should take up the matter and thresh it out. He consulted with friends, who advised against it; his editors were all opposed to the introduction of the unsavory subject into the magazine.

"But it isn't unsavory," argued Bok. "That is just it. We have made it so by making it mysterious, by surrounding it with silence, by making it a forbidden topic. It is the most beautiful story in life."

Mr. Curtis, alone, encouraged his editor. Was he sure he was right? If he was, why not go ahead? Bok called his attention to the fact that a heavy loss in circulation was a foregone conclusion; he could calculate upon 100,000 subscribers, at least, stopping the magazine. "It is a question of right," answered the publisher, "not of circulation."

And so, in 1906, with the subject absolutely prohibited in every periodical and newspaper of any standing, never discussed at a public gathering save at medical meetings, Bok published his first editorial.

The readers of his magazine fairly gasped; they were dumb with astonishment! *The Ladies' Home Journal,* of all magazines, to discuss such a subject! When they had recovered from their astonishment, the parents began to write letters, and one morning Bok was confronted with a large wastebasket full brought in by his two office boys.

"Protests," laconically explained one of his editors. "More than that, the majority threaten to stop their subscription unless you stop."

"All right, that proves I am right," answered Bok. "Write to each one and say that what I have written is nothing as compared in frankness to what is coming, and that we shall be glad to refund the unfulfilled part of their subscriptions."

Day after day, thousands of letters came in. The next issue contained another editorial, stronger than the first. Bok explained that he would not tell the actual story of the beginning of life in the magazine—that

The Editor's Personal Page

The time has come to turn the light on an existing condition touching the American fireside that will appal the average woman and girl. It is the knowledge of this condition that led this magazine, now nearly two years ago, to insist upon a greater parental frankness with children about their physical selves.

The Condition:

BECAUSE of the secrecy with which the whole question is enshrouded it is practically impossible to obtain absolute figures. But so far as the highest authorities have been able, through the most careful inquiries, to secure actual figures, it is a conservative statement to say that at least 80 per cent of all guilty men are today "sowing their wild oats." Of these 80 young men a startling number are either already making or will make a tragedy of marriage. They produce either childless homes: dead-born or blind babies; children with lifelong disease with them; or they will send thousands of women to the operating table. Exactly what percentage of these 80 young men escape the lifelong perils of their early indiscretions it is impossible to tell.

These statements are made not upon theory, but facts that are proved and demonstrated at thousands of domestic bedsides and in the autopsy rooms of hundreds of hospitals. They are facts that are known to every physician.

This frightful condition has been brought about, largely, by two contributing factors:

First, The parental policy of mock-modesty and silence with their sons and daughters about their physical selves, and

Second: The condoning in men what is condemned in women. Fathers and mothers, and, in consequence, girls have condoned in a young man the sowing of his "wild oats" because it was considered a phase of his necessity; that "it would do him good"; that "it would make a man of him;" that "it would show him the world"—all arguments absolutely baseless.

With hundreds of girls the young man who has most promiscuously and profusely scattered his "wild oats" has been looked upon as the most favored one among possible husbands. Too many a girl there is always something alluring to marry a man with a past because it appealed to her vanity to "remake" or "reform" him. The peril to herself she has never known, for silence has been the portion meted out to her by her parents.

The Five Results:

THE FIRST: The lifelong invalidism or the surgical mutilation of thousands of women;

THE SECOND: The death of untold thousands of unborn or new-born babies;

THE THIRD: The lifelong taint of disease upon children who do live;

THE FOURTH: The blindness of over 6 out of every 100 new-born blind babies;

THE FIFTH: The domestic unhappiness of tens of thousands of homes because of the absence of children.

> Over 70 out of every 100 special surgical operations on women are the direct or indirect result of one cause
>
> This statement is made on the highest medical authority

The Remedy:

NOW thousands will not only ask: Is there a remedy for this, except the awful blinking of bell-or and the surgical mutilation of women? There is not only a remedy, but a remedy as potent as it is simple. It is this, and it is distinctly "up to" the parents:

First: We parents must have at all get it into our minds firm and fast to do away with the policy of silence with our children that has done so much to bring about this condition. Our sons and daughters must be told what they are, and they must be told lovingly and frankly. And told they must be.

Second: We fathers of daughters must rid ourselves of the notion that has worked such diabolical havoc of a double moral standard. There can be but one standard: that of moral equality. Instead of being so painfully anxious about the "financial prospects" of a young man who seeks the hand of our daughter in marriage, and making that the first question, it is time that we put health first and money second; that we find out, first of all, if the young man comes to court, as the lawyers say, with clean hands. Let a father ask the young man, as his leading question, whether he is physically clean: insist that he shall go to his family physician, and if he gives him a clean bill of health, then his financial prospects can be gone into. But his physical self first. That mach every father would do in the case of a horse or a dog that he bought with a view to mating. Yet he does less for his daughter: his own flesh and blood.

Once let young men realize that such a question would be asked them by the fathers of the young women whom they would marry: that a physical standard would be demanded—and that knowledge would be more effective for morality among young men than all the preaching and moralizing and exhortations of the past thousand years.

Thus, and thus only, can we save our daughters and their unborn children. But in no other way.

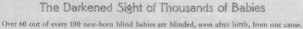

The Darkened Sight of Thousands of Babies

Over 60 out of every 100 new-born blind babies are blinded, soon after birth, from one cause.
One cause kills outright before, or shortly after, birth, 3 out of 4 children affected.

"A child dying, leaving this good world of ours, seems to have had so small a chance for itself. There is something in all of us struggling against oblivion, striving vainly to make a real impress on the current of time, and a child dying can only clutch the hands about it and go down—forever. It seems so merciless, so unfair. Perhaps that is why, all over the world, the little graves are cared for best. It is to the little graves that we turn, and not to the larger mounds, in our keenest anguish: to the little graves that our hearts are drawn in our hours of triumph; and so the child, though dead, lives its appointed time and dies only in the fullness of its years. The little shoes, the little dresses, the 'little tin soldiers, covered with rust,' and the memories sweeter than dreams of a honeymoon—these are life's immortelles that never fade."

—WILLIAM ALLEN WHITE.

Bok's controversial editorial campaign to increase knowledge about sexually transmitted diseases, September 1908

was the prerogative of the parents, and he had no notion of taking it away from either; but that he meant to insist upon putting their duty squarely up to them, that he realized it was a long fight, hence the articles to come would be many and continued; and that those of his readers who did not believe in his policy had better stop the magazine at once. But he reminded them that no solution to any question was ever reached by running away from it. This question had to be faced some time, and now was as good as any.

Thousands of subscriptions were stopped; advertisements gave notice that they would cancel accounts; the greatest pressure was placed upon Mr. Curtis to order his editor to cease, and Bok had the grim experience of seeing his magazine, hitherto proclaimed all over the land as a model advocate of the virtues, refused admittance into thousands of homes, and saw his own friends tear the offending pages out of their periodical before it was allowed to find a place on their home tables.

But the *Journal* kept steadily on. Number after number contained some article on the subject, and finally such men and women as Jane Addams, Cardinal Gibbons, Margaret Deland, Henry van Dyke, President Eliot, the Bishop of London, braved the public storm, came to Bok's aid, and wrote articles for his magazine heartily backing up his lonely fight.

The public, seeing this array of distinguished opinion expressing itself, began to wonder "whether there might be something in what Bok was saying, after all."

At the end of eighteen months, inquiries began to take the place of protests; and Bok knew then that the fight was won. He employed two experts, one man and one woman, to answer the inquiries, and he had published a series of little books, each written by a different author on a different aspect of the question.

This series was known as The Edward Bok Books. They sold for twenty-five cents each, without profit to either editor or publisher. The series was sold into the tens of thousands. Information was, therefore, to be had, in authoritative form, enabling every parent to tell the story to his or her child. Bok now insisted that every parent should do this, and announced that he intended to keep at the subject until the parents did. He explained that the magazine had lost about 75,000 subscribers, and that it might just as well lose some more; but that the insistence should go on.

Slowly but surely the subject became a debatable one. Where, when Bok began, the leading prophylactic society in New York could not secure five speaking dates for its single lecturer during a session, it was now put to it to find open dates for over ten speakers. Mothers' clubs, women's clubs, and organizations of all kinds clamored for authoritative talks; here and there a much-veiled article apologetically crept into print, and occasionally a progressive school board or educational institution experimented with a talk or two.

The Ladies' Home Journal published a full-page editorial declaring that over 70 of every 100 special surgical operations on women were directly or indirectly the result of one cause; that 60 of every 100 newborn blinded babies were blinded soon after birth from this same cause; and that every man knew what this cause was!

Letters from men now began to pour in by the hundreds. With an oath on nearly every line, they told him that their wives, daughters, sisters, or mothers had demanded to know this cause, and that they had to tell them. Bok answered these heated men and told them that was exactly why the *Journal* had published the editorial, and that in the next issue there would be another for those women who might have missed his first. He insisted that the time had come when women should learn the truth, and that, so far as it lay in his power, he intended to see that they did know.

The tide of public opinion at last turned toward the *Journal* and its campaign. Women began to realize that it had a case; that it was working for their best interests and for those of their children, and they decided that the question might as well be faced. Bok now felt that his part in the work was done. He had started something well on its way; the common sense of the public must do the rest.

Bok was now done with health measures for a while, and determined to see what he could do with two or three civic questions he felt needed attention.

XXVII

Adventures in Civics

THE ELECTRIC POWER companies at Niagara Falls were beginning to draw so much water from above the great Horseshoe Falls as to bring into speculation the question of how soon America's greatest asset would be a coal pile with a thin trickle of water crawling down its vast cliffs. Already companies had been given legal permission to utilize one-quarter of the whole flow, and additional companies were asking for further grants. Permission for forty percent of the whole volume of water had been granted. J. Horace McFarland, as president of the American Civic Association, called Bok's attention to the matter, and urged him to agitate it through his magazine so that restrictive legislation might be secured.

Bok went to Washington, conferred with President Roosevelt, and found him cognizant of the matter in all its aspects.

"I can do nothing," said the president, "unless there is an awakened public sentiment that compels action. Give me that, and I'll either put the subject in my next message to Congress or send a special message. I'm from Missouri on this point," continued the president. "Show me that the American people want their Falls preserved, and I'll do the rest. But I've got to be shown." Bok assured the president he could demonstrate this to him.

The next number of his magazine presented a graphic picture of the Horseshoe Falls as they were and the same Falls as they would be if more water was allowed to be taken for power: a barren coal pile with a tiny rivulet of water trickling down its sides. The editorial asked whether the American women were going to allow this? If not, each, if an American, should write to the president, and, if a Canadian, to Earl Grey, then Governor-General of Canada. Very soon after the magazine had reached its subscribers' hands, the letters began to reach the White House; not by dozens, as the president's secretary wrote to Bok, but by the hundreds and then by the thousands. "Is there any way to turn this spigot off?" telegraphed the president's secretary. "We are really being inundated."

Bok went to Washington and was shown the huge pile of letters.

"All right," said the president. "That's all I want. You've proved to me that there is a public sentiment."

The clerks at Rideau Hall, at Ottawa, did not know what had happened one morning when the mail quadrupled in size and thousands of protests came to Earl Grey. He wired the president, the president exchanged views with the governor-general, and the great international campaign to save Niagara Falls had begun. The American Civic Association and scores of other patriotic bodies joined in the clamor.

The Desecration of Niagara

President Roosevelt's Call to the Readers of The Ladies' Home Journal for Help

WE ASKED on this page last September, "Shall we make a coal-pile of Niagara?" The answer to us was a thunderous "No." We asked that our readers would write a personal letter to President Roosevelt and to Governor General Gray

"Get as Many Intelligent Citizens as You Possibly

NOW, help the President. He has spoken. He can do no more until Congress acts. This magazine can do no more. It is now for you, as one of the people, to act. The responsibility is fully upon you who read this anywhere in the

The Magnificent Rapids of Niagara as They are Today. One of the Seven Scenic Wonders of the World

As These Same Rapids Would Look if Only One-Half of the Annual "Grab" is Permitted — An Ugly Mass of Rock and Rubbish

Part of the Journal's *campaign to protect Niagara Falls, January 1906*

The attorney-general and the secretary of state were instructed by the president to look into the legal and diplomatic aspects of the question, and in his next message to Congress President Roosevelt uttered a clarion call to that body to restrict the power-grabbing companies.

The Ladies' Home Journal urged its readers to write to their congressmen and they did by the thousands. Every congressman and senator was overwhelmed. As one senator said: "I have never seen such an avalanche. But thanks to *The Ladies' Home Journal,* I have received these hundreds of letters from my constituents; they have told me what they want done, and they are mostly from those of my people whose wishes I am bound to respect."

The power companies, of course, promptly sent their attorneys and lobbyists to Washington; but the public sentiment aroused was too strong to be disregarded, and on 20 June 1906, the president signed the Burton Bill restricting the use of the water of Niagara Falls.

The matter was then referred to the secretary of war, William Howard Taft, to grant the use of such volume of water as would preserve the beauty of the Falls. McFarland and Bok wanted to be sure that Secretary Taft felt the support of public opinion, for his policy was to be conservative, and tremendous pressure was being brought upon him from every side to permit a more liberal use of water. Bok turned to his readers and asked them to write to Secretary Taft and assure him of the support of the American women in his attitude of conservatism.

The flood of letters that descended upon the secretary almost taxed even his genial nature; and when Mr. McFarland, as the editorial representative of the *Journal,* arose to speak at the public hearing in Washington, the secretary said: "I can assure you that you don't have to say very much. Your case has already been pleaded for you by, I should say at the most conservative estimate, at least 100,000 women. Why, I have had letters from even my wife and my mother."

Secretary Taft adhered to his conservative policy, Sir Wilfred Laurier, premier of Canada, met the overtures of Secretary of State Root, a new international document was drawn up, and Niagara Falls had been saved to the American people.

In 1905 and in previous years the casualties resulting from fireworks on the Fourth of July averaged from 5,000 to 6,000 each year. The humorous weekly *Life* and the *Chicago Tribune* had been for some time agitating a restricted use of fireworks on the national fête day, but nevertheless the list of casualties kept creeping to higher figures. Bok decided to help by arousing the parents of America, in whose hands, after all, lay the remedy. He began a series of articles in the magazine, showing what had happened over a period of years, the criminality of allowing so many young lives to be snuffed out, and suggested how parents could help by prohibiting the deadly firecrackers and cannon, and how organizations could help by influencing the passage of city ordinances. Each recurring January, the *Journal* returned to the subject, looking forward to the coming Fourth. It was a deep-rooted custom to eradicate, and powerful influences in the form of thousands of small storekeepers were at work upon local officials to pay no heed to the agitation. Gradually public opinion changed. The newspapers joined in the cry; women's organizations insisted upon action from local municipal bodies.

Finally, the civic spirit in Cleveland, Ohio, forced the passage of a city ordinance prohibiting the sale or use of fireworks on the Fourth. The following year when Cleveland reported no casualties as compared to an ugly list for the previous Fourth, a distinct impression was made upon other cities. Gradually, other municipalities took action, and year by year the list of Fourth of July casualties grew perceptibly shorter. New York City was now induced to join the list of prohibitive cities, by a personal appeal made to its mayor by Bok, and on the succeeding Fourth of July the city authorities, on behalf of the people of New York City, conferred a gold medal upon Edward Bok for his services in connection with the birth of the new Fourth in that city.

There still remains much to be done in cities as yet unawakened; but a comparison of the list of casualties of 1920 with that of 1905 proves the growth in enlightened public sentiment in fifteen years to have been steadily increasing. It is an instance not of Bok taking the initiative—that had already been taken—

but of throwing the whole force of the magazine with those working in the field to help. It is the American woman who is primarily responsible for the safe and sane Fourth, so far as it already exists in this country today, and it is the American woman who can make it universal.

Mrs. Pennypacker, as president of the Federation of Women's Clubs, now brought to Bok's attention the conditions under which the average rural school teacher lived; the suffering often entailed on her in having to walk miles to the schoolhouse in wintry weather; the discomfort she had to put up with in the farm houses where she was compelled to live, with the natural result, under these conditions, that it was almost impossible to secure the services of capable teachers, or to have good teaching even where efficient teachers were obtained.

Mrs. Pennypacker suggested that Bok undertake the creation of a public sentiment for a residence for the teacher in connection with the schoolhouse. The parson was given a parsonage; why not the teacher a "teacherage"? The *Journal* cooperated with Mrs. Pennypacker and she began the agitation of the subject in the magazine. She also spoke of the subject wherever she went, and induced women's clubs all over the country to join the magazine in its advocacy of the "teacherage."

By personal effort, several "teacherages" were established in connection with new schoolhouses; photographs of these were published and sent personally to school boards all over the country; the members of the women's clubs saw to it that the articles were brought to the attention of members of their local school boards; and the now generally accepted idea that a "teacherage" must accompany a new schoolhouse was well on its way to national recognition.

Just about this time a group of Philadelphia physicians, headed by Doctor Samuel McClintock Hamill,[1] which had formed itself into a hygienic committee for babies, waited upon Bok to ask him to join them in the creation of a permanent organization devoted to the welfare of babies and children. Bok found that he was dealing with a company of representative physicians, and helped to organize "The Child Federation," an organization "to do good on a business basis."

It was to go to the heart of the problem of the baby in the congested districts of Philadelphia, and do a piece of intensive work in the ward having the highest infant mortality, establishing the first health center in the United States actively managed by competent physicians and nurses. This center was to demonstrate to city authorities that the fearful mortality among babies, particularly in summer, could be reduced.

Meanwhile, there was created a "Baby Saving Show," a set of graphic pictures conveying to the eye

---

[1]Samuel McClintock Hamill was a prominent pediatrician, director of welfare for the state of Pennsylvania in 1917-1918, and chairman of the National Welfare Committee of the Council for National Defense. He also served as president of the American Academy of Pediatrics.

methods of sanitation and other too often disregarded essentials of the wise care and feeding of babies; and this traveled, like a theatrical attraction, to different parts of the city. "Little Mothers' Leagues" were organized to teach the little girl of ten or twelve, so often left in charge of a family of children when the mother is at work during the day, and demonstrations were given in various parts of the city.

The Child Federation now undertook one activity after another. Under its auspices, the first municipal Christmas tree ever erected in Philadelphia was shown in the historic Independence Square, and with two bands of music giving concerts every day from Christmas to New Year's Day, attracted over 200,000 persons. A pavilion was erected in City Hall Square, the most central spot in the city, and the "Baby Saving Show" was permanently placed there and visited by over 100,000 visitors from every part of the country on their way to and from Pennsylvania Station.

A searching investigation of the Day Nurseries of Philadelphia probably one of the most admirable pieces of research work ever made in a city—changed the methods in vogue and became a standard guide for similar institutions throughout the country. So successful were the Little Mothers' Leagues that they were introduced into the public schools of Philadelphia, and are today a regular part of the curriculum. The Health Center, its success being proved, was taken over by the city Board of Health, and three others were established.

Today The Child Federation is recognized as one of the practically conducted child welfare agencies in Philadelphia, and its methods have been followed by similar organizations all over the country. It is now rapidly becoming the central medium through which the other agencies in Philadelphia are working, thus avoiding the duplication of infant welfare work in the city. Broadening its scope, it is not unlikely to become one of the greatest indirect influences in the welfare work of Philadelphia and the vicinity, through which other organizations will be able to work.

Bok's interest and knowledge in civic matters had now peculiarly prepared him for a personal adventure into community work. Merion, where he lived, was one of the most beautiful of the many suburbs that surround the Quaker City; but, like hundreds of similar communities, there had been developed in it no civic interest. Some of the most successful business men of Philadelphia lived in Merion; they had beautiful estates, which they maintained without regard to expense, but also without regard to the community as a whole. They were busy men; they came home tired after a day in the city; they considered themselves good citizens if they kept their own places sightly, but the idea of devoting their evenings to the problems of their community had never occurred to them before the evening when two of Bok's neighbors called to ask his help in forming a civic association.

A canvass of the sentiment of the neighborhood revealed the unanimous opinion that the experiment, if attempted, would be a failure—an attitude not by any means confined to the residents of Merion! Bok decided to test it out; he called together twenty of his neighbors, put the suggestion before them and asked for $2,000 as a start, so that a paid secretary might be engaged, since the men themselves were too busy to attend to the details of the work. The amount was immediately subscribed, and in 1913 the Merion Civic Association applied for a charter and began its existence.

The leading men in the community were elected as a board of directors, and a salaried secretary was engaged to carry out the directions of the board. The association adopted the motto: "To be nation right, and state right, we must first be community right." Three objectives were selected with which to attract community interest and membership: safety to life, in the form of proper police protection; safety to property, in the form of adequate hydrant and fire engine service; and safety to health, in careful supervision of the water and milk used in the community.

"The three S's," as they were called, brought an immediate response. They were practical in their appeal, and members began to come in. The police force was increased from one officer at night and none in the day, to three at night and two during the day, and to this the association added two special night officers of its own. A fire hydrant was placed within 700 feet of every house, with the insurance rates reduced from 12.5 percent to 30 percent; the services of three fire engine companies was arranged for. One hundred and fifty new electric light posts specially designed and pronounced by experts as the most beautiful and practical road lamps ever introduced into any community, were erected, making Merion the best-lighted community in its vicinity.

At every corner was erected an artistically designed cast iron road sign; instead of the unsightly wooden ones, cast iron automobile warnings were placed at every dangerous spot; community bulletin boards, preventing the display of notices on trees and poles, were placed at the railroad station; litter cans were distributed over the entire community; a new railroad station and post office were secured; the station grounds were laid out as a garden by a landscape architect; new roads of permanent construction, from curb to curb, were laid down; uniform tree planting along the roads was introduced; bird houses were made and sold, as to attract bird life to the community; toll gates were abolished along the two main arteries of travel; the removal of all telegraph and telephone poles was begun; an efficient Boy Scout troop was organized, as well as an American Legion post; the automobile speed limit was reduced from twenty-four to fifteen miles as a protection to children; roads were regularly swept, cleaned and oiled, and uniform sidewalks advocated and secured.

Within seven years so efficiently had the association functioned that its work attracted attention far beyond its own confines and that of Philadelphia, and

caused Theodore Roosevelt voluntarily to select it as
a subject for a special magazine article in which he
declared it to "stand as a model in civic matters."
Today it may be conservatively said of the Merion
Civic Association that it is pointed out as one of the
most successful suburban civic efforts in the country;
as Dr. Lyman Abbott said in *Outlook*, it has made
"Merion a model suburb, which may standardize
ideal suburban life, certainly for Philadelphia, possibly
for the United States."

When the Armistice was signed in November 1918,
the Association immediately canvassed the neighborhood to erect a suitable Tribute House, as a memor-
ial to the eighty-three Merion boys who had gone into
the Great War: a public building which would com-
prise a community center, with an American Legion
Post room, a Boy Scout house, an auditorium, and a
meeting place for the civic activities of Merion. A subscription was raised, and plans were already drawn
for the Tribute House, when Eldridge R. Johnson,[2]
president of the Victor Talking Machine Company,

---

[2]Eldridge Reeves Johnson developed a hand-cranked spring
motor for gramophone pioneer Emile Berliner, organized the
Victor Talking Machine Company in 1901, absorbed Berliner's
patents, further improved the gramophone, and introduced the
Victrola, a disc-playing machine with an improved tone arm and
speaker horn, in 1906. Through aggressive marketing and record-
ing contracts with leading artists, Johnson built Victor into a
world-wide enterprise and sold it for $40 million when he retired
in 1927 after playing a key role in making disc phonography a mass
consumer industry.

one of the strongest supporters of The Merion Civic Association, presented his entire estate of twelve acres, the finest in Merion, to the community, and agreed to build a Tribute House at his own expense. The grounds represented a figure of $250,000. This building, now about to be erected, will be one of the most beautiful and complete community centers in the United States.

Perhaps no other suburban civic effort proves the efficiency of community cooperation so well as does the seven years' work of The Merion Civic Association. It is a practical demonstration of what a community can do for itself by concerted action. It preached, from the very start, the gospel of united service; it translated into actual practice the doctrine of being one's brother's keeper, and it taught the invaluable habit of collective action. The Association has no legal powers; it rules solely by persuasion; it accomplishes by the power of combination; by a spirit of the community for the community.

When the Merion Civic Association was conceived, the spirit of local pride was seemingly not present in the community. As a matter of fact, it was there as it is in practically every neighborhood; it was simply dormant; it had to be awakened, and its value brought vividly to the community consciousness.

XXVIII

A Bewildered Bok

O NE OF THE misfortunes of Edward Bok's training, which he realized more clearly as time went on, was that music had little or no place in his life. His mother did not play; and aside from the fact that his father and mother were patrons of the opera during their residence in The Netherlands, the musical atmosphere was lacking in his home. He realized how welcome an outlet music might be in his now busy life. So what he lacked himself and realized as a distinct omission in his own life he decided to make possible for others.

The Ladies' Home Journal began to strike a definite musical note. It first caught the eye and ear of its public by presenting the popular new marches by John Philip Sousa; and when the comic opera of "Robin Hood" became the favorite of the day, it secured all the new compositions by Reginald de Koven. Following these, it introduced its readers to new compositions by Sir Arthur Sullivan, Tosti, Moscowski, Richard Strauss, Paderewski, Josef Hofmann, Edouard Strauss, and Mascagni. Bok induced Josef Hofmann to give a series of piano lessons in his magazine, and Madame Marchesi a series of vocal lessons. The *Journal* introduced its readers to all the great instrumental and

At Work on a New Composition

With Josef Hofmann at the Piano

A Few Carefully-Prepared Lessons by Josef Hofmann

III—How to Play "in Style"

BY PLAYING a piece of music "in style" is understood a certain manner which points to its creation in regard to the correct manner of expression. Now the true manner of expression must be sought and found for each piece individually, even though a number of different pieces may be written by one and the same composer. Our first endeavor should be to search out the peculiarity of the piece in hand and rather than the peculiarity of the composer in general. If you have succeeded in playing one work by Chopin in style, it does not follow, by any means, that you

individual; it rests with those many and complex qualities which are usually summarized by the term "talent," and this must be preoccupied with a player who aspires to artistic work.

On the other hand, talent alone cannot lift the veil that hides the spiritual content of a composition if its possessor neglects to examine the latter carefully as to its purely musical ingredients. He may be possessor of the widest talent, sensuously speaking, but he can never play the piece in style.

these defects, one by one, and in so doing you will come nearer and nearer to the spiritual essence of the work in hand.

As to the remaining "purely technical task" (as I said before), it must not be underestimated. To transmit one's matured conception to one's auditors requires a considerable degree of mechanical skill; and this skill, in turn, must be incorporated in the work of the writer. Of course, after the foregoing—this does not mean that everybody who has a good and well-controlled technique can interpret

Josef Hofmann, who offered piano lessons through

356

The Philadelphia Orchestra in 1899, about the time that Bok became involved with its administration

Courtesy The Philadelphia Orchestra Association

vocal artists of the day through articles; it offered prizes for the best piano and vocal compositions; it had the leading critics of New York, Boston, and Chicago write articles explanatory of orchestral music and how to listen to music.

Meanwhile, Bok's marriage had brought music directly into his domestic circle. Mrs. Bok loved music, was a pianist herself, and she sought to acquaint her husband with what his former training had omitted. Hofmann and Bok had become strong friends outside of the editorial relation, and the pianist frequently visited the Bok home. But it was some time, even with these influences surrounding him, before music began to play any real part in Bok's own life.

He attended the opera occasionally; more or less under protest, because of its length, and because his mind was too practical for the indirect operatic form. He could not remain patient at a recital. The Philadelphia Orchestra gave a symphony concert each Saturday evening, and Bok dreaded the coming of that evening for fear of being taken to hear music he was convinced was "over his head."

Like many men of his practical nature, he had made up his mind on this point without ever having heard such a concert. Then, too, in the back of his mind there was a feeling that, while he was perfectly willing to offer the best that the musical world afforded in his magazine, his readers were primarily women, and the appeal of music, after all, he felt was largely, if not wholly, to the feminine nature.

In order to have first-hand information, Bok attended the concert that Saturday evening. The symphony, Dvorak's *New World Symphony*, amazed Bok by its beauty; he was more astonished that he could so easily grasp any music in symphonic form. He was equally surprised at his own perfectly absorbed attention during Hofmann's playing of a rather long concerto.

The pianist's performance was so beautiful that the audience was uproarious in its approval; it had calculated, of course, upon an encore. But earlier, Leopold Stokowski, the young conductor of the orchestra, had determined to eliminate encores, and had personally enlisted Bok's help in this. So, although the pianist appeared and bowed his thanks several times, there was no encore; the stage hands appeared and moved the piano to one side, and the audience relapsed into unsatisfied and rather bewildered silence.

Then followed Bok's publicity work in the newspapers, beginning the next day, exonerating Hofmann and explaining the situation. The following week, with Mischa Elman as soloist, the audience once more tried to have its way and its cherished encore, but again none was forthcoming. Once more the newspapers explained; the battle was won, and the no-encore rule has prevailed at the Philadelphia Orchestra concerts from that day to this.

But the bewildered Bok could not make out exactly what had happened to his preconceived notion about symphonic music. He attended another concert the following Saturday; he listened to a Brahms symphony that pleased him even more than had *The New World,* and when, two weeks later, he heard the Tschaikovsky *Pathetique* and later the *Unfinished* symphony, by Schumann,[1] and a Beethoven symphony, attracted by each in turn, he realized that his prejudice against the whole question of symphonic music had been both wrongly conceived and baseless.

He now began to see the possibility of a whole world of beauty which up to that time had been closed to him, and he made up his mind that he would enter it. Somehow or other, he found the appeal of music did not confine itself to women; it seemed to have a message for men. After a busy week, he discovered that nothing he had ever experienced served to quiet him so much as these end-of-the-week concerts.

Bok concluded he would not read the articles he had published on the meaning of different "sections" of a symphony orchestra, or the books issued on that subject. He would try to solve the mechanism of an orchestra for himself, and ascertain as he went along the relation that each portion bore to the other. When, therefore, in 1913, the president of the Philadelphia Orchestra Association asked him to become a member of its Board of Directors, his acceptance was a natural step in the gradual development of his interest in orchestral music.

The public support given to orchestras now greatly

[1]Bok errs in attributing the *Unfinished Symphony* to Robert Schumann; it was composed by Franz Schubert.

interested Bok. He was surprised to find that every symphony orchestra had a yearly deficit. This he immediately attributed to faulty management; but on investigating the whole question, he then learned that a symphony orchestra could not possibly operate at a profit or even on a self-sustaining basis, because of its weekly change of program, the incessant rehearsals required, and the limited number of times it could actually play within a contracted season. An annual deficit was inevitable.

He found that the Philadelphia Orchestra had a small but faithful group of guarantors who each year made good the deficit in addition to paying for its concert seats. This did not seem to Bok a sound business plan; it made of the orchestra a necessarily exclusive organization, maintained by a few; and it gave out this impression to the general public, which felt that it did not "belong," whereas the true relation of public and orchestras, he found, was mutual dependence. On the other hand, the Boston Symphony and the New York Philharmonic had their deficits met by one individual patron in each case. This, to Bok's mind, was an even worse system, since it entirely excluded the public, making the orchestra dependent on the continued interest and life of a single man.

In 1916, Bok sought Mr. Alexander Van Rensselaer, the president of the Philadelphia Orchestra Association, and proposed that he, himself, should guarantee the deficit of the orchestra for five years, provided that during that period an endowment fund should be raised, contributed by a large number of subscribers, and sufficient in amount to meet, from its interest, the annual deficit. It was agreed that the donor should remain in strict anonymity, an understanding which has been adhered to until the present writing.

The offer from the "anonymous donor," presented by the president, was accepted by the Orchestra Association. A subscription to an endowment fund was shortly afterward begun; and the amount had been brought to $800,000 when the Great War interrupted any further additions. In the autumn of 1919, however, a citywide campaign for an addition of $1 million to the endowment fund was launched. The amount was not only secured, but oversubscribed. Thus, instead of a guarantee fund, contributed by 1,300 subscribers, with the necessity for annual collection, an endowment fund of $1.8 million, contributed by 14,000 subscribers, had been secured; and the Philadelphia Orchestra has been promoted from a privately maintained organization to a public institution in which 14,000 residents of Philadelphia feel a proprietary interest. It has become in fact, as well as in name, "our orchestra."

XXIX

How Millions of People Are Reached

THE SUCCESS OF *The Ladies' Home Journal* went steadily forward. The circulation had passed the previously unheard of figure for a monthly magazine of 1.5 million copies per month; it had now touched 1.75 million.

And not only was the figure so high, but the circulation was absolutely free from "water." The public could not obtain the magazine through what are known as clubbing rates, since no subscriber was permitted to include any other magazine with it; years ago it had abandoned the practice of offering premiums or consideration of any kind to induce subscriptions; the news dealers were not allowed to return unsold copies of the periodical. Hence every copy was either purchased by the public at the full price at a newsstand, or subscribed for at its stated subscription price. It was, in short, an authoritative circulation. And on every hand the question was being asked: "How is it done? How is such a high circulation obtained?"

Bok's invariable answer was that he gave his readers the very best of the reading that he believed would interest them, and that he spared neither effort nor expense to obtain it for them. When Mr. Howells once asked him how he classified his audience, Bok replied: "We appeal to the intelligent American woman rather than to the intellectual type." And he gave her the best he could obtain. As he knew her to be fond of the personal type of literature, he gave her in succession Jane Addams's story of "My Fifteen Years at Hull House," and the remarkable narration of Helen Keller's "Story of My Life"; he invited Henry Van Dyke,[1] who had never been in the Holy Land, to go there, camp out in a tent, and then write a series of sketches, "Out of Doors in the Holy Land"; he induced Lyman Abbott to tell the story of "My Fifty Years as a Minister." He asked Gene Stratton Porter[2] to tell of her bird experiences in the series: "What I Have Done with Birds"; he persuaded Dean Hodges[3] to turn from his work of training young clergymen at the Episcopal Seminary, at Cambridge, and write one the most successful series of Bible stories for children ever printed; and then he supplemented this feature for children by publish-

---

[1]Henry Van Dyke was pastor of United Congregational Church at Newport, Rhode Island, and the Brick Presbyterian Church in New York, as well as a prolific author and poet who became particularly famous for such stories as "The Fourth Wise Man"; he also was renowned as a public speaker.

[2]Gene Stratton Porter, pseudonym of Geneva Grace Stratton Porter, was an American writer, photographer, illustrator, nature lover, and novelist whose most famous work, *A Girl of the Limberlost,* was published in 1909.

[3]George Hodges, a prominent Episcopal clergyman and prolific author, was dean of Episcopal Theological School (now Episcopal Divinity School), Cambridge, Massachusetts, from 1894 to 1919.

ing Rudyard Kipling's "Just So" stories and his "Puck of Pook's Hill." He induced F. Hopkinson Smith[4] to tell the best stories he had ever heard in his wide travels in "The Man in the Arm Chair"; he got Kate Douglas Wiggin[5] to tell a country church experience of hers in "The Old Peabody Pew"; and Jean Webster[6] her knowledge of almshouse life in "Daddy Long Legs."

The readers of the *Journal* realized that it searched the whole field of endeavor in literature and art to secure what would interest them, and they responded with their support. Another of Bok's methods in editing was to do the common thing in an uncommon way. He had the faculty of putting old wine in new bottles and the public liked it. His ideas were not new; he knew there were not new ideas, but he presented his ideas in such a way that they seemed new. It is a significant fact, too, that a large public will respond more

[4]Francis Hopkinson Smith was an artist, novelist, and mechanical engineer who designed the star-shaped base of the Statue of Liberty, wrote a long list of novels and stories, and created award-winning paintings. Scribner's published a twenty-three volume set of his works between 1902 and 1915.

[5]Kate Douglas (Smith) Wiggin was an American pioneer in kindergarten education who used reading aloud, dramatics, and music in teaching and training young children, some of whom came from severely disadvantaged circumstances. A superb story teller, she wrote tales for children, including her most famous book, *Rebecca of Sunnybrook Farm* (1903).

[6]Jean Webster, pseudonym of Alice Jane Chandler, was a popular writer of stories for young women. Her best-known work, *Daddy-Long-Legs* (1912), has never gone out of print.

quickly to an idea than it will to just simply a name.

This the *Journal* proved again and again. Its most pronounced success, from the point of view of circulation, were those in which the idea was the sole and central appeal. For instance, when it gave American women an opportunity to look into a hundred homes and see how they were furnished, it added 100,000 copies to the circulation. There was nothing new in publishing pictures of rooms and, had it merely done this, it is questionable whether success could have followed the effort. It was the way in which it was done. The note struck entered into the feminine desire, reflected it, piqued curiosity, and won success.

Again, when the *Journal* decided to show good taste and bad taste in furniture, in comparative pictures, another 100,000 circulation came to it. There was certainly nothing new in the comparative idea; but applied to a question of taste, which could not be explained so clearly in words, it seemed new.

Had it simply presented masterpieces of art as such, the series might have attracted little attention. But when it announced that these masterpieces had always been kept in private galleries, and seen only by the favored few; that the public had never been allowed to get any closer to them than to read of the fabulous prices paid by their millionaire owners; and that now the magazine would open the doors of those exclusive galleries and let the public in—public curiosity was at once piqued, and over 150,000 persons who had never bought the magazine were added.

In not one of these instances, nor in the case of other successful series, did the appeal to the public depend upon the names of contributors; there were none: it was the idea which the public liked and to which it responded.

The editorial Edward Bok enjoyed this hugely; the real Edward Bok did not. The one was bottled up in the other. It was a case of absolute self effacement. The man behind the editor knew that if he followed his own personal tastes and expressed them in his magazine, a limited audience would be his instead of the enormous clientele that he was now reaching. It was the man behind the editor who had sought expression in the idea of *Country Life,* the magazine which his company sold to Doubleday, Page & Company, and which he would personally have enjoyed editing.

It was in 1913 that the real Edward Bok, bottled up for twenty-five years, again came to the surface. The majority stockholders of the *Century Magazine* wanted to dispose of their interest in the periodical. Overtures were made to The Curtis Publishing Company, but its hands were already full, and the matter was presented for Bok's personal consideration. The idea did interest him, as he saw in the *Century* a chance for his self expression. He entered into negotiations, looked carefully into the property itself and over the field which such a magazine might fill, decided to buy it, and install an active editor while he, as a close adviser, served as the propelling power.

Bok figured out that there was room for one of the trio of what was, and still is, called the standard-sized magazine, namely *Scribner's, Harper's,* and the *Century.* He believed, as he does today, that any one of these magazine could be so edited as to preserve all its traditions and yet be so ingrafted with the new progressive, modern spirit as to dominate the field and constitute itself the leader in that particular group. He believed that there was a field which would produce a circulation in the neighborhood of a quarter of a million copies a month for one of those magazines so that it would be considered not, as now, one of three, but *the* one.

What Bok saw in the possibilities of the standard illustrated magazine has been excellently carried out by Mr. Ellery Sedgwick in the *Atlantic Monthly;* every tradition has been respected, and yet the new progressive note introduced has given it a position and a circulation never before attained by a nonillustrated magazine of the highest class.

As Bok studied the field, his confidence in the proposition, as he saw it, grew. For his own amusement, he made up some six issues of the *Century* as he visualized it, and saw that the articles he had included were all obtainable. He selected a business manager and publisher who would relieve him of the manufacturing problems; but before the contract was actually closed Bok wanted to consult Mr. Curtis, who was just returning from abroad, as to this proposed sharing of his editor.

For one man to edit two magazines inevitably meant a distribution of effort, and this Mr. Curtis counseled against. He did not believe that any man could successfully serve two masters; it would also mean a division of public association; it might result in Bok's physical undoing, as already he was overworked. Mr. Curtis's arguments, of course, prevailed; the negotiations were immediately called off, and for the second time—for some wise reason, undoubtedly—the real Edward Bok was subdued. He went back into the bottle!

A cardinal point in Edward Bok's code of editing was not to commit his magazine to unwritten material, or to accept and print articles or stories simply because they were the work of well known persons. And as his acquaintance with authors multiplied, he found that the greater the man the more willing he was that his work should stand or fall on its merit, and that the editor should retain his prerogative on declination—if he deemed it wise to exercise it.

Rudyard Kipling was, and is, a notable example of this broad and just policy. His work is never imposed upon an editor; it is invariably submitted, in its completed form, for acceptance or declination. "Wait until it's done," said Kipling once to Bok as he outlined a story to him which the author liked, "and see whether you want it. You can't tell until then." (What a difference from the author who insists that an editor must take his or her story before a line is written!)

"I told Watt to send you," he writes to Bok, "the

first four of my child stories (you see I hadn't forgotten my promise), and they may serve to amuse you for a while personally, even if you don't use them for publication. Frankly, I don't myself see how they can be used for the L.H.J.; but they're part of a scheme of mine for trying to give children *not* a notion of history, but a notion of the time sense which is at the bottom of all knowledge of history; and history, rightly understood, means the love of one's fellow men and the land one lives in."

A turning point in his editing which Bok always kept in view was his rule that the editor must always be given the privilege of revising or editing a manuscript. Bok's invariable rule was, of course, to submit his editing for approval, but here again the bigger the personality back of the material, the more willing the author was to have his manuscript "blue-pencilled," if he were convinced that the deletions or condensations improved or at least did not detract from his arguments. It was the small author who ever resented the touch of the editorial pencil upon his precious effusions.

As a matter of fact there are few authors who cannot be edited with advantage, and it would be infinitely better for our reading if this truth was applied to some of the literature of today.

Bok had once under his hand a story by Mark Twain, which he believed contained passages that should be deleted. They represented a goodly portion of the manuscript. They were, however, taken out, and the result submitted to the humorist. The answer was curious. Twain evidently saw that Bok was right, for he wrote: "Of course, I want every single line and word of it left out," and then added: "Do me the favor to call the next time you are again in Hartford. I want to say things which—well, I want to argue with you." Bok never knew what those "things" were, for at the next meeting they were not referred to.

It is, perhaps, a curious coincidence that all of the presidents of the United States whose work Bok had occasion to publish were uniformly liberal with regard to having their material edited.

Colonel Roosevelt was always ready to concede improvement: "Fine," he wrote; "the changes are much for the better, I never object to my work being improved, where it needs it, so long as the sense is not altered."

William Howard Taft wrote, after being subjected to editorial revision: "You have done very well by my article. You have made it more readable by your rearrangement."

It was always interesting to Bok, as a study of mental processes, to note how differently he and some author with whom he would talk it over would see the method of treating some theme. He was discussing the growing unrest among American women with Rudyard Kipling at the latter's English home, and expressed the desire that the novelist should treat the subject and its causes.

They talked until the early hours, when it was

agreed that each should write out a plan, suggest the best treatment, and come together the next morning. When they did so, Kipling had mapped out the scenario of a novel; Bok had sketched out the headings of a series of analytical articles. Neither one could see the other's viewpoint, Kipling contending for the greater power of fiction and Bok strongly arguing for the value of the direct essay. In this instance, the point was never settled, for the work failed to materialize in any form!

If the readers of *The Ladies' Home Journal* were quick to support its editor when he presented an idea that appealed to them, they were equally quick to tell him when he gave them something of which they did not approve. An illustration of this occurred during the dance craze that preceded the Great War. In 1914, America was dance mad, and the character of the dances rapidly grew more and more offensive. Bok's readers, by the hundred, urged him to come out against the tendency.

The editor looked around and found that the country's terpsichorean idols were Mr. and Mrs. Vernon Castle; he decided that, with their cooperation, he might, by thus going to the fountainhead, effect an improvement through the introduction, by the Castles, of better and more decorous dances. Bok could see no reason why the people should not dance, if they wanted to, so long as they kept within the boundaries of decency.

He found the Castles willing and eager to cooperate, not only because of the publicity it would mean for them, but because they were themselves not in favor of the new mode. They had little sympathy for the elimination of the graceful dance by the introduction of what they called the "shuffle" or the "bunny-hug," "turkey-trot," and other ungraceful dances. It was decided that the Castles should, through Bok's magazine and their own public exhibitions, revive the gavotte, the polka, and finally the waltz. They would evolve these into new forms and Bok would present them pictorially. A series of three double-page presentations was decided upon, allowing for large photographs so that the steps could be easily seen and learned from the printed page.

The magazine containing the first "lesson" was no sooner published than protests began to come in by the hundreds. Bok had not stated his object, and the public misconstrued his effort and purpose into an acknowledgement that he had fallen a victim to the prevailing craze. He explained in letters, but to no purpose. Try as he might, Bok could not rid the pages of the savor of the cabaret. He published the three dances as agreed, but he realized he had made a mistake, and was as much disgusted as were his readers. Nor did he, in the slightest degree, improve the dance situation. The public refused to try the new Castle dances, and kept on turkey-trotting and bunny-hugging.

The *Journal* followed the Castle lessons with a series of the most beautiful dances of Madam Pavlova, the Russian dancer, hoping to remove the unfavorable impression of the former series. But it was only partially successful. Bok had made a mistake in recognizing the craze at all; he should have ignored it, as he had so often in the past ignored other temporary, superficial hysterics of the public. The *Journal* readers knew the magazine had made a mistake and frankly said so.

Which shows that, even after having been for over twenty-five years in the editorial chair, Edward Bok was by no means infallible in his judgment of what the public wanted or would accept.

No man is, for that matter.

XXX

A War Magazine and War Activities

W HEN, early in 1917, events began to shape themselves as directly to point to the entrance of the
United States into the Great War, Edward Bok set
upon himself to formulate a policy for *The Ladies'
Home Journal.* He knew that he was in an almost in-
surmountably difficult position. The huge edition ne-
cessitated going to press fully six weeks in advance of
publication, and the preparation of material fully four
weeks prior to that. He could not, therefore, get much
closer than ten weeks to the date when his readers received the magazine. And he knew that events, in war
time, had a way of moving rapidly.

Late in January he went to Washington, consulted
those authorities who could indicate possibilities to
him better than anyone else, and found, as he had sus-
pected, that the entry of the United States into the war
was a practical certainty; it was only a question of time.

Bok went south for a month's holiday to get ready
for the fray, and in the saddle and on the golf links he
formulated a policy. The newspapers and weeklies
would send innumerable correspondents to the front,
and obviously, with the necessity for going to press so
far in advance, the *Journal* could not compete with
them. They would depict every activity in the field.

There was but one logical thing for him to do: ignore the "front" entirely, refuse all the offers of correspondents, men and women, who wanted to go with the armies for his magazine, and cover fully and practically the results of the war as they would affect the women left behind. He went carefully over the ground to see what these would be, along what particular lines women's activities would be most likely to go, and then went home and back to Washington.

It was now March. He conferred with the president,[1] had his fears confirmed, and offered all of the resources of his magazine to the government. His diagnosis of the situation was verified in every detail by the authorities whom he consulted. The *Journal* could best serve by keeping up the morale at home and by helping to meet the problems that would confront the women.

A year before, Bok had opened a separate editorial office in Washington and had secured Dudley Harmon, the Washington correspondent for the *New York Sun,* as his editor-in-charge. The purpose was to bring the women of the country into a clearer understanding of their government and a closer relation with it. This work had been so successful as to necessitate a force of four offices and twenty stenographers. Bok now placed this Washington office on a war-time basis, bringing it into close relation with every department of the government connected with war activities.

[1]A reference to Woodrow Wilson.

Bok learned that the country's first act would be to recruit for the navy, so as to get this branch of the service into a state of preparedness. He therefore secured Franklin D. Roosevelt, assistant secretary of the navy, to write an article explaining to mothers why they should let their boys volunteer for the navy and what it would mean to them.

He made arrangements at the American Red Cross Headquarters for an official department to begin at once in the magazine, telling women the first steps that would be taken by the Red Cross and how they could help. He secured former President William Howard Taft, as chairman of the Central Committee of the Red Cross, for the editor of this department.

He cabled to Viscount Northcliffe[2] and Ian Hay[3] for articles showing what the English women had done at the outbreak of the war, the mistakes they had made, what errors the American women should avoid.

And so it happened that when the first war issue of the *Journal* appeared on 20 April, only three weeks after the president's declaration, it was the only

[2]Viscount Northcliffe (Alfred Harmsworth) was one of the most important newspaper publishers in British history. In 1896, he established the *Daily Mail,* which became a sensational success. By the end of the century, Harmsworth, a supporter of the Conservative Party, had become one of the most powerful men in Great Britain. During World War I, Harmsworth became minister of information, which is why Bok was writing him for material relating to the roles played by British women in that conflict.

[3]Ian Hay, pseudonym of Sir John Hay Beith, was a British writer of short stories, novels, plays, and nonfictional books.

monthly that recognized the existence of war, and its pages had already begun to indicate practical lines along which women could help.

The editor had been told that the question of food would come to be of paramount importance. The Food Administration was no sooner organized than Bok made arrangements for an authoritative department to be conducted in his magazine, reflecting the plans and desires of the Food Administration, and Herbert Hoover's first public declaration as food administrator to the women of America was published in the *Journal*. Bok now placed all the resources of his four-color press work at Mr. Hoover's disposal. The food administration's domestic experts, in conjunction with the full culinary staff of the magazine, had prepared the new war dishes and presented them appetizingly in full colors.

Doctor Anna Howard Shaw had been appointed chairman of the National Committee of the Women's Council of National Defense, and Bok arranged at once with her that she should help edit a department page in his magazine, setting forth the plans of the committee and how the women of America could cooperate therewith. The magazine had thus practically become the semiofficial mouthpiece of all the various government war bureaus and war-work bodies.

The magazine reflected in full-color pictures the life and activities of the boys in the American camps, and William C. Gorgas, surgeon-general of the United States, was the spokesman in the magazine for the

"For God's Sake Send Food:
Thousands of Little Ones are Starving"

THIS is the fearful cry that comes over the cable from one of the most conservative of American men on the spot in Belgium.

Never before in the history of the world has there been a condition to compare with it. No language has words to describe it. Women and children are without shelter, food or clothing. Babies are dying by the hundreds. There never was such a thing. It is unutterable and incomprehensible.

The American Ambassador at London, Walter H. Page, cables to me personally:

"There Never Was Such Dire Want in Any Land
at Any Time in the History of the World"

That is why Her Majesty the Queen of the Belgians brushes aside all precedent and etiquette, and from her heart, as a woman and a mother, cables to a great magazine an appeal to the mothers and women of America to help her starving people.

Her cry is not that of a Queen, but that of a woman and a mother; and her appeal should bring forth the greatest response ever given to a woman.

So let every man and woman open his or her heart, and give! If you have perhaps given already to a local Belgian fund, give again to this Queen of the Belgians Fund. Don't think you can give too much. Listen, again, to what Ambassador Page cables:

"It Will Require Five Millions of Dollars Each Month
for All Winter Just for Food"

Give at this happy Christmastime. Give what you intended for presents. Go without your own Christmas. Give your Christmas money that you may receive.

But give: Give what you can and all you can: in large amounts or small.

Other neutral countries are doing their share, but it is great, rich and generous America that must do the larger part. Shall the Queen and her starving mothers and children look to us in vain? No, a thousand times, No!

A special buying committee composed of well-known merchants has been organized in Philadelphia, that will at once translate your money into foodstuffs—flour, peas, beans, yeast, salt, bacon, barley, etc—buying at wholesale at the lowest prices. And under the supervision of the Ambassadors and Ministers abroad the food will be distributed directly to the stricken Belgians. All our arrangements are perfected for the work.

We are ready to buy. Will you give?

Let the noble Queen of the Belgians, herself in the trenches and on the firing line with her husband, receive the greatest outpouring of affection from the women of America that any woman has ever experienced.

Read carefully, on page 7, how and where to send your money. But send it generously and quickly, for the need is urgent.

Without America thousands of children will starve; with America they shall not!

Do your part and do all you can: large and small.

The War is Not Ours,
But a Starving Child Touches All of Us

I will personally see that every penny you send is wisely spent and for the right foods.

Edward Bok

Editor of The Ladies' Home Journal and Vice-President of the Belgian Relief Fund.

Bok's efforts in the Journal to assist children
in war-torn Belgium, January 1915

health of the boys. The president of the United States, in a special message to women, wrote in behalf of the subsequent Loan; Bernard Baruch, as chairman of the War Industries Board, made clear the need for war time thrift; and Elizabeth, queen of the Belgians, explained the plight of the babies and children of Belgium, and made a plea to the women of the magazine to help. So straight to the point did the queen write, and so well did she present her case that within six months there had been sent to her, through the *Journal,* 248,000 cans of condensed milk, 72,000 cans of pork and beans, 5,000 cans of infants' prepared food, 80,000 cans of beef soup, and nearly 4,000 bushels of wheat, purchased with the money donated by the magazine readers.

The Committee on Public Information now sought the magazine for the issuance of a series of official announcements explanatory of matters to women. When the "meatless" and the "wheatless" days were inaugurated, the women of America found that the magazine had anticipated their coming. The issue that appeared on the first of these days, as publicly announced by the Food Administration, presented pages of substitutes in full colors.

Of course, miscellaneous articles on the war there were, without number. Before the war was ended, the magazine did send a representative to the front in Catherine Van Dyke, who did most effective work for the magazine in articles of a general nature. The full-page battle pictures, painted from data furnished by those who took actual part, were universally commended and exhausted even the largest editions that could be printed. A source of continual astonishment was the number of copies of the magazine found among the boys in France; it became the third in the official War Department list of the most desired American periodicals, evidently representing a tie between the boys and their home folks.

Considering the difficulties to be surmounted, due to the advance preparation of material, and considering that, at the best, most of its advance information, even by the highest authorities, could only be in the nature of surmise, the comprehensive manner in which the *Journal* covered every activity of women during the Great War will always remain one of the magazine's most noteworthy achievements. This can be said without reserve here, since the credit is due to no single person; it was the combined, careful work of its entire staff, weighing every step before it was taken, and always seeking the most authoritative sources of information.

With the establishment of the various war boards in Washington, Bok received overtures to associate himself exclusively with them and move to the capital. He sought the best advice and with his own instincts pointing in the same way, he decided that he could give his fullest service by retaining his editorial position and adding to that such activities as his leisure allowed. He undertook several private commissions for the United States government, and then he was elected vice-president of the Philadelphia Belgian Relief Commission.

With the Belgian consul-general for the United States, Mr. Paul Hagemans, as the president of the commission, and guided by his intimate knowledge of the Belgian people, Bok selected a committee of the ablest buyers and merchants in the special lines of foods which he would have to handle. The commission raised hundreds of thousands of dollars, with which it purchased foods and chartered ships. The quantities of food ran into prodigious figures; Bok felt that he was feeding the world; and yet when the holds of the ships began to take in the thousands of crates of canned goods, the bags of peas and beans, and the endless tins of condensed milk, it was amazing how the piled-up boxes melted from the piers and the ship-holds yawned for more. Flour was sent in seemingly endless hundreds of barrels.

Each line of goods was bought by a specialist on the committee at the lowest quantity prices; and the result was that the succession of ships leaving the port of Philadelphia was a credit to the generosity of the people of the city and the commonwealth. The commission delegated one of its members to go to Belgium and personally see that the food actually reached the Belgian people.

In September 1917, word was received from John R. Mott that Bok had been appointed state chairman for the Y.M.C.A. War Work Council for Pennsylvania; that a countrywide campaign for $25 million would be launched six weeks hence, and that Pennsylvania's quota was $3 million. He was to set up an organization throughout the state, conduct the drive from Philadelphia, speak at various centers in Pennsylvania, and secure the allocated quota. Bok knew little or nothing about the work of the Y.M.C.A.; he accordingly went to New York headquarters and familiarized himself with the work being done and proposed; and then began to set up his state machinery. The drive came off as scheduled, Pennsylvania doubled its quota, subscribing $6 million instead of $3 million, and of this was collected $5,829,000.

Bok, who was now put on the National War Work Council of the Y.M.C.A. at New York, was asked to take part in the creation of the machinery necessary for the gigantic piece of work that the organization had been called upon by the president of the United States to do. It was a herculean task; practically impossible with any large degree of efficiency in view of the almost insurmountable obstacles to be contended with. But step by step the imperfect machinery was set up, and it began to function in the home camps. Then the overseas work was introduced by the first troops going to France, and the difficulties increased.

But Bok's knowledge of the workings of the government departments at Washington, the war boards, and the other war-work organizations soon convinced him that the Y.M.C.A. was not the only body asked to set up an organization almost overnight, that was staggering under its load and falling down as often as it was functioning.

The need for Y.M.C.A. secretaries overseas and in the camps soon became acute, and Bok was appointed chairman of the Philadelphia Recruiting Committee. As in the case of his Belgian relief work, he at once surrounded himself with an able committee: this time composed of business and professional men trained in a knowledge of human nature in the large, and of wide acquaintance in the city. Simultaneously, Bok secured the release of one of the ablest men in the Y.M.C.A. service in New York, Edward S. Wilkinson, who became the permanent secretary of the Philadelphia committee. Bok organized a separate committee composed of automobile manufacturers to recruit for chauffeurs and mechanicians; another separate committee recruited for physical directors, and later a third committee recruited for women.

The work was difficult because the field of selection was limited. No men between the military ages could be recruited; the War Boards at Washington had drawn heavily upon the best men of the city; the slightest physical defect barred out a man, on account of the exposure and strain of the Y.M.C.A. work; the residue was not large.

It was scarcely to be wondered at that so many incompetent secretaries had been passed and sent over to France. How could it have been otherwise with the restricted selection? But the Philadelphia committee was determined, nevertheless, that its men should be of the best, and it decided that to get a hundred men of unquestioned ability would be to do a greater job than to send over 200 men of indifferent quality.

Bok took large advertising spaces in the Philadelphia newspapers, asking for men of exceptional character to go to France in the service of the Y.M.C.A. Members of the committee spoke before different commercial bodies at their noon luncheons. The applicants now began to come, and the committee began its discriminating selection. Each applicant was carefully questioned by the secretary before he appeared before the committee, which held sittings twice a week. Hence, of over 2,500 applicants, only 300 appeared before the committee, of whom 258 were passed and sent overseas.

The committee's work was exceptionally successful; it soon proved of so excellent a quality as to elicit a cabled request from Paris headquarters to send more men of the Philadelphia type. The secret of this lay in the sterling personnel of the committee itself, and its interpretation of the standards required; and so well did it work that when Bok left for the front to be absent from Philadelphia for ten weeks, his committee did some of its best work.

The after-results, according to the report of the New York headquarters, showed that no Y.M.C.A. recruiting committee had equaled the work of the Philadelphia committee in that its men, in point of service, had proved 100 percent secretaries. With two exceptions, the entire 258 men passed, brought back

100 percent records, some of them having been placed in the most important posts abroad and having given the difficult service. The work of the other Philadelphia committees, particularly that of the Women's Committee, was equally good.

To do away with the multiplicity of "drives," rapidly becoming a drain upon the efforts of the men engaged in them, a War Chest Committee was now formed in Philadelphia and vicinity to collect money for all the war-work agencies. Bok was made a member of the Executive Committee, and chairman of the Publicity Committee. In May 1918, a campaign for $20 million was started; the amount was subscribed, and although much of it had to be collected after the Armistice, since the subscriptions were in twelve monthly payments, a total of $15.5 million was paid in total and turned over to the different agencies.

Bok, who had been appointed one of the Boy Scout commissioners in his home district of Merion, saw the possibilities of the Boy Scouts in the Liberty Loan and other campaigns. Although only "gleaners" in most of the campaigns—that is, working only in the last three days after the regular committees had scoured the neighborhood—the Merion Boy Scouts sold over $1.4 million in Liberty Bonds, and raised enough money in the Y.M.C.A. campaign to erect one of the largest huts in France for the army boys, and a Y.M.C.A. gymnasium at the League Island Navy Yard accommodating 2,000 sailor boys.

In the summer of 1918, the eight leading war-work

agencies, excepting the Red Cross, were merged, for the purpose of one drive for funds, into the United War Work Campaign, and Bok was made chairman for Pennsylvania. In November, a countrywide campaign was launched, the quota for Pennsylvania being $20 million—the largest amount ever asked of the commonwealth. Bok organized a committee of the representative men of Pennsylvania, and proceeded to set up the machinery to secure the huge sum. He had no sooner done this, however, than he had to sail for France, returning only a month before the beginning of the campaign.

But the efficient committee had done its work; upon his return Bok found the organization complete. On the first day of the campaign, the false rumor that an armistice had been signed made the raising of the large amount seem almost hopeless; furthermore, owing to the influenza raging throughout the commonwealth,[4] no public meetings had been permitted or held. Still, despite all these obstacles, not only was the $20 million subscribed but oversubscribed to the extent of nearly $1 million; and in face of the fact that every penny of this large total had to be collected after the signing of the Armistice late in 1918, $20 million

[4]Beginning in September 1918, the worst influenza pandemic in history swept around the world. According to a recent study by Gina Kolata, a science reporter for the *New York Times,* "Estimates [of the number killed by the disease] range from 20 million to 100 million, but the true number can never be known." It killed 2.5 percent of its victims as opposed to .001 percent in ordinary influenzas, making it 25 times as lethal.

was paid in and been turned over to the war agencies.

He had now seen and come into personal knowledge of the work of the Y.M.C.A. from his Philadelphia point of vantage, with his official connection with it at New York headquarters; he had seen the work as it was done in the London and Paris headquarters; and he had seen the actual work in the American camps, the English rest camps, back of the French lines, in the trenches, and as near the firing line as he had been permitted to go.

He had, in short, seen the Y.M.C.A. function from every angle, but he had also seen the work of the other organizations in England and France, back of the lines and in the trenches. He found them all faulty—necessarily so. Each had endeavored to create an organization within an incredibly short space of time and in the face of adverse circumstances.

The Y.W.C.A. made little claim about its work in France, since the United States government would not, until nearly at the close of the war, allow women to be sent over in the uniforms of any of the war-work organizations. But no one can gainsay for a single moment the efficient service rendered by the Y.W.C.A. in its hostess-house work in the American camps; that work alone would have entitled it to the support of the American people. That of the Y.M.C.A. was on so large a scale that naturally its inefficiency was often in proportion to its magnitude.

Bok was in France when a large storm of criticism against the Y.M.C.A. broke out, and, since he was state

What I Have Seen

A Personal Message From the Western Front to the Readers of The Ladies' Home Journal: By the Editor

I AM writing this "somewhere in France." I have spent days in the battle area between the base ports and the British and French front. I have traversed hundreds of miles through tracts of devastation that forbid description. We were the first civilians to penetrate into certain front-line spots of the Amiens-Béthune, Albert-Péronne, Bapaume-Soissons and Saint Mihiel sections within two weeks after their evacuation by the Germans, where débris lay at a depth of six feet in the streets and the German dead were still unburied. The scenes of absolutely complete devastation and wreckage of village after village and city after city will live in my memory, in all their stark and vivid horror, so long as memory lives. Describe them, I cannot. Before coming here I had visioned, as the reader doubtless has, a village here and there destroyed. Now I know. Not a village, or several villages, or even many villages, but rather a wave of villages, a chain, a continuous succession of not only villages but cities, and all so completely annihilated that the mind staggers in contemplation of them and the futility of words to describe their devastation.

ONE, for two hours, I motored through village after village wherein not a single house is standing to-day. Indeed, it is almost incomprehensible that any human force could be so complete in its power of destruction. I have seen piles of mud that to-day that yesterday was a village: areas of wreckages that once meant communities, but that to-day defy the belief that communities ever were here; spots of devastation that once were cities of three and four thousand happy men and women and children where not a house stands to-day: areas that once were forests where not a tree lifts its arms to God: ghastly fingers of masonry that once were cathedral spires: simple homes of the peasantry and stately châteaux of the rich wherein one cannot, in what is left of them, trace the walls of the rooms and apartments.

Nor was there any military reason for the destruction: nor was it, save in some small part, the unavoidable result of shell fire. It was due to the mine explosions of the retreating Germans, prompted by the military order that not a structure should be left standing. Never, even in the ruthless days of barbaric antiquity, was such despotic vandalism achieved!

YESTERDAY I rode through the heart of that marvelous battlefield of the Somme, fifty miles in length and one hundred in width, between Amiens and Péronne,—a battlefield that has been fought over, four times,—and in that vast area to-day not a house, not a barn, not even a tree remains. What was, less than five years ago, a magnificent stretch of populous and fertile land and superb forest is to-day a succession of gaping craters, of shell holes and of graves, each with its little unnamed cross simply. I saw, do that never-to-be-forgotten ride, acres of orchards, all beyond the range of the guns, yet all wantonly destroyed: and I personally saw what before I had hesitated to believe—entire cemeteries destroyed by mines which had been deliberately placed in vaults and tombs until to-day scores of these resting places of the dead gape wide open, with caskets shattered and corpses stark to the eye of the passer-by.

Never before has the world seen such wholesale destruction, reaching out even to the dead, who have not been allowed to sleep on in peace.

AT HOME we had spoken with an easy readiness of the rebuilding of these devastated districts of France: but when one confronts the frightful spectacle, face to face,—the completeness of the devastation and its awful extent,—when one realizes that cities that prided themselves upon four or five thousand houses are to-day mere piles of red dust, absolutely beyond repair or rebuilding, the mind becomes numb before the task, and the realization is for the first time brought home of the stupendous nature of the undertaking, and that years, and not months, will be required for its accomplishment.

And even then we cannot give back to these people their centuries-old cathedrals, their châteaux of historic and tender family association, nor yet the real "houses" that are gone forever.

One wonders, as he stands amid the ruins, where have gone those who dwelt here, and what will be their emotions when they return at last, to find everything that they had held dear reduced to red dirt and ashes.

I have seen the first of these refugees, aged and sorrow-bent, trekking back to what remains. I asked two or three of them where they were going, and each replied, with a smile: "Back home!" I could say nothing; but, O God, the anguish that will be theirs when they reach "home"!

BEFORE these indescribable scenes of fearful and deliberate destruction the great Army of the New World now stands with a grim determination to avenge these deliberate and wanton wrongs inflicted upon the homes and lives of these unfortunate people. And never was an army better fitted for its task, and never before has a nation sent forth such an army as is to-day the admiration of three peoples here.

During the past days I have seen thousands of our boys, and have sat beside British and French officers as they have viewed with unsfeigned admiration these young giants of physical fitness, well fed, well clothed, every one of them holding an attitude of thought and action toward morality that is absolutely austere, every eye alert, clear and dancing with merriment, each heart overflowing with a buoyant cheerfulness that has made the conservative Englishman, for the first time in his life, use superlatives when he speaks of the American Army; while the faces of the French officer and poilu positively radiate their delight.

The American Army is the most popular army that has ever gone upon a foreign battlefield: it is so positively and literally beloved that at this Christmastime the American woman may well feel a sense of glowing pride in having a part in such an army with such a mission to perform, and cherish a perfect ease of mind with regard to her boy who is "over here."

She need have no anxiety as to whether he is well looked after: he is the envy of every British and French soldier.

She need not worry about whether he is warmly clothed: no other army is so adequately equipped.

She need not ask herself whether he is well fed: his rations are the amazement of his Allied companions.

She need not worry as to his habits: intoxication simply does not exist and venereal diseases are negligible. The world has never before seen an army so clean of habit.

And if her boy is wounded the American woman need have no anxiety as to the care he will receive. I have visited base hospital after base hospital: I have walked through their wards. I have seen the boys carried in from the hospital trains. I have talked with them on their cots, and I have marveled at the completeness of every preparation and at the thoroughness of every detail. Indeed, no part of the American Army over here is such a triumph in the hospital service; it is nothing short of marvelous.

A WONDERFUL Christmas faces "Our Boys," whether they are in trench, dugout, on shipboard or in hospital. Nothing will be left undone to bring to each and every one of them the highest cheer of an American Christmas, as is becoming to the finest body of lads that any nation ever sent to fight for the most righteous cause in history.

And those of us "back home" may, at this Christmastime, cherish only one feeling: that of supreme confidence in their well-being, and in that superb body of men and women who are looking after their every necessity and their every comfort.

Edward Bok

Your Boy: By Henry van Dyke

YOUR boy has fallen on the field of honor, a brave defender of righteousness, humanity and freedom. May a stranger, who is also a friend, venture into the sacred quiet of your sorrow to say a word of sympathy and comfort?

He was your baby, your own, flesh of your flesh, bone of your bone—a long time you carried him under your heart. But all the while you wanted him to be a man, true and fearless. He was. He heard his country's call. He counted not his own life dear, but offered it gladly to defend the world from the menace of Prussian paganism.

Weep for him, yes: but do not forget to be proud of him, and to rejoice in him. No possible ending of his earthly life could have been more glorious, more rewarding for all that you have done for him, than this. He went forth, an American boy—your boy—to fight for the liberty and the peace of the world. You made him and you sent him. It is your right and duty to be proud of him.

Do not be anxious about his lot in the unseen world. Leave that to the Righteous God who is the Father of us all, and to Christ who said: "He that loveth his life for my sake shall find it." Self-sacrifice is the key to heaven.

You will never forget your boy. Do not think of him as dead, but as living—living! Be sure that he will look down from fields of eternal peace upon that victory over the German war lords which is surely coming, and which he helped to win. Be sure that you will see him again in a better world—

"Where loyal hearts and true
Stand ever in the light,
All rapture through and through,
In God's most holy sight."

chairman for Pennsylvania, it became his duty to meet the outcry when it came to the United States. That the work of the Y.M.C.A. was faulty no one can deny. Bok saw the "holes" long before they were called to the attention of the public, but he also saw the almost impossible task, in face of prevailing difficulties, of caulking them up. No one who was not in France can form any conception of the practically insurmountable obstacles against which all the war-work organizations worked; and the larger the work the greater were the obstacles, naturally. That the Y.M.C.A. and the other similar agencies made mistakes is not the wonder so much as that they did not make more. The real marvel is that they did so much efficient work.

What was actually accomplished was nothing short of marvellous; and it is this fact that must be borne in mind; not the omissions, but the commissions. And when the American public gets that point of view—as it will, and, for that matter, is already beginning to do—the work of the American Y.M.C.A. will no longer suffer for its omissions, but will amaze and gladden by its accomplishments. As an American officer of high rank said to Bok: "The mind cannot take in what the war would have been without the 'Y'." And that, in time, will be the universal American opinion, extended, in proportion to their work, to all the war-work agencies and the men and women who endured, suffered, and were killed in their service.

XXXI

At the Battle Fronts of the Great War

I<small>T WAS</small> in the summer of 1918 that Edward Bok received from the British government through its department of public information, of which the Lord Beaverbrook[1] was the minister, an invitation to join a party of thirteen American editors to visit Great Britain and France. The British government, not versed in publicity methods, was anxious that selected parties of American publicists should see, personally, what Great Britain had done, and was doing in the war; and it had decided to ask a few individuals to pay personal visits to its munitions factories, great aerodomes, the Great Fleet,[2] which lay in the Firth of Forth, and to the battlefields. It was understood that

[1] Lord Beaverbrook (William Maxwell Aitken) was a Canadian millionaire who moved to England in 1910. He was elected to Parliament in that same year as a Conservative. In 1916, he gained control of the London *Daily Express,* followed by the *Sunday Express* (1918) and *Evening Standard* (1923). All of these newspapers gained mass circulation and vigorously espoused his political and economic views, which were strongly in favor of private enterprise and imperial free trade. During World War II Beaverbrook served in Winston Churchill's cabinet as minister of aircraft production, minister of supply, and Lord Privy Seal, and was British lend-lease administrator in the United States in 1942.

[2] Bok refers to the British Grand Fleet, the principal fleet of the Royal Navy.

no specific obligation rested upon any member of the party to write of what he saw: he was asked simply to observe and then, with discretion, use his observations for his own guidance and information in future writing. In fact, each member was explicitly told that much of what he would see could not be revealed either personally or in print.

The party embarked in August amid all the attendant secrecy of war conditions. The steamer was known only by number, although later it turned out to be the White Star liner, *Adriatic*. Preceded by a powerful United States cruiser, flanked by destroyers, guided overhead by observation balloons, the *Adriatic* was found to be the first ship in a convoy of sixteen other ships with 30,000 United States troops on board.

It was a veritable armada that steamed out of lower New York on that early August morning, heading straight into the rising sun. But it was a voyage of unpleasant war reminders, with life savers carried every moment of the day, with every light out at night, with every window and door as if hermetically sealed so the stuffy cabins deprived of sleep those accustomed to fresh air, with over sixty army men and civilians on watch at night, with life drills each day, with lessons to behavior in lifeboats; and with a fleet of eighteen British destroyers meeting the convoy upon its approach to the Irish Coast after a thirteen days' voyage of constant anxiety. No one could say he traveled across the Atlantic Ocean in war days for pleasure, and no one did.

Once ashore, the party began a series of inspections of munition plants, shipyards, aeroplane factories and of meetings with the different members of the English war cabinet. Luncheons and dinners were the order of each day until broken by a journey to Edinburgh to see the amazing Great Fleet, with the addition of six of the foremost fighting machines of the United States Navy, all straining like dogs at leash, awaiting an expected dash from the bottled-up German fleet. It was a formidable sight, perhaps never equaled: those lines of huge, menacing, and yet protecting fighting machines stretching down the river for miles, all conveying the single thought of the power and extent of the British Navy and its formidable character as a fighting unit.

It was upon his return to London that Bok learned, through the confidence of a member of the British "inner circle," the amazing news that the war was practically over: that Bulgaria had capitulated and was suing for peace; that two of the Central Power provinces had indicated their strong desire that the war should end; and that the first peace intimations had gone to the president of the United States. All diplomatic eyes were turned toward Washington. Yet not a hint of the impending events had reached the public. The Germans were being beaten back, that was known; it was evident that the morale of the German army was broken; that Foch[3] had turned the tide

[3]Ferdinand Foch, marshal of France, became supreme commander of Allied armies in 1918 after a German offensive under

toward victory; but even the best-informed military authorities, outside of the inner diplomatic circles, predicted that the war would last until the spring of 1919, when a final "drive" would end it. Yet, at that very moment, the end of the war was in sight!

Next Bok went to France to visit the battlefields. It was arranged that the party should first, under guidance of British officers, visit back of the British lines; and then, successively, be turned over to the American and French governments, and visit the operations back of their armies.

It is an amusing fact that although each detail of officers delegated to escort the party "to the front" received the most explicit instructions from superior officers to take the party only to quiet sectors where there was no fighting going on, each detail from the three governments successively brought the party directly under shell fire, and each on the first day of the "inspection." It was unconsciously done: the officers were as much amazed to find themselves under fire as were the members of the party. The officers, in each case, were plainly worried: the editors were intensely interested.

There were depressing trips through miles and miles of devastated villages and small cities. From two

---

Erich von Ludendorff threatened to overwhelm the French-British-American forces defending the Western Front. After stopping the German drive, Foch organized a counter-offensive that recovered almost all of occupied France and part of Belgium before the Armistice of 11 November 1918.

to three days each were spent in front-line posts. Often, the party was the first civilian group to enter a town evacuated only a week before, and all the horrible evidence of bloody warfare was fresh and plain. Bodies of German soldiers lay in the trenches where they had fallen; wired bombs were on every hand, so that no object could be touched that lay on the battlefields; the streets of some of the towns were still mined, so that no automobiles could enter; the towns were deserted, the streets desolate. It was an appalling panorama of the most frightful results of war.

The picturesqueness and romance of the war of picture books were missing. To stand beside an English battery of thirty guns laying a barrage as they fired their shells to a point ten miles distant, made one feel as if one were an actual part of real warfare, and yet far removed from it, until the battery was located from the enemy's "sausage observation";[4] then the shells from the enemy fired a return salvo, and the better part of valor was discretion a few miles farther back.

The amazing part of the "show," however, was the American doughboy. Never was there a more cheerful, laughing, good natured set of boys in the world; never a more homesick, lonely, and complaining set. But good nature predominated, and the smile was always uppermost, even when the moment looked the blackest and the privations were worst.

Bok had been talking to a boy who lived near his

[4]Refers to German observation balloons.

own home, who was on his way to the front and "over the top" in the Argonne mess. Three days afterward, at a hospital base where a hospital train was just discharging its load of wounded, Bok walked among the boys as they lay on their stretchers on the railroad platform waiting for bearers to carry them into the huts. As he approached one stretcher, a cheery voice called, "Hello, Mr. Bok. Here I am again."

It was the boy he had left just seventy-two hours before hearty and well.

"Well, my boy, you weren't in it long, were you?"

"No, sir," answered the boy. "Fritzie sure got me first thing. Hadn't gone a hundred yards over the top. Got a cigarette (the invariable question)?"

Bok handed a cigarette to the boy, who then said:

"Mind sticking it in my mouth?" Bok did so and then offered him a light; the boy continued, all with his wonderful smile: "If you don't mind, would you just light it. You see, Fritzie kept both of my hooks as souvenirs."

With both arms amputated, the boy could still jest and smile!

It was the same boy who on his hospital cot the next day said: "Don't you think you could do something for the chap next to me, there on my left? He's really suffering: cried like hell all last night. It would be a Godsend if you could get Doc to do something."

A promise was given that the surgeon should be seen at once, but the boy was asked: "How about you?"

"Oh," came the cheerful answer, "I'm all right. I haven't anything to hurt. My wounded members are gone—just plain gone. But that chap has got something—he got the real thing!"

What was the real thing according to such a boy's idea?

There were beautiful stories that one heard "over there." One of the most beautiful acts of consideration was told, later, of a lovable boy whose throat had been practically shot away. During his convalescence he had learned the art of making beaded bags. It kept him from talking, the main prescription. But one day he sold the bag which he had first made to a visitor, and with his face radiant with glee he sought the nurse-mother to tell her all about his good fortune. Of course, nothing but a series of the most horrible guttural sounds came from the boy; not a word could be understood. It was his first venture into the world with the loss of his member, and the nurse-mother could not find it in her heart to tell the boy that not a word which he spoke was understandable. With eyes full of tears she placed both of her hands on the boy's shoulders and said to him: "I am so sorry, my boy. I cannot understand a word you say to me. You evidently do not know that I am totally deaf. Won't you write what you want to tell me?"

A look of deepest compassion swept the face of the boy. To think that one could be so afflicted, and yet so beautifully tender and always so radiantly cheerful, he wrote her.

Pathos and humor followed rapidly one upon the other "at the front" in those gruesome days, and Bok was to have his spirits lightened somewhat by an incident the next day.

He found himself in one of the numerous little towns where our doughboys were billeted, some in the homes of the peasants, others in stables, barns, outhouses, lean-tos, and what not. These were the troops on their way to the front where the fighting in the Argonne Forest was at that time going on. As Bok was walking with an American officer, the latter pointed to a doughboy crossing the road, followed by as disreputable a specimen of a pig as he had ever seen.

Catching Bok's smile, the officer said: "That's Pinney and his porker. Where you see the one you see the other."

Bok caught up with the boy, and said: "Found a friend, I see, buddy?"

"I sure have," grinned the doughboy, "and it sticks closer than a poor relation, too."

"Where did you pick it up?"

"Oh, in there," said the soldier, pointing to a dilapidated barn.

"Why in there?"

"My home," grinned the boy.

"Let me see," said Bok, and the doughboy took him in with the pig following close behind. "Billeted here—been here six days. The pig was here when we came, and the first night I lay down and slept, it came up to me and stuck its snout in my face and woke me up. Kind enough, all right, but not very comfortable: it stinks so."

"Yes; it certainly does. What did you do?"

"Oh, I got some grub I had and gave it to eat: thought it might be hungry, you know. I guess that sort of settled it, for the next night it came again and stuck its snout right in my mug. I turned around, but it just climbed over me and there it was."

"Well, what did you do then? Chase it out?"

"Chase it out?" said the doughboy, looking into Bok's face with the most unaffected astonishment. "Why, mister, that's a mother pig, that is. She's going to have young ones in a few days. How could I chase her out?"

"You're quite right, buddy," said Bok. "You couldn't do that."

"Oh, no," said the boy. "The worst of it is, what am I going to do with her when we move up within a day or two? I can't take her along to the front, and I hate to leave her here. Someone might treat her rough."

"Captain," said Bok, hailing the officer, "you can attend to that, can't you, when the time comes?"

"I sure can, and I sure will," answered the captain. And with a quick salute, Pinney and his porker went off across the road!

Bok was standing talking to the commandant of one of the great French army supply depots one morning. He was a man of forty; a colonel in the regular French army. An erect, sturdy-looking man with white hair and mustache, and who wore the single star of a subaltern on his sleeve, came up, saluted, delivered a message, and then asked: "Are there any more orders, sir?"

"No," was the reply. He brought his heels together with a click, saluted again, and went away.

The commandant turned to Bok with a peculiar smile on his face and asked: "Do you know who that man is?"

"No," was the reply.

"That is my father," was the answer.

The father was then exactly seventy-two years old. He was a retired business man when the war broke out. After two years of the heroic struggle he decided that he couldn't keep out of it. He was too old to fight, but after long insistence he secured a commission. By one of the many curious coincidences of the war he was assigned to serve under his own son.

When under the most trying conditions, the Americans never lost their sense of fun. On the staff of a prison hospital in Germany, where a number of captured American soldiers were being treated, a German sergeant became quite friendly with the prisoners under his care. One day he told them that he had been ordered to active service on the front. He felt convinced that he would be captured by the English, and asked the Americans if they could give him some sort of testimonial which he could show if he were taken prisoner, so that he would not be ill treated.

The Americans were much amused at this idea,

and concocted a note of introduction, written in English. The German sergeant knew no English and could not understand his testimonial, but he tucked it in his pocket, well satisfied.

In due time, he was sent to the front and was captured by "the ladies from hell," as the Germans called the Scotch kilties. He at once presented his introduction, and his captors laughed when they read:

"This is L_____. He is not a bad sort of chap. Don't shoot him; torture him slowly to death."

One evening as Bok was strolling out after dinner a Red Cross nurse came to him, explained that she had two severely wounded boys in what remained of an old hut: that they were both from Pennsylvania and had expressed a great desire to see him as a resident of their state.

"Neither can possibly survive the night," said the nurse.

"They know that?" asked Bok.

"Oh, yes, but like all our boys they are lying there joking with each other."

Bok was taken into what remained of a room in a badly shelled farmhouse, and there, on two roughly constructed cots, lay the two boys. Their faces had been bandaged so that nothing was visible except the eyes of each boy. A candle in a bottle standing on a box gave out the only light. But the eyes of the boys were smiling as Bok came in and sat down on the box on which the nurse had been sitting.

He talked with the boys, got as much of their stories

from them as he could, and told them such home news as he thought might interest them.

After half an hour he arose to leave, when the nurse said: "There is no one here, Mr. Bok, to say the last words to these boys. Will you do it?" Bok stood transfixed. In sending men over in the service of the Y.M.C.A. he had several times told them to be ready for any act that they might be asked to render, even the most sacred one. And here he stood himself before that duty. He felt as if he stood stripped before his Maker. Through the glassless window the sky lit up constantly with the flashes of a shell as it landed.

"Yes, won't you sir?" asked the boy on the right cot as he held out his hand. Bok took it, and then the hand of the other boy reached out.

What to say, he did not know. Then, to his surprise, he heard himself repeating extract after extract from a book by Lyman Abbott called *The Other Room,* a message to the bereaved declaring the nonexistence of death, but that we merely move from this earth to another: from one room to another, as it were. Bok had not read the book for years, but here was the subconscious self supplying the material for him in his moment of greatest need. Then he remembered that just before leaving home he had heard sung at matins, after the prayer for the president, a beautiful song called "Passing Souls." He had asked the rector for a copy of it; and, wondering why, he had put it in his wallet that he carried with him. He took it out now and holding the hand of the boy at his right, read to them:

For the passing souls we pray,
Savior, meet them on their way;
Let their trust lay hold on Thee
Ere they touch eternity.

Holy counsels long forgot
Breathe again 'mid shell and shot;
Through the mist of life's last pain
None shall look to Thee in vain.

To the hearts that know Thee, Lord,
Thou will speak through flood or sword;
Just beyond the cannon's roar,
Thou art on the farther shore.

For the passing souls we pray,
Savior, meet them on their way;
Thou wilt hear our yearning call,
Who last loved and died for all.

Absolute stiffness reigned in the room save for the half-suppressed sob from the nurse and the distant booming of the cannon. As Bok finished, he heard the boy at his right say slowly: "Savior—meet—me—on—my—way": with a little emphasis on the word "my." The hand in his relaxed slowly, and then fell on the cot; and he saw that the soul of another brave American boy had "gone west."

Bok glanced at the other boy, reached for his hand, shook it, and looking deep into his eyes, he left the little hut.

He little knew where and how he was to look into those eyes again!

Feeling the need of air in order to get hold of himself after one of the most solemn moments of his visit to the front, Bok strolled out, and soon found himself on what only a few days before had been a field of carnage where the American boys had driven back the Germans. Walking in the trenches and looking out, in the clear moonlight, over the field of desolation and ruin, and thinking of the inferno that had been enacted there only so recently, he suddenly felt his foot rest on what seemed to be a soft object. Taking his "ever-ready" flash from his pocket, he shot a ray at his feet, only to realize that his foot was resting on the face of a dead German!

Bok had had enough for one evening! In fact, he had had enough of war in all its aspects; and he felt a sigh of relief when, a few days, thereafter, he boarded *The Empress of Asia* for home, after a ten-week absence.

He hoped never again to see, at first hand, what war meant!

XXXII

The End of Thirty Years Editorship

ON THE voyage home, Edward Bok decided that, now that the war was over, he would ask his company to release him from the editorship of *The Ladies' Home Journal.* His original plan had been to retire at the end of a quarter of a century of editorship, when in his fiftieth year. He was, therefore, six years behind his schedule. In October 1919, he would reach his thirtieth anniversary as editor, and he fixed upon this as an appropriate time for the relinquishment of his duties.

He considered carefully where he would leave an institution which the public had so thoroughly associated with his personality, and he felt that at no point in its history could he so safely transfer it to other hands. The position of the magazine in the public estimation was unquestioned; it had never been so strong. Its circulation not only had outstripped that of any other monthly periodical, but it was still growing so rapidly that it was only a question of a few months when it would reach the almost incredible mark of 2 million copies per month. With its advertising patronage exceeding that of any other monthly, the periodical had become, probably, the most valuable and profitable piece of magazine property in the world.

Moreover, he wished to say goodbye to his public

before it decided, for some reason or other, to say goodbye to him. He had no desire to outstay his welcome. That public had been wonderfully indulgent toward his shortcomings, lenient with his errors, and tremendously inspiring to his best endeavor. He would not ask too much of it. Thirty years was a long tenure of office, one of the longest, in point of consecutively active editorship, in American magazines.

He had helped to create and to put into the life of the American home a magazine of peculiar distinction. From its beginning it had been unlike any other periodical; it had always retained its individuality as a magazine apart from the others. It had sought to be something more than a mere assemblage of stories and articles. It had consistently stood for ideals; and, save in one or two instances, it had carried through what it undertook to achieve. It had a record of worthy accomplishment; a more fruitful record than many imagined. It had become a national institution such as no other magazine had ever been.

Edward Bok was content to leave it at this point.

He explained all this in December 1918, to the board of directors, and asked that his resignation be considered. It was understood that he was to serve out his thirty years, thus remaining with the magazine for the best part of another year.

In the material which the *Journal* now included in its contents, it began to point the way to the problems which would face women during the reconstruction period. Bok scanned the rather crowded field of thought very carefully, and selected for discussion in the magazine such questions as seemed to him most important for the public to understand in order to face and solve its impending problems. The outstanding question he saw which would immediately face men and women of the country was the problem of Americanization. The war and its after-effects had clearly demonstrated this to be the most vital need in the life of the nation, not only for the foreign-born but for the American as well.

The more one studied the problem the clearer it became that the vast majority of American-born needed a refreshing, and, in many cases, a new conception of American ideals as much as did the foreign-born, and that the latter could never be taught what America and its institutions stood for until they were more clearly defined in the mind of the men and women of American birth.

Bok went to Washington, consulted with Franklin K. Lane, secretary of the interior, of whose department the Government Bureau of Americanization was a part. A comprehensive series of articles was outlined; the most expert writer, Esther Everett Lape,[1] who had several years of actual experience in Americanization work, was selected.

With the full and direct cooperation of the Federal Bureau of Americanization, the material was then

[1] Esther Everett Lape was a well-known writer on conflict resolution, medicine, and world peace.

assembled and worked up with the result that, in the opinion of the director of the Federal Bureau, the series proved to be the most comprehensive exposition of practical Americanization adapted to city, town, and village thus far published.

The work on this series was one of the last acts of Edward Bok's editorship; and it was peculiarly gratifying to him that his editorial work should end with the exposition of that Americanization of which he himself was a product. It seemed a fitting close to the career of a foreign-born Americanized editor.

The scope of the reconstruction articles now published, and the clarity of vision shown in the selection of the subjects, gave a fresh impetus to the circulation of the magazine; and now that the government's embargo on the use of paper had been removed, the full editions of the periodical could again be printed.

The result reached phenomenal figures. The last number under Bok's full editorial control was the issue of October 1919. This number was oversold with a printed edition of 2 million copies—a record never before achieved by any magazine. This same issue presented another record unattained in any single number of any periodical in the world. It carried between its covers the amazing total of over $1 million in advertisements.

This was the psychological point at which to stop. And Edward Bok did. Although his official relation as editor did not terminate until January 1920, when the number which contained his valedictory editorial was issued, his actual editorship ceased on 22 September 1919. On that day he handed over the reins to his successor.

As Bok was, on that day, about to leave his desk for the last time, it was announced that a young soldier whom he "had met and befriended in France" was waiting to see him. When the soldier walked into the office he was to Bok only one of the many whom he had met on the other side. But as the boy shook hands with him and said: "I guess you do not remember me, Mr. Bok," there was something in those eyes into which he looked that startled him. And then, in a flash, the circumstances under which he had last seen those eyes came to him.

"Good heavens, my boy, you are not one of those two boys in the little hut that I—"

"To whom you read the poem 'Passing Souls,' that evening. Yes, sir, I'm the boy who had hold of your left hand. My bunkie, Ben, went west that same evening, you remember."

"Yes," replied the editor, "I remember; I remember only too well," and again Bok felt the hand in his relax, drop from his own, and heard the words: "Savior—meet—me—on—my—way."

The boy's voice brought Bok back to the moment.

"It's wonderful you should remember me; my face was all bound up—I guess you couldn't see anything but my eyes."

"Just the eyes, that's right," said Bok. "But they burned into me all right, my boy."

"I don't think I get you, sir," said the boy.

"No, you wouldn't," Bok replied. "You couldn't, boy, not until you're older. But, tell me, how in the world did you ever get out of it?"

"Well, sir," answered the boy, with that shyness which we all have come to know in the boys who actually did, "I guess it was a close call, all right. But just as you left us, a hospital corps happened to come along on its way to the back and Miss Nelson—the nurse, you remember?—she asked them to take me along. They took me to a wonderful hospital, gave me fine care, and then after a few weeks they sent me back to the States, and I've been in a hospital over here ever since. Now except for this thickness of my voice that you notice, which Doc says will be all right soon, I'm fit again. The government has given me a job, and I came here on leave just to see my parents upstate, and I thought I'd like you to know that I didn't go west after all."

Fifteen minutes later, Edward Bok left his editorial office for the last time.

But as he went home his thoughts were not of his last day at the office, nor of his last acts as editor, but of his last caller—the soldier boy whom he had left seemingly so surely on his way "west," and whose eyes had burned into his memory. Strange that this boy should have been his last visitor!

As John Drinkwater, in his play,[2] makes Abraham Lincoln say to General Grant: "It's a queer world!"

[2]Reference to *Abraham Lincoln*, written by John Drinkwater, an English poet and dramatist, in 1918.

XXXIII

The Third Period

THE ANNOUNCEMENT of Edward Bok's retirement came as a great surprise to his friends. Save for one here and there, who had a clearer vision, the feeling was general that he had made a mistake. He was fifty-six, in the prime of life, never in better health, with "success lying easily upon him"—said one; "at the very summit of his career," said another—and all agreed it was "queer," "strange,"—unless, they argued, he was really ill. Even the most acute students of human affairs among his friends wondered. It seemed incomprehensible that any man should want to give up before he was, for some reason, compelled to do so. A man should go on until he "dropped in the harness," they argued.

Bok agreed that any man had a perfect right to work until he *did* "drop in the harness." But, he argued, if he conceded this right to others, why should they not concede to him the privilege of dropping with the blinders off?

"But," continued the argument, "a man degenerates when he retires from active affairs." And then, instances were pointed out as notable examples. "A year of retirement and he was through," was the picture given of one retired man. "In two years, he was glad to

411

come back," and so the examples ran on. "No big man ever retired from active business and did great work afterwards," Bok was told.

"No?" he answered. "Not even Cyrus W. Field or Herbert Hoover?"[1]

And all this time Edward Bok's failure to be entirely Americanized was brought home to his consciousness. After fifty years, he was still not an American! He had deliberately planned, and then had carried out his plan, to retire while he still had the mental and physical capacity to enjoy the fruits of his years of labor! For foreign to the American way of thinking it certainly was: the protestations and arguments of his friends proved that to him. After all, he

---

[1] Cyrus West Field amassed a fortune in the paper industry and retired at age thirty-three in search of new challenges. After crossing the Andes Mountains and bringing back a live jaguar, he became inspired by a British engineer's plan to link Newfoundland and the Canadian mainland with an underwater telegraph cable. Despite having no prior knowledge of electrical technology, Field succeeded in laying a cable between St. John's and New York. He then conceived the audacious project of connecting Newfoundland with Europe by cable. After repeated failures, he succeeded in 1858, only to have the connection go dead in less than a month. Field finally triumphed in July 1865 when the *Great Eastern,* the world's largest steamship, finally brought the first permanent transatlantic cable to Newfoundland. Herbert Hoover also was an early retiree who went on to greater achievements. In August 1914, he abandoned a lucrative career as a mining engineer to head relief efforts in World War I. He was secretary of commerce under presidents Harding and Coolidge, president of the United States, and longtime elder statesman of the Republican Party. He also directed two commissions to streamline the work of the United States government under presidents Truman and Eisenhower.

was still Dutch; he had held on to the lesson which his people had learned years ago; that the people of other European countries had learned; that the English had discovered: that the Great Adventure of Life was something more than material work, and that the time to go is while the going is good!

For it cannot be denied that the pathetic picture we so often see is found in American business life more frequently than in that of any other land: men unable to let go—not only for their own good, but to give the younger men behind them an opportunity. Not that a man should stop work, for man was born to work, and in work he should find his greatest refreshment. But so often it does not occur to the man in a pivotal position to question the possibility that at sixty or seventy he can keep steadily in touch with a generation whose ideas are controlled by men twenty years younger. Unconsciously he hangs on beyond his greatest usefulness and efficiency.

Such a man in a position of importance seems often not to see that he has it within his power to advance the fortunes of younger men by stepping out when he has served his time, while by refusing to let go he often works dire injustice and even disaster to his younger associates.

The sad fact is that in all too many instances the average American business man is actually afraid to let go because he realizes that out of business he should not know what to do. For years he has so excluded all other interests that at fifty or sixty or seventy he finds himself a slave to his business, with positively no inner resources. Retirement from the one thing he does know would naturally leave such a man useless to himself and his family, and his community: worse than useless, as a matter of fact, for he would become a burden to himself, a nuisance to his family, and, when he would begin to write "letters" to the newspapers, a bore to the community.

It is significant that a European or English business man rarely reaches middle age devoid of acquaintance with other matters; he always lets the breezes from other worlds of thought blow through his ideas, with the result that when he is ready to retire from business he has other interests to fall back upon.

A man must unquestionably prepare years ahead for his retirement, not alone financially, but mentally as well. Bok noticed as a curious fact that nearly every business man who told him he had made a mistake in his retirement, and that the proper life for a man is to stick to the game and see it through—"hold her nozzle agin the bank" as Jim Bludso would say—was a man with no resources outside his business. Naturally a retirement is a mistake in the eyes of such a man; but oh, the pathos of such a position: that in a world of so much interest, in an age so fascinatingly full of things worth doing, a man should have allowed himself to become a slave to his business, and should imagine no other man happy without the same claims!

It is this lesson that the American business man has still to learn: that no man can be wholly efficient in his life, that he is not living a four-squared existence, if he concentrates every waking thought on his material affairs. He has still to learn that man cannot live by bread alone. The making of money, the accumulation of material power, is not all there is to living. Life is something more than these, and the man who misses this truth misses the greatest joy and satisfaction that can come into his life—service for others.

Some men argue that they can give this service and be in business, too. But service with such men generally means drawing a check for some worthy cause, and nothing more. Edward Bok never belittled the giving of contributions—he solicited too much money himself for the causes in which he was interested—but it is a poor nature that can satisfy itself that it is serving humanity by merely signing checks. There is no form of service more comfortable or so cheap. Real service, however, demands that a man give himself with his check. And that the average man cannot do if he remains in affairs.

Particularly true is this today, when every problem of business is so engrossing, demanding a man's full time and thought. It is the rare man who can devote himself to business and be fresh for service of others afterward. No man can, with efficiency, serve two masters so exacting as are these. Besides, if his business has seemed important enough to demand his entire attention, are not the great uplift questions equally worth his exclusive thought? Are they easier of solution than the material problems?

A man can live a full life-square only when he divides it into three periods:

First: that of education, acquiring the fullest and best within his reach and power;

Second: that of achievement, achieving for himself and his family, and discharging the first duty of any man, that in case of his incapacity those who are closest to him are provided for. But each provision does not mean an accumulation that becomes to those he leaves behind him an embarrassment rather than a protection. To prevent this, the next period confronts him;

Third: Service for others. That is the acid test where many a man falls short: to know when he has enough, and to be willing not only to let well enough alone, but to give a helping hand to the other fellow; to recognize in a practical way, that we are our brother's keeper; that a brotherhood of man does exist outside after-dinner speeches. Too many men make the mistake, when they reach the point of enough, of going on pursuing the same old game: accumulating more money, grasping for more power until either a nervous breakdown overtakes them and a sad incapacity results, or they drop "in the harness," which is, of course, only calling an early grave by another name. They cannot seem to get the truth into their heads that as they have been helped by others so should they now help others: as their means have come from the public, so now they owe something in turn to that public.

Edward W. Bok, after retirement

417

If You are a Man) bold

read this book ☉ If you have a son, hand it to him ☉ Never fear but that he'll read it if he only scans the first page ☉ If you are a woman, get the book and learn what kind of a man it was who led the feminine thought of this nation for 30 years. It is far & away the most interesting autobiography I have ever read " — tells this from a woman writer in the Birmingham, Alabama, Age-Herald about

The Americanization of Edward Bok
The Story of a Dutch Boy 50 years later

Three Editions Within The Past ~~Two~~ Five Weeks)

Seventh Edition Now Printing

"The most marvelously human book of the last 20 years".
The ~~whole~~ Washington Post.

Illustrated ~ $5.00

Charles Scribner's Sons, New York

full line
with dash
and no score

Copy written by Edward Bok to advertise
The Americanization of Edward Bok

Courtesy Bruccoli Clark Layman, Inc.

418

No man has a right to leave the world no better than he found it. He must add something to it: either he must make its people better and happier, or he must make the face of the world fairer to look at. And the one really means the other.

"Idealism," immediately say some. Of course, it is. But what is the matter with idealism? What really is idealism? Do one-tenth of those who use the phrase so glibly know its true meaning, the part it has played in the world? The worthy interpretation of an ideal is that it embodies an idea—a conception of the imagination. All ideas are at first ideals. They must be. The producer brings forth an idea, but some dreamer has dreamed it before him either in whole or in part.

The idealist, particularly today when there is so great need of him, is not to be scoffed at. It is through him and only through him that the world will see a new and clear vision of what is right. It is he who has the power of going out himself—that self in which too many are nowadays so deeply imbedded; it is he who, in seeking the ideal, will, through his own clearer perception or that of others, transform the ideal into the real.

"Where there is no vision, the people perish."

It was his remark that he retired because he wanted "to play" that Edward Bok's friends most completely misunderstood. "Play" in their minds meant tennis, golf, horseback, polo, travel, etc.—(curious that scarcely one mentioned reading!). It so happens that no one enjoys some of these play forms more than

Bok; but "God forbid," he said, "that I should spend the rest of my days in a bunker or in the saddle. In moderation," he added, "yes; most decidedly." But the phrase of "play" meant more to him than all this. Play is diversion: exertion of the mind as well as of the body. There is such a thing as mental play as well as physical play. We ask of play that it shall rest, refresh, exhilarate. Is there any form of mental activity that secures all these ends so thoroughly and so directly as doing something that a man really likes to do, doing it with all his heart, all the time conscious that he is helping to make the world better for some one else?

Our cities, towns, communities of all sizes and kinds, urban and rural, cry out for men to solve their problems. There is room and to spare for the man of any bent. The old Romans looked forward, on coming to the age of retirement, which was definitely fixed by rule, to a rural life, when they hied themselves to a little home in the country, had open house for their friends, and "kept bees." While bee-keeping is unquestionably interesting, there are today other and more vital occupations awaiting the retired American.

The main thing is to secure that freedom of movement that lets a man go where he will and do what he thinks he can do best, and prove to himself and to others that the acquirement of the dollar is not all there is to life. No man can realize, until on awakening some morning he feels the exhilaration, can sense the freedom that comes from knowing he can choose his own doings and control his own goings. Time is of more value than money, and it is that which the man who retires feels that he possesses. Hamilton Mabie once said, after his retirement from an active editorial position: "I am so happy that the time has come when I elect what I shall do," which is true; but then he added: "I have rubbed out the word 'must' from my vocabulary," which was not true. No man ever reaches that point. Duty of some sort confronts a man in business or out of business, and duty spells "must." But there is less "must" in the vocabulary of the retired man; and it is this lessened quantity that gives the tang of joy to the new day.

It is a wonderful inner personal satisfaction to reach the point when a man can say: "I have enough." His soul and character are refreshed by it: he is made over by it. He begins a new life! He gets a sense of new joy; he feels, for the first time, what a priceless possession is that thing that he never knew before, freedom. And if he seeks that freedom at the right time, when he is at the summit of his years and powers and at the most opportune moment in his affairs, he has that supreme satisfaction denied to so many men, the opposite of which comes home with such cruel force to them: that they overstayed their time and wore out their welcome.

There is no satisfaction that so thoroughly satisfies as that of going while the going is good.

Still—

The friends of Edward Bok may be right when they said he made a mistake in his retirement.

However—

As Mr. Dooley says: "It's a good thing, sometimes, to have people size ye up wrong, Hinnessey: it's whin they've got ye'er measure ye're in danger."[2]

Edward Bok's friends failed to get his measure—yet!

They still have to learn what he has learned and is learning every day: "the joy," as Charles Lamb so aptly put it upon his retirement, "of walking about and around instead of to and fro."

The question now naturally arises, having read this record thus far: To what extent, with his unusual opportunities of fifty years, has the Americanization of Edward Bok gone? How far is he, today, an American? These questions, so direct and personal in their nature, are perhaps best answered in a way more direct and personal than the method thus far adopted in this chronicle. We, therefore, let Edward Bok answer these questions for himself, in closing this record of his Americanization.

[2]Mr. Dooley was the pen name of Finley Peter Dunne, a satirist who catapulted to fame after 1893 by writing astute commentary as "Mr. Dooley," lampooning political leaders in an Irish dialect.

XXXIV

Where America Fell Short with Me

WHEN I came to the United States as a lad of six, the most needful lesson for me, as a boy, was the necessity for thrift. I had been taught in my home across the sea that thrift was one of the fundamentals in a successful life. My family had come from a land (The Netherlands) noted for its thrift; but we had been in the United States only a few days before the realization came home strongly to my father and mother that they had brought their children to a land of waste.

Where the Dutchman saved, the American wasted. There was waste, and the most prodigal waste, on every hand. In every street car and on every ferry boat the floors and seats were littered with newspapers that had been read and thrown away or left behind. If I went to a grocery store to buy a peck of potatoes, and a potato rolled off the heaping measure, the grocery-man, instead of picking it up, kicked it into the gutter for the wheels of his wagon to run over. The butcher's waste filled my mother's soul with dismay. If I bought a scuttle of coal at the corner grocery, the coal that missed the scuttle, instead of being shoveled up and put back into the bin, was swept into the street. My young eyes quickly saw this; in the evening I gathered up the coal thus swept away, and during the course of a week I collected a scuttleful. The first time my mother saw the garbage pail of a family almost as poor as our own, with the wife and husband constantly complaining that they could not get along, she could scarcely believe her eyes. A half pan of hominy of the preceding day's breakfast lay in the pail next to a third of a loaf of bread. In later years, when I saw, daily, a scow loaded with the garbage of Brooklyn house-holders being towed through New York harbor out to sea, it was an easy calculation that what was thrown away in a week's time from Brooklyn homes would feed the poor of The Netherlands.

At school, I quickly learned that to "save money" was to be "stingy"; as a young man, I soon found that the American disliked the word "economy," and on every hand as plenty grew spending grew. There was literally nothing in American life to teach me thrift or economy; everything to teach me to spend and to waste.

I saw men who had earned good salaries in their prime, reach the years of incapacity as dependents. I saw families on every hand either living quite up to their means or beyond them; rarely within them. The more a man earned, the more he—or his wife—spent. I saw fathers and mothers and their children dressed beyond their incomes. The proportion of families who ran into debt was far greater than those who saved. When a panic came, the families "pulled in"; when the panic was over, they "let out." But the end of one year found them precisely where they were at the close of the previous year, unless they were deeper in debt.

It was in this atmosphere of prodigal expenditures and culpable waste that I was to practice thrift: a fundamental in life! And it is into this atmosphere that the foreign-born comes now, with every inducement to spend and no encouragement to save. For as it was in the days of my boyhood, so it is today—only worse.

Is it any wonder, then, that in this, one of the essentials in life and in all success, America fell short with me, as it is continuing to fall short with every foreign-born who comes to its shores?

As a Dutch boy, one of the cardinal truths taught me was that whatever was worth doing was worth doing well: that next to honesty came thoroughness as a factor in success. It was not enough that anything should be done: it was not done at all if it was not done well. I came to America to be taught exactly the opposite. The two infernal Americanisms "That's good enough" and "That will do" were early taught me, together with the maxim of quantity rather than quality.

It was not the boy at school who could write the words in his copy book who received the praise of the teacher; it was the boy who could write the largest number of words in a given time. As I grew into young manhood, and went into business, I found on every hand that quantity counted for more than quality. The emphasis was almost always placed on how much work one could do in a day, rather than upon how well the work was done. Thoroughness was at a discount on every hand; production at a premium. It made no difference in what direction I went, the result was the same: the cry was always for quantity, quantity! Into this atmosphere of almost utter disregard for quality I brought my ideas of Dutch thoroughness and my conviction that doing well whatever I did was to count as a cardinal principle in life.

During my years of editorship, save in one or two conspicuous instances, I was never able to assign to an American writer work which called for painstaking research. In every instance, the work came back to me either incorrect in statement or otherwise obviously lacking in careful preparation.

One of the most successful departments I ever conducted in *The Ladies' Home Journal* called for infinite reading and patient digging, with the actual results sometimes almost negligible. I made a study of my associates by turning the department over to one after another, and always with the same result: absolute lack of a capacity for patient research. As one of my editors, typically American, said to me: "It isn't worth all the trouble that you put into it." Yet no single department ever repaid the searcher more for his pains. Save for assistance derived from a single person, I had to do the work myself for all the years that the department continued.

Here again, in one of the most important matters in life, did America fall short with me; and, what is more important, she is falling short with every foreigner that comes to her shores.

In the matter of education, America fell short in what should be the strongest of all her institutions: the public school. A more inadequate, incompetent method of teaching, as I look back over my seven years of attendance at three different public schools, it is difficult to conceive. If there is one thing that I, as a foreign-born child, should have been carefully taught, it is the English language. The individual effort to teach this, if effort there was, and I remember none, was negligible. It was left for my father to teach me, or for me to dig it out myself. There was absolutely no indication on the part of the teacher or principal of responsibility for seeing that a foreign-born boy should acquire the English language correctly. I was taught as if I were American-born, and, of course, I was left dangling in the air, with no conception of what I was trying to do.

My father worked with me evening after evening; I plunged my young mind deep into the bewildering confusions of the language—and no one realizes the confusions of the English language as does the foreign-born—and got what I could through these joint efforts. But I gained nothing from the much-vaunted public school system which the United States had borrowed from my own country, and then had rendered incompetent—either by disregard for the thoroughness that makes Dutch schools the admiration of the world, or by too close a regard for politics.

Thus, in her most important institution to the foreign-born, America fell short. And while I am ready to believe that the public school may have increased in efficiency since that day, it is, indeed, a question for the American to ponder, just how far the system is efficient for the education of the child who comes to its school without a knowledge of the first word in the English language. Without a detailed knowledge of the subject, I know enough of conditions in the average public school today to warrant at least the suspicion that Americans would not be particularly proud of the system, and of what it gives for which annually they pay millions of dollars in taxes.

I am aware in making this statement that I shall be met with convincing instances of intelligent effort being made with the foreign-born children in special classes. No one has a higher respect for those efforts than I have—few, other than educators, know of them better than I do, since I did not make my five-year study of the American public school system for naught. But I am not referring to the exceptional instance here and there.

As a Dutch boy I was taught a wholesome respect for law and for authority. The fact was impressed upon me that laws of themselves were futile unless the people for whom they were made respected them, and obeyed them in spirit more even than in the letter. I came to America to feel, on every hand, that exactly the opposite was true. Laws were passed, but were not enforced; the spirit to enforce them was lacking in the people. There was little respect for the law; there was scarcely any for those appointed to enforce it.

As I grew into manhood, the newspapers rang on every side with disrespect for those in authority. Under the special dispensation of the liberty of the press, which was construed into the license of the press, no man was too high to escape editorial vituperation if his politics did not suit the management, or if his action ran counter to what the proprietors believed it should be. It was not a criticism of his acts, it was personal attack upon the official; whether supervisor, mayor, governor, or president, it mattered not.

At the most vital part of my life, when I was to become an American citizen and exercise the right of suffrage, America fell entirely short. It reached out not even the suggestion of a hand.

When the presidential conventions had been held in the year I reached my legal majority, and I knew I could vote, I endeavored to find out whether, being foreign-born, I was entitled to suffrage. No one could tell me; and not until I had visited six different municipal departments, being referred from one to yet another, was it explained that, through my father's naturalization, I became, automatically, as his son, an American citizen. I decided to read up on the platforms of the Republican and Democratic parties, but I could not secure copies anywhere, although a week had passed since they had been adopted.

I was told the newspapers had printed them. It occurred to me there must be many others besides me who were very anxious to secure the platforms of the two parties in some more convenient form. With the eye of necessity ever upon a chance to earn an honest penny, I went to a newspaper office, cut out from its files the two platforms, had them printed in a small pocket edition, sold one edition to the American News Company and another to the News Company controlling the Elevated Railroad bookstands in New York City, where they sold at ten cents each. So great was the demand which I had only partially guessed, that within three weeks I had sold such huge editions of the little books that I had cleared over a thousand dollars.

But it seemed to me strange that it should depend on a foreign-born American to supply an eager public with what should have been supplied through the agency of the political parties or through some educational source.

I now tried to find out what a vote actually meant. It must be recalled that I was only twenty-one years old, with scant education, and with no civic agency offering me the information I was seeking. I went to the headquarters of each of the political parties and put my query. I was regarded with puzzled looks.

"What does it mean to vote?" asked one chairman. "Why, on Election Day you go up to the ballot box and put your ballot in, and that's all there is to it."

But I knew very well that that was not all there was to it, and was determined to find out the significance of the franchise. I met with dense ignorance on every hand. I went to the Brooklyn Library and was frankly told by the librarian that he did not know of a book that would tell me what I wanted to know. This was in 1884.

As the campaign increased in intensity, I found myself a desired person in the eyes of the local campaign managers, but not one of them could tell me the significance and meaning of the privilege I was for the first time to exercise.

Finally, I spent an evening with Seth Low,[1] and, of course, got the desired information.

But fancy the quest I had been compelled to make to acquire the simple information that should have been placed in my hands or made readily accessible to me. And how many foreign-born would take equal pains to ascertain what I was determined to find out?

Surely America fell short here at the moment most sacred to me: that of my first vote!

Is it any easier today for the foreign citizen to acquire this information when he approaches his first vote? I wonder! Not that I do not believe there are agencies for this purpose. You know there are, and so do I. But how about the foreign-born? Does he know it? Is it not perhaps like the owner of the bulldog who assured the friend calling on him that it never attacked

---

[1] Seth Low helped draft the charter of the newly consolidated New York City, and, after being defeated in his first attempt to be elected mayor, served a two-year term in that office from 1901 to 1903. He was also chairman of the New York City Chamber of Commerce.

friends of the family? "Yes," said the friend, "that's all right. You know and I know that I am a friend of the family, but does the dog know?"

Is it today made known to the foreign-born, about to exercise his privilege of suffrage for the first time, where he can be told what that privilege means: is the means to know made readily accessible to him: is it, in fact, as it should be, brought to him?

It was not to me; is it to him?

One fundamental trouble with the present desire for Americanization is that the American is anxious to Americanize two classes—if he is a reformer, the foreign-born; if he is an employer, his employees. It never occurs to him that he himself may be in need of Americanization. He seems to take it for granted that because he is American-born, he is an American in spirit and has a right understanding of American ideals. But that, by no means, always follows. There are thousands of the American-born who need Americanization just as much as do the foreign-born. There are hundreds of American employers who know far less of American ideals than do some of their employees. In fact, there are those actually engaged today in the work of Americanization, men at the top of the movement, who sadly need a better conception of true Americanism.

An excellent illustration of this came to my knowledge when I attended a large Americanization Conference in Washington. One of the principal speakers was an educator of high standing and considerable influence in one of the most important sections of the United States. In a speech setting forth his ideas of Americanization, he dwelt with much emphasis and at considerable length upon instilling into the mind of the foreign-born the highest respect for American institutions.

After the conference he asked me whether he could see me that afternoon at my hotel; he wanted to talk about contributing to the magazine. When he came, before approaching the object of his talk, he launched out on a tirade against the president of the United States; the weakness of the cabinet, the inefficiency of the Congress, and the stupidity of the Senate. If words could have killed, there would have not remained a single living member of the administration at Washington.

After fifteen minutes of this, I reminded him of his speech and the emphasis which he had placed upon the necessity of inculcating in the foreign-born respect for American institutions.

Yet this man was a power in his community, a strong influence upon others; he believed he could Americanize others, when he himself, according to his own statements, lacked the fundamental principle of Americanization. What is true of this man is, in lesser or greater degree, true of hundreds of others. Their Americanization consists of lip service; the real spirit, the only factor which counts in the successful teaching of any doctrine, is absolutely missing.

We certainly cannot teach anything approaching a

true Americanism until we ourselves feel and believe and practice in our own lives what we are teaching others. No law, no lip service, no effort, however well intentioned, will amount to anything worth while in inculcating the true American spirit in our foreign-born citizens until we are sure that the American spirit is understood by ourselves and is warp and woof of our own being.

To the American, part and parcel of his country, these particulars in which his country falls short with the foreign-born are, perhaps, not so evident; they may even seem not so very important. But to the foreign-born they seem distinct tasks; they loom large; they form serious handicaps which, in many cases, are never surmounted; they are a menace to that Americanization which is, today, more than ever our fondest dream, and which we now realize more keenly than before is our most vital need.

It is for this reason that I have put them down here as a concrete instance of where and how America fell short in my own Americanization, and, what is far more serious to me, where she is falling short in her Americanization of thousands of other foreign-born.

"Yet you succeeded," it will be argued.

That may be; but you, on the other hand, must admit that I did not succeed by reason of these short-comings; it was in spite of them, by overcoming them—a result that all might not achieve.

XXXV

What I Owe to America

Whatever shortcomings I may have found during my fifty-year period of Americanization; however America may have failed to help my transition from a foreigner into an American, I owe to her the most priceless gift that any nation can offer, and that is opportunity.

As the world stands today, no nation offers opportunity in the degree that America does to the foreign-born. Russia may, in the future, as I like to believe she will, prove a second United States of America in this respect. She has the same limitless area; her people the same potentialities. But, as things are today, the United States offers, as does no other nation, a limitless opportunity: here a man can go as far as his abilities will carry him. It may be that the foreign-born, as in my own case, must hold on to some of the ideals and ideas of the land of his birth; it may be that he must develop and mould his character by overcoming the habits resulting from national shortcomings. But into the best that the foreign-born can retain, America can graft such a wealth of inspiration, so high a national idealism, so great an opportunity for the highest endeavor, as to make him the fortunate man of the earth today.

He can go where he will: no traditions hamper him; no limitations are set except those within himself. The larger the area he chooses in which to work, the larger the vision he demonstrates, the more eager the people are to give support to his undertakings if they are convinced that he has their best welfare as his goal. There is no public confidence equal to that of the American public, once it is obtained. It is fickle, of course, as are all publics, but fickle only toward the man who cannot maintain an achieved success.

A man in America cannot complacently lean back upon victories won, as he can in the older European countries, and depend upon the glamour of the past to sustain him or the momentum of success to carry him. Probably the most alert public in the world, it requires of its leaders that they be alert. Its appetite for variety is insatiable, but its appreciation, when given, is full handed and whole hearted. The American public never holds back from the man to whom it gives; it never bestows in a niggardly way; it gives all or it gives nothing.

What is not generally understood of the American people is their wonderful idealism. Nothing so completely surprises the foreign-born as the discovery of this trait in American character. The impression is current in European countries—perhaps less generally since the war—that America is given over solely to a worship of the American dollar. While between nations as between individuals, comparisons are valueless, it may not be amiss to say, from Bok's personal knowledge, that the Dutch worship the gulden infinitely more than do Americans the dollar.

I do not claim that the American is always conscious of this idealism; often he is not. But let a great convulsion touching moral questions occur, and the result always shows how close to the surface is his idealism. And the fact that so frequently he puts over it a thick veneer of materialism does not affect its quality. The truest approach, indeed the only approach in reality, to the American character is, as Sir James Bryce[1] has so well said, through its idealism.

It is this quality which gives the truest inspiration to the foreign-born in his endeavor to serve the people of his adopted country. He is mentally sluggish, indeed, who does not discover that America will make good with him if he makes good with her.

"The sky is the limit" to the foreign-born who comes to America endowed with honest endeavor, ceaseless industry, and the ability to carry through. In any honest endeavor, the way is wide open to the will to succeed. Every path beckons, every vista invites, every talent is called forth, and every efficient effort finds its due reward. In no land is the way so clear and so free.

---

[1]James Bryce was an eminent British author and statesman. In 1870, he made the first of three visits to the United States. On each visit he tried to learn the customs and laws of the people, leading in 1888 to the publication of *The American Commonwealth,* a three-volume work modeled on Alexis de Tocqueville's *Democracy in America.*

How good an American has the process of Americanization made me? That I cannot say. Who *can* say that of himself? But when I look around me at the American-born I have come to know as my close friends, I wonder whether, after all, the foreign-born does not make in some sense a better American—whether he is not able to get a truer perspective; whether his is not the deeper desire to see America greater; whether he is not less content to let its faulty institutions be as they are; whether in seeing faults more clearly he does not make a more decided effort to have America reach those ideals or those fundamentals of his own land which he feels are in his nature, and the best of which he is anxious to graft into the character of his adopted land?

It is naturally with a feeling of deep satisfaction that I remember two presidents of the United States considered me a sufficiently typical American to wish to send me to my native land as the accredited minister of my adopted country. And yet when I analyze the reasons for my choice in both these instances, I derive a deeper satisfaction from the fact that my strong desire to work in America for America led me to ask to be permitted to remain here.

It is this strong impulse that my Americanization has made the driving power of my life. And I ask no greater privilege than to be allowed to live to see my potential America become actual: the America that I like to think of as the America of Abraham Lincoln and of Theodore Roosevelt—not faultless, but less faulty. It is a part in trying to shape America, and an opportunity to work in that America when it comes, that I ask in return for what I owe to her. A greater privilege no man could have.

Edward W. Bok

Index

INDEX

List of The Lakeside Classics

The Lakeside Classics

DESIGNED, TYPESET, PRINTED, BOUND, AND DISTRIBUTED BY
R.R. DONNELLEY & SONS COMPANY

COMPOSITION:
ALLENTOWN DIGITAL SERVICES,
ALLENTOWN, PENNSYLVANIA

SCANNING, COMPUTER TO PLATES, PRESSWORK, AND BINDING:
CRAWFORDSVILLE, INDIANA, BOOK MANUFACTURING DIVISION

IMAGE PROOFING (KODAK APPROVAL XP4):
LANCASTER, PENNSYLVANIA, PREMEDIA CENTER,
NORTHEAST DIVISION

WORLDWIDE DISTRIBUTION:
DONNELLEY LOGISTICS SERVICES

E-BOOK VERSION:
HTML CONVERSION, ALLENTOWN DIGITAL SERVICES
SITE MAINTENANCE, TECHNOLOGY CENTER,
DOWNERS GROVE, ILLINOIS
www.rrdonnelley.com/elakeside

BODY TYPEFACE:
11/12 POINT BULMER

PAPER STOCK:
50-POUND WHITE LAKESIDE CLASSICS OPAQUE,
50-PERCENT RECYCLED SHEET, BY GLATFELTER

CLOTH:
ROXITE C VELLUM CHOCOLATE BROWN,
BY HOLLISTON MILLS, INC.